Chemical War *and* Casualty Management

Chemical War *and* Casualty Management

Col. (Retd.) S. C. Narang

Prashant Publishing House
DELHI - 110094 (INDIA)

PRASHANT PUBLISHING HOUSE
C-34, 28 Foota Road, Gali No. 3
West Karawal Nagar, Delhi-110094
Phone : 9810396373, 22963970

Chemical War and Casualty Management

First Published : 2009

ISBN : 978-81-908282-0-8

PRINTED IN INDIA

Published by Mr. R. K. Jha M/s. Prashant Publishing House, Delhi and Printed at H.S. Offset Press, Delhi.

PREFACE

At the height of the Cold War, arms control was a bitterly disputed topic, but few questioned its importance. Today more than a decade after the end of the Cold War, arms control remains bitterly disputed, but the disputes have largely vanished from the front page and many question whether it really matters how they are resolved. The most obvious reason for this change is that few today, East or West, North or South, fear an outbreak of nuclear war or even a catastrophic nonnuclear war like those of the early twentieth century. To a considerable extent this absence of fear is well founded.

Unfortunately, one cannot make so optimistic an assessment of much of the rest of the world. Developing nations do not today command the kinds of resources available to the former Cold Warriors, so the danger of a world war arising from disputes outside of Europe is vanishingly small. This does not, however, mean that the human suffering now or in the decades to come resulting from quarrels in developing regions is negligible. And, unlike Europe, institutions to deal with inter-State or internal violence remain inadequate, whether at the national, regional, or global level.

Meanwhile, those institutions that are beginning to develop lack the arms control underpinnings that the Cold War, for all its evils, effectively bequeathed to Europe. There remain, moreover, certain dangers in or from the North. The agreements at the end of the Cold War were "arms control," not "disarmament." They thus left an enormous nuclear "overhang," especially in the United States and Russia, and these nuclear stockpiles remain dangerous, both to their possessors and to others. Chemical and biological weapons are widely banned but not yet eradicated, and very large conventional military power remains in the hands of a number of countries, especially the United States.

— *Author*

Contents

Preface

1. Introduction 1
2. Chemical Weapon Proliferation 14
3. Chemical Warfare in World War I 46
4. Types of Chemical Weapons 129
5. Chemical Decontamination 177
6. Chemical Detection Equipment 191
7. Chemical Warfare Agents 203
8. Chemical Warfare Mass Casualty Management 223
9. Reigle Report on Chemical War 259

Bibliography 283

Index 285

1 Introduction

Chemical warfare involves using the toxic properties of chemical substances to kill, injure or incapacitate an enemy. Chemical warfare is different from the use of conventional weapons or nuclear weapons because the destructive effects of chemical weapons are not primarily due to any explosive force. The offensive use of living organisms (such as anthrax) is considered to be biological warfare rather than chemical warfare; the use of nonliving toxic products produced by living organisms (e.g., toxins such as botulinum toxin, ricin, or saxitoxin) *is* considered chemical warfare under the provisions of the Chemical Weapons Convention. Under this Convention, any toxic chemical, regardless of its origin, is considered as a chemical weapon unless it is used for purposes that are not prohibited (an important legal definition, known as the General Purpose Criterion).

About 70 different chemicals have been used or stockpiled as Chemical Warfare (CW) agents during the 20th century. Chemical weapons are classified as weapons of mass destruction by the United Nations, and their production and stockpiling was outlawed by the Chemical Weapons Convention of 1993. Under the Convention, chemicals that are toxic enough to be used as chemical weapons, or may be used to manufacture such chemicals, are divided into three groups according to their purpose and treatment:

- Schedule 1 – Have few, if any, legitimate uses. These may only be produced or used for research, medical, pharmaceutical or protective purposes (i.e. testing of chemical weapons sensors and protective clothing). Examples include nerve agents, ricin, lewisite and mustard gas. Any production over 100 g must be notified to the OPCW and a country can have a stockpile of no more than one tonne of these chemicals.

- Schedule 2 – Have no large-scale industrial uses, but may have legitimate small-scale uses. Examples include dimethyl methylphosphonate, a precursor to sarin but which is also used as a flame retardant and Thiodiglycol which is a precursor chemical used in the manufacture of mustard gas but is also widely used as a solvent in inks.
- Schedule 3 – Have legitimate large-scale industrial uses. Examples include phosgene and chloropicrin. Both have been used as chemical weapons but phosgene is an important precursor in the manufacture of plastics and chloropicrin is used as a fumigant. Any plant producing more than 30 tonnes per year must be notified to, and can be inspected by, the OPCW.

TECHNOLOGY

Although crude chemical warfare has been employed in many parts of the world for thousands of years, "modern" chemical warfare began during World War I (see main article - Poison gas in World War I). Initially, only well-known commercially available chemicals and their variants were used. These included chlorine and phosgene gas. The methods of dispersing these agents during battle were relatively unrefined and inefficient.

Germany, the first side to employ chemical warfare on the battlefield, simply opened canisters of chlorine upwind of the opposing side and let the prevailing winds do the dissemination. Soon after, the French modified artillery munitions to contain phosgene – a much more effective method that became the principal means of delivery.

Since the development of modern chemical warfare in World War I, nations have pursued research and development on chemical weapons that falls into four major categories: new and more deadly agents; more efficient methods of delivering agents to the target (dissemination); more reliable means of defense against chemical weapons; and more sensitive and accurate means of detecting chemical agents.

Chemical warfare technology timeline				
	Agents	***Dissemination***	***Protection***	***Detection***
1900s	Chlorine Chloropicrin Phosgene Mustard gas	Wind dispersal		Smell
1910s	Lewisite	Chemical shells	Gas mask Rosin oil clothing	
1920s		Projectiles w/ central bursters	CC-2 clothing	
1930s	G-series nerve agents	Aircraft bombs		Blister agent detectors Color change paper
1940s		Missile warheads Spray tanks	Protective ointment (mustard) Collective protection Gas mask w/ Whetlerite	
1950s				
1960s	V-series nerve agents	Aerodynamic	Gas mask w/ water supply	Nerve gas alarm
1970s				
1980s		Binary munitions	Improved gas masks (protection, fit, comfort)	Laser detection
1990s	Novichok nerve agents			

CHEMICAL WARFARE AGENTS

A chemical used in warfare is called a *chemical warfare agent* (*CWA*). About 70 different chemicals have been used or stockpiled as chemical warfare agents during the 20th century and the 21st century. These agents may be in liquid, gas or solid form. Liquid agents are generally designed to evaporate quickly; such liquids are said to be *volatile* or have a *high vapor pressure*. Many chemical agents are made volatile so they can be dispersed over a large region quickly.

The earliest target of chemical warfare agent research was not toxicity, but development of agents that can affect a target through the skin and clothing, rendering protective gas masks useless. In July 1917, the Germans first employed mustard gas, the first agent that circumvented gas masks. Mustard gas easily penetrates leather and fabric to inflict painful burns on the skin.

Chemical warfare agents are divided into *lethal* and *incapacitating* categories. A substance is classified as incapacitating if less than 1/100 of the lethal dose causes incapacitation, e.g., through nausea or visual problems. The distinction between lethal and incapacitating substances is not fixed, but relies on a statistical average called the LD_{50}.

Persistency

One way to classify chemical warfare agents is according to their *persistency*, a measure of the length of time that a chemical agent remains effective after dissemination. Chemical agents are classified as *persistent* or *nonpersistent*.

Agents classified as *nonpersistent* lose effectiveness after only a few minutes or hours. Purely gaseous agents such as chlorine are nonpersistent, as are highly volatile agents such as sarin and most other nerve agents. Tactically, nonpersistent agents are very useful against targets that are to be taken over and controlled very quickly. Generally speaking, nonpersistent agents present only an inhalation hazard.

By contrast, *persistent* agents tend to remain in the environment for as long as a week, complicating decontamination. Defense against persistent agents requires shielding for extended periods of time. Non-volatile liquid agents, such as blister agents and the oily VX nerve agent, do not easily evaporate into a gas, and therefore present primarily a contact hazard.

Classes

Chemical warfare agents are organized into several categories according to the manner in which they affect the human body. The names and number of categories varies slightly from source to source, but in general, types of chemical warfare agents are as follows:

> There are other chemicals used militarily that are not scheduled by the Chemical Weapons Convention, and thus are not controlled under the CWC treaties.
>
> These include:
>
> Defoliants that destroy vegetation, but are not immediately toxic to human beings. Some batches of Agent Orange, for instance, used by the United States in Vietnam, contained dioxins as manufacturing impurities. Dioxins, rather than Agent Orange itself, have long-term cancer effects and for causing genetic damage leading to serious birth deformities.

Incendiary or explosive chemicals (such as napalm, extensively used by the United States in Vietnam, or dynamite) because their destructive effects are primarily due to fire or explosive force, and not direct chemical action.

Viruses, bacteria, or other organisms. Their use is classified as biological warfare. Toxins produced by living organisms are considered chemical weapons, although the boundary is blurry. Toxins are covered by the Biological Weapons Convention.

Designations

Most chemical weapons are assigned a one- to three-letter "NATO weapon designation" in addition to, or in place of, a common name.

Binary munitions, in which precursors for chemical warfare agents are automatically mixed in shell to produce the agent just prior to its use, are indicated by a "-2" following the agent's designation (for example, GB-2 and VX-2).

Some examples are given below:

Blood agents:	***Vesicants:***
Cyanogen chloride: CK Hydrogen cyanide: AC	Lewisite: L Sulfur mustard: H, HD, HS, HT
Pulmonary agents:	***Incapacitating agents:***
• Phosgene: CG	• Quinuclidinyl benzilate: BZ
Lachrymatory agents:	***Nerve agents:***
• Pepper spray: OC • Tear gas: CN, CS, CR	• Sarin: GB • VE, VG, VM, VX

Delivery

The most important factor in the effectiveness of chemical weapons is the efficiency of its delivery, or *dissemination,* to a target. The most common techniques include *munitions* (such as bombs, projectiles, warheads) that allow dissemination at a distance and *spray tanks* which disseminate from low-flying aircraft. Developments in the techniques of filling and storage of munitions have also been important.

Although there have been many advances in chemical weapon delivery since World War I, it is still difficult to achieve effective dispersion. The dissemination is highly dependent on atmospheric conditions because many chemical agents act in gaseous form. Thus, weather observations and forecasting are essential to optimize weapon delivery and reduce the risk of injuring friendly forces.

PAST CHEMICAL WARS

Dispersion is the simplest technique of delivering an agent to its target. It consists of placing the chemical agent upon or adjacent to a target immediately before dissemination, so that the material is most efficiently used.

World War I saw the earliest implementation of this technique, when German forces at Ypres simply opened cylinders of chlorine and allowed the wind to carry the gas across enemy lines. While simple, this technique had numerous disadvantages. Moving large numbers of heavy gas cylinders to the front-line positions from where the gas would be released was a lengthy and difficult logistical task. Stockpiles of cylinders had to be stored at the front line, posing a great risk if hit by artillery shells. Gas delivery depended greatly on wind speed and direction. If the wind was fickle, as at Loos, the gas could blow back, causing friendly casualties. Gas clouds gave plenty of warning, allowing the enemy time to protect themselves, though many soldiers found the sight of a creeping gas cloud unnerving. This made the gas doubly effective, as, in addition to damaging the enemy physically, it also had a psychological effect on the intended victims. Also gas clouds had limited penetration, capable only of affecting the front-line trenches before dissipating. Although it produced limited results in World War I, this technique shows how simple chemical weapon dissemination *can* be.

Shortly after this "open canister" dissemination, French forces developed a technique for delivery of phosgene in a non-explosive artillery shell. This technique overcame many of the risks of dealing with gas in cylinders. First, gas shells were independent of the wind and increased the effective range of gas, making any target within reach of guns vulnerable. Second, gas shells could be delivered without warning, especially the clear, nearly odorless phosgene — there are numerous accounts of gas shells, landing with a "plop" rather than exploding, being initially dismissed as dud high explosive or shrapnel shells, giving the gas time to work before the soldiers were alerted and took precautions.

The major drawback of artillery delivery was the difficulty of achieving a killing concentration. Each shell had a small gas payload and an area would have to be subjected to saturation bombardment to produce a cloud to match cylinder delivery. A British solution to the problem was the Livens Projector. This was effectively a large-bore mortar, dug into the ground that used the gas cylinders themselves as projectiles - firing a 14 kg cylinder up to 1500 m. This combined the gas volume of cylinders with the range of artillery.

Over the years, there were some refinements in this technique. In the 1950s and early 1960s, chemical artillery rockets and cluster bombs contained a multitude of submunitions, so that a large number of small clouds of the chemical agent would form directly on the target.

THERMAL DISSEMINATION

Thermal dissemination is the use of explosives or pyrotechnics to deliver chemical agents. This technique, developed in the 1920s, was a major improvement over earlier dispersal techniques, in that it allowed significant quantities of an agent to be disseminated over a considerable distance. Thermal dissemination remains the principal method of disseminating chemical agents today.

Most thermal dissemination devices consist of a bomb or projectile shell that contains a chemical agent and a central "burster" charge; when the burster detonates, the agent is expelled laterally.

Thermal dissemination devices, though common, are not particularly efficient. First, a percentage of the agent is lost by incineration in the initial blast and by being forced onto the ground. Second, the sizes of the particles vary greatly because explosive dissemination produces a mixture of liquid droplets of variable and difficult to control sizes.

The efficacy of thermal detonation is greatly limited by the flammability of some agents. For flammable aerosols, the cloud is sometimes totally or partially ignited by the disseminating explosion in a phenomenon called *flashing*. Explosively disseminated VX will ignite roughly one third of the time. Despite a great deal of study, flashing is still not fully understood, and a solution to the problem would be a major technological advance.

Despite the limitations of central bursters, most nations use this method in the early stages of chemical weapon development, in part because standard munitions can be adapted to carry the agents.

AERODYNAMIC DISSEMINATION

Aerodynamic dissemination is the non-explosive delivery of a chemical agent from an aircraft, allowing aerodynamic stress to disseminate the agent. This technique is the most recent major development in chemical agent dissemination, originating in the mid-1960s.

This technique eliminates many of the limitations of thermal dissemination by eliminating the flashing effect and theoretically allowing precise control of particle size. In actuality, the altitude of dissemination, wind direction and velocity, and the direction and velocity of the aircraft greatly influence particle size. There are other drawbacks as well; ideal deployment requires precise knowledge of aerodynamics and fluid dynamics, and because the agent must usually be dispersed within the boundary layer (less than 200–300 ft above the ground), it puts pilots at risk.

Significant research is still being applied toward this technique. For example, by modifying the properties of the liquid, its breakup when subjected to aerodynamic stress can be controlled and an idealized particle distribution achieved, even at supersonic speed. Additionally, advances in fluid dynamics, computer modeling, and weather forecasting allow an ideal direction, speed, and altitude to be calculated, such that warfare agent of a predetermined particle size can predictably and reliably hit a target.

PROTECTION AGAINST CHEMICAL WARFARE

Ideal protection begins with nonproliferation treaties such as the Chemical Weapons Convention, and detecting, very early, the *signatures* of someone building a chemical weapons capability. These include a wide range of intelligence disciplines, such as economic analysis of exports of dual-use chemicals and equipment, human intelligence (HUMINT) such as diplomatic, refugee, and agent reports; photography from satellites, aircraft and drones (IMINT); examination of captured equipment (TECHINT); communications intercepts (COMINT); and detection of chemical manufacturing and chemical agents themselves (MASINT).

If all the preventive measures fail and there is a clear and present danger, then there is a need for detection of chemical attacks, collective protection, and decontamination. Since industrial accidents can cause dangerous chemical releases (e.g., the Bhopal disaster), these activities are things that civilian, as well as military, organizations must be prepared to carry out. In civilian situations in developed countries, these are duties of HAZMAT organizations, which most commonly are part of fire departments.

Detection has been referred to above, as a technical MASINT discipline; specific military procedures, which are usually the model for civilian procedures, depend on the equipment, expertise, and personnel available. When chemical agents are detected, an alarm needs to sound, with specific warnings over emergency broadcasts and the like.

There may be a warning to expect an attack. If, for example, the captain of a US Navy ship believes there is a serious threat of chemical, biological, or radiological attack, the crew may be ordered to set Circle William, which means closing all openings to outside air, running breathing air through filters, and possibly starting a system that continually washes down the exterior surfaces.

Civilian authorities dealing with an attack or a toxic chemical accident will invoke the Incident Command System, or local equivalent, to coordinate defensive measures.

Individual protection starts with a gas mask and, depending on the nature of the threat, through various levels of protective clothing up to a complete chemical-resistant suit with a self-contained air supply. The US military defines various levels of MOPP (mission-oriented protective posture) from mask to full chemical resistant suits; Hazmat suits are the civilian equivalent, but go farther to include a fully independent air supply, rather than the filters of a gas mask.

Collective protection allows continued functioning of groups of people in buildings or shelters, the latter which may be fixed, mobile, or improvised. With ordinary buildings, this may be as basic as plastic sheeting and tape, although if the protection needs to be continued for any appreciable length of time, there will need to be an air supply, typically a scaled-up version of a gas mask.

Decontamination varies with the particular chemical agent used. Some *nonpersistent* agents, such as most pulmonary agents such as chlorine and phosgene, blood gases, and nonpersistent nerve gases (e.g., GB) will dissipate from open areas, although powerful exhaust fans may be needed to clear out building where they have accumulated.

In some cases, it might be necessary to neutralize them chemically, as with ammonia as a neutralizer for hydrogen cyanide or chlorine. Riot control agents such as CS will dissipate in an open area, but things contaminated with CS powder need to be aired out, washed by people wearing protective gear, or safely discarded.

Mass decontamination is a less common requirement for people than equipment, since people may be immediately affected and treatment is the action required. It is a requirement when people have been contaminated with persistent agents. Treatment and decontamination may need to be simultaneous, with the medical personnel protecting themselves so they can function.

There may need to be immediate intervention to prevent death, such as injection of atropine for nerve agents. Decontamination is especially important for people contaminated with persistent agents; many of the fatalities after the explosion of a WWII US ammunition ship carrying mustard gas, in the harbor of Bari, Italy, after a German bombing on 2 December 1943, came when rescue workers, not knowing of the contamination, bundled cold, wet seamen in tight-fitting blankets.

For decontaminating equipment and buildings exposed to persistent agents, such as blister agents, VX or other agents made persistent by mixing with a thickener, special equipment and materials might be needed.

Some type of neutralizing agent will be needed; e.g. in the form of a spraying device with neutralizing agents such as Chlorine, Fichlor, strong alkaline solutions or enzymes . In other cases, a specific chemical decontaminant will be required.

Sociopolitical Climate

While the study of chemicals and their military uses was widespread in China, the use of toxic materials has historically been viewed with mixed emotions and some disdain in the West.

One of the earliest reactions to the use of chemical agents was from Rome. Struggling to defend themselves from the Roman legions, Germanic tribes poisoned the wells of their enemies, with Roman jurists having been recorded as declaring "armis bella non venenis geri", meaning "war is fought with weapons, not with poisons."

Before 1915 the use of poisonous chemicals in battle was typically the result of local initiative, and not the result of an active government chemical weapons program. There are many reports of the isolated use of chemical agents in individual battles or sieges, but there was no true tradition of their use outside of incendiaries and smoke. Despite this tendency, there have been several attempts to initiate large-scale implementation of poison gas in several wars, but with the notable exception of World War I, the responsible authorities generally rejected the proposals for ethical reasons.

For example, in 1854 Lyon Playfair, a British chemist, proposed using a cyanide-filled artillery shell against enemy ships during the Crimean War. The British Ordnance Department rejected the proposal as "as bad a mode of warfare as poisoning the wells of the enemy."

Efforts to Eradicate Chemical Weapons

- August 27, 1874: The Brussels Declaration Concerning the Laws and Customs of War is signed, specifically forbidding the "employment of poison or poisoned weapons."
- September 4, 1900: The Hague Conference, which includes a declaration banning the "use of projectiles the object of which is the diffusion of asphyxiating or deleterious gases," enters into force.
- February 6, 1922: After World War I, the Washington Arms Conference Treaty prohibited the use of asphyxiating, poisonous or other gases. It was signed by the United States, Britain, Japan, France, and Italy, but France objected to other provisions in the treaty and it never went into effect.
- September 7, 1929: The Geneva Protocol enters into force, prohibiting the use of poison gas.

Nation	*CW Possession*	*Signed CWC*	*Ratified CWC*
Albania	Known	January 14, 1993	May 11, 1994
Burma (Myanmar)	Possible	January 13, 1993	No
the People's Republic of China	Probable	January 13, 1993	April 4, 1997
Egypt	Probable	No	No
France	Probable	January 13, 1993	March 2, 1995
India	Known	January 14, 1993	September 3, 1996
Iran	Known	January 13, 1993	November 3, 1997
Israel	Probable	January 13, 1993	No
Japan	Probable	January 13, 1993	September 15, 1995
Libya	Known	No	January 6, 2004 (acceded)
North Korea	Known	No	No
Pakistan	Probable	January 13, 1993	October 28, 1997
Russia	Known	January 13, 1993	November 5, 1997
Serbia and Montenegro	Probable	No	April 20, 2000 (acceded)
Sudan	Possible	No	May 24, 1999 (acceded)
Syria	Known	No	No
Taiwan	Possible	n/a	n/a
United States	Known	January 13, 1993	April 25, 1997
Vietnam	Probable	January 13, 1993	September 30, 1998

2

Chemical Weapon Proliferation

Despite numerous efforts to reduce or eliminate them, some nations continue to research and/or stockpile chemical warfare agents. To the right is a summary of the nations that have either declared weapon stockpiles or are suspected of secretly stockpiling or possessing CW research programs. Notable examples include China.

According to the testimony of Assistant Secretary of State for Intelligence and Research Carl W. Ford before the Senate Committee on Foreign Relations, it is very probable that China has an advanced chemical warfare program, including research and development, production, and weaponization capabilities. Furthermore, there is considerable concern from the US regarding China's contact and sharing of chemical weapons expertise with other states of proliferation concern, including Syria and Iran.

HISTORY

Ancient to Medieval Times

Chemical weapons have been used for millennia in the form of poisoned arrows, but evidence can be found for the existence of more advanced forms of chemical weapons in ancient and classical times.

A good example of early chemical warfare was the late Stone Age (10 000 BC) hunter-gatherer societies in Southern Africa, known as the San. They used poisoned arrows, tipping the wood, bone and stone tips of their arrows with poisons obtained from their natural environment. These poisons were mainly derived from scorpion or snake venom, but it is believed that some poisonous plants were also utilized. The arrow was fired into the target of choice, usually an antelope (the favourite being an eland), with the hunter then tracking the doomed animal until the poison caused its collapse.

The earliest surviving references to toxic warfare are possibly those in the Indian epics *Ramayana* and *Mahabharata.* The Manusmriti book of laws also forbids use of poison weapons.

Dating from the 4th century BC, writings of the Mohist sect in China describe the use of bellows to pump smoke from burning balls of mustard and other toxic vegetables into tunnels being dug by a besieging army. Even older Chinese writings dating back to about 1000 BC contain hundreds of recipes for the production of poisonous or irritating smokes for use in war along with numerous accounts of their use. From these accounts we know of the arsenic-containing "soul-hunting fog", and the use of finely divided lime dispersed into the air to suppress a peasant revolt in AD 178.

The earliest recorded use of gas warfare in the West dates back to the 5th century BC, during the Peloponnesian War between Athens and Sparta. Spartan forces besieging an Athenian city placed a lighted mixture of wood, pitch, and sulfur under the walls hoping that the noxious smoke would incapacitate the Athenians, so that they would not be able to resist the assault that followed. Sparta wasn't alone in its use of unconventional tactics during these wars: Solon of Athens is said to have used hellebore roots to poison the water in an aqueduct leading from the Pleistrus River around 590 BC during the siege of Cirrha.

Chemical weapons were known and used in ancient and medieval China. Polish chronicler Jan D³ugosz mentions usage of poisonous gas by the Mongol army in 1241 in the Battle of Legnica.

Rediscovery

During the Renaissance, people again considered using chemical warfare. One of the earliest such references is from Leonardo da Vinci, who proposed a powder of sulfide of arsenic and verdigris in the 15th century:

> throw poison in the form of powder upon galleys. Chalk, fine sulfide of arsenic, and powdered verdegris may be thrown among enemy ships by means of small

mangonels, and all those who, as they breathe, inhale the powder into their lungs will become asphyxiated.

It is unknown whether this powder was ever actually used.

In the 17th century during sieges, armies attempted to start fires by launching incendiary shells filled with sulphur, tallow, rosin, turpentine, saltpeter, and/or antimony. Even when fires were not started, the resulting smoke and fumes provided a considerable distraction. Although their primary function was never abandoned, a variety of fills for shells were developed to maximize the effects of the smoke.

In 1672, during his siege of the city of Groningen, Christoph Bernhard van Galen, the Bishop of Münster, employed several different explosive and incendiary devices, some of which had a fill that included belladonna, intended to produce toxic fumes. Just three years later, August 27, 1675, the French and the Germans concluded the Strasbourg Agreement, which included an article banning the use of "perfidious and odious" toxic devices.

In 1854, Lyon Playfair, a British chemist, proposed a cacodyl cyanide artillery shell for use against enemy ships as way to solve the stalemate during the siege of Sevastopol. The proposal was backed by Admiral Thomas Cochrane of the Royal Navy. It was considered by the Prime Minister, Lord Palmerston, but the British Ordnance Department rejected the proposal as "as bad a mode of warfare as poisoning the wells of the enemy." Playfair's response was used to justify chemical warfare into the next century:

> There was no sense in this objection. It is considered a legitimate mode of warfare to fill shells with molten metal which scatters among the enemy, and produced the most frightful modes of death. Why a poisonous vapor which would kill men without suffering is to be considered illegitimate warfare is incomprehensible. War is destruction, and the more destructive it can be made with the least suffering the sooner will be ended that barbarous method of protecting national rights. No doubt in time chemistry will be used to lessen the suffering of combatants, and even of criminals condemned to death.

Later, during the American Civil War, New York school teacher John Doughty proposed the offensive use of chlorine gas, delivered by filling a 10 inch (254 millimeter) artillery shell with 2 to 3 quarts (2 to 3 liters) of liquid chlorine, which could produce many cubic feet (a few cubic meters) of chlorine gas. Doughty's plan was apparently never acted on, as it was probably presented to Brigadier General James Wolfe Ripley, Chief of Ordnance, who was described as being congenitally immune to new ideas.

A general concern over the use of poison gas manifested itself in 1899 at the Hague Conference with a proposal prohibiting shells filled with asphyxiating gas. The proposal was passed, despite a single dissenting vote from the United States. The American representative, Navy Captain Alfred Thayer Mahan, justified voting against the measure on the grounds that "the inventiveness of Americans should not be restricted in the development of new weapons."

WORLD WAR I

The Hague Declaration of 1899 and the Hague Convention of 1907 forbade the use of "poison or poisonous weapons" in warfare, yet more than 124,000 tons of gas were produced by the end of World War I. The French were the first to use chemical weapons during the First World War, using tear gas. The German's first use of chemical weapons were shells containing xylyl bromide that were fired at the Russians near the town of Bolimów, Poland in January 1915. The first full-scale deployment of chemical warfare agents was during World War I, originating in the Second Battle of Ypres, April 22, 1915, when the Germans attacked French, Canadian and Algerian troops with chlorine gas. Deaths were light, though casualties relatively heavy. A total 50,965 tons of pulmonary, lachrymatory, and vesicant agents were deployed by both sides of the conflict, including chlorine, phosgene and mustard gas. Official figures declare about 1,176,500 non-fatal casualties and 85,000 fatalities directly caused by chemical warfare agents during the course of the war.

To this day unexploded WWI-era chemical ammunition is still frequently uncovered when the ground is dug in former battle or depot areas and continues to pose a threat to the civilian population in Belgium and France and less commonly in other countries. The French and Belgian governments have had to launch special programs for treating discovered ammunition.

After the war, most of the unused German chemical warfare agents were dumped into the Baltic Sea, a common disposal method among all the participants in several bodies of water. Over time, the salt water causes the shell casings to corrode, and mustard gas occasionally leaks from these containers and washes onto shore as a wax-like solid resembling ambergris. Even in this solidified form, the agent is active enough to cause severe contact burns to anybody coming into contact with it.

Interwar Years

After World War I chemical agents were occasionally used to subdue populations and suppress rebellion. Following the defeat of the Ottoman Empire in 1917, the Ottoman government collapsed completely, and the former empire was divided amongst the victorious powers in the Treaty of Sèvres. The British occupied Mesopotamia (present-day Iraq) and established a colonial government.

In 1920, the Arab and Kurdish people of Mesopotamia revolted against the British occupation, which cost the British dearly. As the Mesopotamian resistance gained strength, the British resorted to increasingly repressive measures. Much speculation was made about aerial bombardment of major cities with gas in Mesopotamia, with Winston Churchill, then-Secretary of State at the British War Office, arguing in favor of it.[13] In the 1920s generals reported that poison had never won a battle. The soldiers said they hated it and hated the gas masks. Only the chemists spoke out to say it was a good weapon.

In 1925, sixteen of the world's major nations signed the Geneva Protocol, thereby pledging never to use gas in warfare again. Notably, in the United States, the Protocol languished in the Senate until 1975, when it was finally ratified.

The Bolsheviks also employed poison gas in 1921 during the Tambov Rebellion. An order signed by military commanders Tukhachevsky and Vladimir Antonov-Ovseenko stipulated: *"The forests where the bandits are hiding are to be cleared by the use of poison gas. This must be carefully calculated, so that the layer of gas penetrates the forests and kills everyone hiding there."*

During the Rif War in Spanish Morocco in 1921–1927, combined Spanish and French forces dropped mustard gas bombs in an attempt to put down the Berber rebellion.

In 1935 Fascist Italy used mustard gas during the invasion of Ethiopia in the Second Italo-Abyssinian War. Ignoring the Geneva Protocol, which it signed seven years earlier, the Italian military dropped mustard gas in bombs, sprayed it from airplanes, and spread it in powdered form on the ground. 15,000 chemical casualties were reported, mostly from mustard gas.

WORLD WAR II

Despite article 171 of the Versailles Peace Treaty and a resolution adopted against Japan by the League of nations on 14 May 1938, the Imperial Japanese Army frequently used chemical weapons. Because of fear of retaliation however, those weapons were never used against Westerners but against other Asians judged "inferior" by the imperial propaganda. According to historians Yoshiaki Yoshimi and Seiya Matsuno, the chemical weapons were authorized by specific orders given by emperor Showa himself, transmitted by the chief of staff of the army. For example, the Emperor authorized the use of toxic gas on 375 separate occasions during the battle of Wuhan from August to October 1938. They were also profusely used during the invasion of Changde. Those orders were transmitted either by prince Kotohito Kan'in or general Hajime Sugiyama.

The Imperial Japanese Army used mustard gas and the recently-developed blister agent Lewisite against Chinese troops and guerrillas. Experiments involving chemical weapons were conducted on live prisoners (Unit 731 and Unit 516). The Japanese also carried chemical weapons as they swept through Southeast Asia towards Australia. Some of these items were captured and analyzed by the Allies. Greatly concerned, Australia covertly imported 1,000,000 chemical weapons from the United Kingdom from 1942 onwards 23 456 7. As of 2005, 60 years after the end of the war, canisters that were abandoned by Japan in their hasty retreat are still being dug up on construction sites, causing injuries and allegedly even deaths. Shortly after the end of World War I, Germany's General Staff enthusiastically pursued a recapture of their preeminent position in chemical warfare.

In 1923, Hans von Seeckt pointed the way, by suggesting that German poison gas research move in the direction of delivery by aircraft in support of mobile warfare. Also in 1923, at the behest of the German army, poison gas expert Dr. Hugo Stolzenberg negotiated with the USSR to built a huge chemical weapons plant at Trotsk, on the Volga river. Collaboration between Germany and the USSR in poison gas continued on and off through the 1920s. In 1924, German officers debated the use of poison gas versus non-lethal chemical weapons against civilians.

Even before World War II, chemical warfare was revolutionized by Nazi Germany's discovery of the nerve agents tabun (in 1937) and sarin (in 1938) by Gerhard Schrader, a chemist of IG Farben. IG Farben was Germany's premier poison gas manufacturer during World War I, so the weaponization of these agents can not be considered accidental. Both were turned over to the German Army Weapons Office prior to the outbreak of the war. The nerve agent soman was later discovered by Nobel Prize laureate Richard Kuhn and his collaborator Konrad Henkel at the Kaiser Wilhelm Institute for Medical Research in Heidelberg in spring of 1944. The Nazis developed and manufactured large quantities of several agents, but chemical warfare was not extensively used by either side. Chemical troops were set up (in Germany since 1934) and delivery technology was actively developed. Recovered Nazi documents suggest that German intelligence incorrectly thought that the Allies also knew of these compounds, interpreting their lack of mention in the Allies' scientific journals as evidence that information about them was being suppressed. Germany ultimately decided not to use the new nerve agents, fearing a potentially devastating Allied retaliatory nerve agent deployment. Fisk, Robert (December 30, 2000). "Poison gas from Germany". *Independent*.

William L. Shirer, in *The Rise and Fall of the Third Reich*, writes that the British high command considered the use of chemical weapons as a last-ditch defensive measure in the event of a Nazi invasion of Britain.

On the night of December 2, 1943, German Ju 88 bombers attacked the port of Bari in Southern Italy, sinking several American ships — among them SS *John Harvey*, which was carrying mustard gas intended for use in retaliation by the Allies if German forces initiated gas warfare. The presence of the gas was highly classified, and authorities ashore had no knowledge of it — which increased the number of fatalities, since physicians, who had no idea that they were dealing with the effects of mustard gas, prescribed treatment improper for those suffering from exposure and immersion.

The whole affair was kept secret at the time and for many years after the war (in the opinion of some, there was a deliberate and systematic cover-up). According to the U.S. military account, "Sixty-nine deaths were attributed in whole or in part to the mustard gas, most of them American merchant seamen" out of 628 mustard gas military casualties.[22] The large number of civilian casualties among the Italian population were not recorded. Part of the confusion and controversy derives from the fact that the German attack was highly destructive and lethal in itself, also apart from the accidental additional effects of the gas (it was nicknamed "The Little Pearl Harbor"), and attribution of the causes of death between the gas and other causes is far from easy.

Rick Atkinson, in his book *The Day of Battle,* describes the intelligence that prompted Allied leaders to deploy mustard gas to Italy. This included Italian intelligence that Adolf Hitler had threatened to use gas against Italy if she changed sides, and prisoner of war interrogations suggesting that preparations were being made to use a "new, egregiously potent gas" if the war turned decisively against Germany. Atkinson concludes that "No commander in 1943 could be cavalier about a manifest threat by Germany to use gas."

The Grand Mufti of Jerusalem, Amin al-Husayni, the senior Islamic religious authority of the Palestinian Arabs and ally of Adolf Hitler was accused of sponsoring an unsuccessful chemical warfare assault on the Jewish community in Tel-Aviv during 1944 by The David S. Wyman Institute for Holocaust Studies. Allegations suggest that five parachutists were supplied with maps of Tel Aviv, canisters of a German–manufactured "fine white powder," and instructions from the Mufti to dump chemicals into the Tel Aviv water system. District police commander Fayiz Bey Idrissi later recalled, "The laboratory report stated that each container held enough poison to kill 25,000 people, and there were at least ten containers."

COLD WAR

After World War II, the Allies recovered German artillery shells containing the three German nerve agents of the day (tabun, sarin, and soman), prompting further research into nerve agents by all of the former Allies. Although the threat of global thermonuclear war was foremost in the minds of most during the Cold War, both the Soviet and Western governments put enormous resources into developing chemical and biological weapons.

Developments by the Western Governments

In 1952, researchers in Porton Down, England, invented the VX nerve agent but soon abandoned the project. In 1958 the British government traded their VX technology with the United States in exchange for information on thermonuclear weapons; by 1961 the U.S. was producing large amounts of VX and performing its own nerve agent research. This research produced at least three more agents; the four agents (VE, VG, VM, VX) are collectively known as the "V-Series" class of nerve agents.

Also in 1952 the U.S. Army patented a process for the "Preparation of Toxic Ricin", publishing a method of producing this powerful toxin.

During the 1960s, the U.S. explored the use of anticholinergic deleriant incapacitating agents. One of these agents, assigned the weapon designation BZ, was allegedly used experimentally in the Vietnam War. These allegations inspired the 1990 fictional film *Jacob's Ladder*.

Between 1967 and 1968, the U.S. decided to dispose of obsolete chemical weapons in an operation called Operation CHASE, which stood for "cut holes and sink 'em." Several shiploads of chemical and conventional weapons were put aboard old Liberty ships and sunk at sea. In 1969, 23 U.S. servicemen and one U.S. civilian stationed in Okinawa, Japan, were exposed to low levels of the nerve agent sarin while repainting the depots' buildings. The weapons had been kept secret from Japan, sparking a furor in that country and an international incident. These munitions were moved in 1971 to Johnston Atoll under Operation Red Hat.

A UN working group began work on chemical disarmament in 1980. On April 4, 1984, U.S. President Ronald Reagan called for an international ban on chemical weapons. U.S. President George H.W. Bush and Soviet Union leader Mikhail Gorbachev signed a bilateral treaty on June 1, 1990, to end chemical weapon production and start destroying each of their nation's stockpiles. The multilateral Chemical Weapons Convention (CWC) was signed in 1993 and entered into force (EIF) in 1997.

In December, 2001, the United States Department of Health and Human Services, CDC, NIOSH, National Personal Protective Technology Laboratory (NPPTL), along with the U.S. Army Research, Development Engineering Command Edgewood Chemical/Biological Center (ECBC), and the U.S. Department of Commerce National Institute for Standards and Technology (NIST) published the first of six technical performance standards and test procedures designed to evaluate and certify respirators intended for use by civilian emergency responders to a chemical, biological, radiological, or nuclear weapon release, detonation, or terrorism incident.

To date NIOSH/NPPTL has published six new respirator performance standards based on a tiered approach that relies on traditional industrial respirator certification policy, next generation emergency response respirator performance requirements, and special live chemical warfare agent testing requirements of the classes of respirators identified to offer respiratory protection against chemical, biological, radiological, and nuclear (CBRN) agent inhalation hazards.

United States Senate Report

A 1994 United States Senate Report, entitled "Is military research hazardous to veterans health? Lessons spanning a half century," detailed the United States Department of Defense's practice of experimenting on animal and human subjects, often without their knowledge or consent. This included:

- Approximately 60,000 US military personnel were used as human subjects in the 1940s to test the chemical agents mustard gas and lewisite. "Mustard" section,
- Between the 1950s through the 1970s, at least 2,200 military personnel were subjected to various biological agents, referred to as Operation Whitecoat. Unlike most of the studies discussed in this report, Operation Whitecoat was truly voluntary. "Seventh" section,
- Between 1951 and 1969, Dugway Proving Ground was the site of testing for various chemical and biological agents, including an open air aerodynamic dissemination test in 1968 that accidentally killed, on neighboring farms, approximately 6,400 sheep by an unspecified nerve agent."Dugway" section,

DEVELOPMENTS BY THE SOVIET GOVERNMENT

Due to the secrecy of the Soviet Union's government, very little information was available about the direction and progress of the Soviet chemical weapons until relatively recently. After the fall of the Soviet Union, Russian chemist Vil Mirzayanov published articles revealing illegal chemical weapons experimentation in Russia. In 1993, Mirzayanov was imprisoned and fired from his job at the State Research Institute of Organic Chemistry and Technology, where he had worked for 26 years. In March 1994, after a major campaign by U.S. scientists on his behalf, Mirzayanov was released.

Among the information related by Vil Mirzayanov was the direction of Soviet research into the development of even more toxic nerve agents, which saw most of its success during the mid-1980s. Several highly toxic agents were developed during this period; the only unclassified information regarding these agents is that they are known in the open literature only as "Foliant" agents (named after the program under which they were developed) and by various code designations, such as A-230 and A-232.

According to Mirzayanov, the Soviets also developed agents that were safer to handle, leading to the development of the binary weapons, in which precursors for the nerve agents are mixed in a munition to produce the agent just prior to its use. Because the precursors are generally significantly less hazardous than the agents themselves, this technique makes handling and transporting the munitions a great deal simpler.

Additionally, precursors to the agents are usually much easier to stabilize than the agents themselves, so this technique also made it possible to increase the shelf life of the agents a great deal. During the 1980s and 1990s, binary versions of several Soviet agents were developed and are designated as "Novichok" agents (after the Russian word for "newcomer"). Together with Lev Fedorov, he told the secret Novichok story exposed in the newspaper Moscow News.

IRAN–IRAQ WAR

Chemical weapons which had been delivered to Saddam Hussein killed and injured numerous Iranians, and even Iraqis. According to Iraqi documents, assistance in developing chemical weapons was obtained from firms in many countries, including the United States, West Germany, the Netherlands, the United Kingdom, France and China.

The Iran–Iraq War began in 1980 when Iraq attacked Iran. Early in the conflict, Iraq began to employ mustard gas and tabun delivered by bombs dropped from airplanes; approximately 5% of all Iranian casualties are directly attributable to the use of these agents.

About 100,000 Iranian soldiers were victims of Iraq's chemical attacks. Many were hit by mustard gas. The official estimate does not include the civilian population contaminated in bordering towns or the children and relatives of veterans, many of whom have developed blood, lung and skin complications, according to the Organization for Veterans. Nerve gas agents killed about 20,000 Iranian soldiers immediately, according to official reports. Of the 80,000 survivors, some 5,000 seek medical treatment regularly and about 1,000 are still hospitalized with severe, chronic conditions. Iraq also targeted Iranian civilians with chemical weapons. Many thousands were killed in attacks on populations in villages and towns, as well as front-line hospitals. Many still suffer from the severe effects.

Despite the removal of Saddam and his regime by Coalition forces, there is deep resentment and anger in Iran that it was Western companies based in the Netherlands, West Germany, France, and the U.S. that helped Iraq develop its chemical weapons arsenal in the first place, and that the world did nothing to punish Iraq for its use of chemical weapons throughout the war.

Shortly before war ended in 1988, the Iraqi Kurdish village of Halabja was exposed to multiple chemical agents, killing about 5,000 of the town's 50,000 residents. After the incident, traces of mustard gas and the nerve agents sarin, tabun and VX were discovered. While it appears that Iraqi government forces are to blame, some debate continues over the question of whether Iraq was really the responsible party, and whether this was a deliberate or accidental act. (see *Halabja poison gas attack*)

During the Persian Gulf War in 1991, Coalition forces began a ground war in Iraq. Despite the fact that they did possess chemical weapons, Iraq did not use any chemical agents against coalition forces. The commander of the Allied Forces, Gen. H. Norman Schwarzkopf, suggested this may have been due to Iraqi fear of retaliation with nuclear weapons.

FALKLANDS WAR

Technically, the employment of tear gas by Argentine forces during the 1982 invasion of the Falkland Islands constitutes chemical warfare. However, the tear gas grenades were employed as nonlethal weapons to avoid British casualties. (In the hope that Britain would more easily accept the loss of territory in the conflict) The barrack buildings the weapons were used on proved to be deserted in any case.

TERRORISM

For many terrorist organizations, chemical weapons might be considered an ideal choice for a mode of attack, if they are available: they are cheap, relatively accessible, and easy to transport. A skilled chemist can readily synthesize most chemical agents if the precursors are available.

The earliest successful use of chemical agents in a non-combat setting was in 1946, motivated by a desire to obtain revenge on

Germans for the Holocaust. Three members of a Jewish group calling themselves Dahm Y'Israel Nokeam ("Avenging Israel's Blood") hid in a bakery in the Stalag 13 prison camp near Nuremberg, Germany, where several thousand SS troops were being detained. The three applied an arsenic-containing mixture to loaves of bread, sickening more than 2,000 prisoners, of whom more than 200 required hospitalization.

In July 1974, a group calling themselves the Aliens of America successfully firebombed the houses of a judge, two police commissioners, and one of the commissioner's cars, burned down two apartment buildings, and bombed the Pan Am Terminal at Los Angeles International Airport, killing three people and injuring eight. The organization, which turned out to be a single resident alien named Muharem Kurbegovic, claimed to have developed and possessed a supply of sarin, as well as 4 unique nerve agents named AA1, AA2, AA3, and AA4S. Although no agents were found at the time he was arrested in August 1974, he had reportedly acquired "all but one" of the ingredients required to produce a nerve agent. A search of his apartment turned up a variety of materials, including precursors for phosgene and a drum containing 25 pounds of sodium cyanide.

The first successful use of chemical agents by terrorists against a general civilian population was on March 20, 1995. Aum Shinrikyo, an apocalyptic group based in Japan that believed it necessary to destroy the planet, released sarin into the Tokyo subway system killing 12 and injuring over 5,000. The group had attempted biological and chemical attacks on at least 10 prior occasions, but managed to affect only cult members. The group did manage to successfully release sarin outside an apartment building in Matsumoto in June 1994; this use was directed at a few specific individuals living in the building and was not an attack on the general population.

In 2001, after carrying out the attacks in New York City on September 11, the organization Al Qaeda announced that they were attempting to acquire radiological, biological and chemical weapons. This threat was lent a great deal of credibility when a large archive of videotapes was obtained by the cable television network CNN in August 2002 showing, among other things, the killing of three dogs by an apparent nerve agent. On October 26, 2002, Russian special forces used a chemical agent (presumably KOLOKOL-1, an aerosolized fentanyl derivative), as a precursor to an assault on Chechen terrorists, ending the Moscow theater hostage crisis. All 42 of the terrorists and 120 of the hostages were killed during the raid; all but one hostage, who was killed, died from the effects of the agent.

In early 2007 multiple terrorist bombings have been reported in Iraq using chlorine gas. These attacks have wounded or sickened more than 350 people. Reportedly the bombers are affiliated with Al-Qaeda in Iraq and have used bombs of various sizes up to chlorine tanker trucks. United Nations Secretary-General Ban Ki-moon condemned the attacks as, "clearly intended to cause panic and instability in the country."

HISTORY OF CHEMICAL AND BIOLOGICAL WEAPONS

Ancient Times to the 19th Century

> The ancients practiced a variant of biological warfare not common today, an example of which is Hannibal's use of pots filled with snakes in a battle in 184 B.C. with the Navy of King Eumenes of Pergamon. The pots were hurled onto the decks of the ships, where they broke, forcing the Pergamene to fight against both the snakes and Hannibal's forces. (Hannibal won.)

The Romans used bees and hornets by catapaulting them at their enemies - to the extent that some historians blame this use for a shortage of hives during the latter years of the Roman Empire.

Evidence can be found for the existence of forms of chemical and biological warfare in ancient and classical times. The evidence for chemical and toxin warfare is the clearest. Solon of Athens is said to have used hellebore roots (a purgative) to poison the water in an aqueduct leading from the Pleistrus River around 590 B.C. during the siege of Cirrha.1 Writings of the Mohist sect in China dating from the Fourth Century B.C. tell of the use of ox-hide bellows to pump smoke from furnaces in which balls of mustard and other toxic vegetable matter were being burnt into tunnels being dug by a beseiging army to discourage the diggers. The use of a toxic cacodyl (arsenic trioxide) smoke is also mentioned in early Chinese manuscripts. Sparta used the toxic smoke generated by burning wood dipped in a mixture of tar and sulfur during one of its periodic wars with Athens.

Many early accounts portray outbreaks of disease in invading armies or among conquerers as divine intervention, perhaps an indication of the terrible effects of disease coupled with the lack of understanding of its causes. This confusion between divine and secular causes does make it difficult to distinguish when an outbreak was natural and when it was, so to speak, assisted. The misfortunes of the Philistines after they captured the Ark of the Covenant from the Israelites more than three thousand years ago (told of in I Samuel 4:10 to 6:12) provide an example. The Philistines conveyed the Ark to the city of Ashdod (the home of one of the rulers of the Philistines) and placed it beside the statue of their god, Dagon, in the temple there.

In short order, the statue of Dagon fell down (twice) and the population was afflicted with "tumors." The people of Ashdod then decided that the best thing to do was send the Ark, the arrival of which had seemed to precipitate their problems, to Gath (the capital city of a different Philistine ruler). No sooner did the Ark arrive in Gath than "the people of the city, both young and old, were afflicted with an outbreak of tumors". The people of Gath quickly decided that the best thing to do was to send the Ark to Ekron (the capital of yet another of the rulers of the Philistines), where we are told that, as the Ark was brought into the town, the people cried out that "They have brought the ark of the god of Israel around to us to kill us..." A plague of tumors also broke out in Ekron, and it is perhaps not surprising at this point that the Philistines decided to send the Ark back (or at least out of Philistine territory), accompanied by an unusual guilt offering (five gold tumors and five gold rats, the apparent association of the disease with the rats causing many modern scholars to suggest that the tumors were the buboes of bubonic plague).

The story as related suggests that the disease appeared by intention (albeit it not the intention of men), although the coincidence of the plague breaking out along the Ark's travels may, of course, also be explained by a natural outbreak, possibly carried from city to city by the escort of the Ark. Diseases that are considered major potential biological weapons in modern times have been known since antiquity. Smallpox is probably the oldest - it is thought to have existed at least since 10,000 B.C., when the first farming settlements were founded in northeastern Africa. It was first described in the West as the Great Plague of Athens in 430 B.C. The Great Plague would help lead to the downfall of Periclean Athens and thereby demonstrate the effectiveness of disease in influencing human events.

Anthrax and the plague have been implicated as the fifth plague of Egypt in the fifteenth century B.C.

It is difficult to be certain about the exact identifications as these diseases affect the soft tissues that decay rapidly after death.

Knowledge of the Chinese application of noxious smokes was not hidden from Europe. Formulas for "fire lances" in the Chinese style may be found in Biringucio's 1540 treatise Pirotechnia.

Based on surviving accounts, it is clear that the Chinese were the original masters of chemical warfare. It has been suggested that the pursuit of chemical weapons may have originated in the fumigation of dwellings to eliminate fleas (known to have been practiced by the Chinese as long ago as the Seventh century B.C.) or from the Chinese philosophical view that all matter faded into a more tenuous form, which lead them to take special interest in the study of vapors.

Whatever the case, Chinese writings contain literally hundreds of recipes for the production of poisonous or irritating smokes for use in war, and many accounts of their use. Thus we know of the arsenic-containing "soul-hunting fog" and the irritating "five-league fog" (formed from a slow-burning gunpowder to which a variety of ingredients, including the excrement of wolves, was added to produce an irritating smoke).

The use of a sort of riot control agent (finely divided lime dispersed into the air) is described in a Chinese account of the suppresion of a peasant revolt in 178 A.D. Nor did they neglect delivery systems - descriptions of weapons with such poetic names as the "poison fog magic smoke eruptor" may be found in the artillery manuals of the Chinese army.

ARMIS BELLA NON VENENIS GERI

"War is fought with weapons, not with poisons."

A declaration of Roman jurists.

The declaration above was made in reaction to the poisoning of wells by their enemies as the Romans tried to conquer the Germanic tribes. In the west, the use of toxic materials was generally viewed with mixed emotions and some disdain (especially when your enemies were doing it). There was also a strong tendency to keep useful knowledge, especially militarily useful knowledge, from wide dissemination. After all, if the knowledge was held by an individual, he could advance himself economically by retaining the secret and offering his services, while states tended to hold knowledge closely to prevent others from using it against them. Nor was there any philosophical reason to investigate vapors and smokes. This meant that, in contrast to China, where the study of chemicals including their military uses was widespread, in Europe the use of chemicals in battle (with the exception of incendiaries of various sorts and, of course, the use of wet vegetable matter to generate smoke screens) was usually the result of an independent local initiative, rather than the result of a logical building on prior experience. While there are many reports of the isolated use of chemical agents in individual battles or sieges, there was no general tradition of their use (again, with the exception of incendiaries and smoke).

The secret of Greek fire, the great incendiary weapon of the Byzantines, was held so closely that its composition has been lost to history. Those knowing the secret often responded to inquiries by saying that the formulation had been revealed by an angel to the Constantines, and that any attempt to discover it would provoke the vengeance of God.

It may even have been lost to the Byzantines - when Constantinople fell into the hands of the Crusaders in 1204 A.D., Greek fire was nowhere to be found.

Wells have been poisoned by various chemicals or by the simple expedient of dropping human and animal corpses into them for millenia. The Romans, despite the declaration of their Jurists, were not above poisoning wells when it suited them. For instance, when, after defeating Aristonicus in Asia Minor (Caria), the Romans were faced with guerrilla warfare by the remnants of Aristonicus' army, they poisoned the wells that the guerillas and their supporters used. The result was the end of the war leaving Rome in control of the region.

Poisoning of wells also occurred in the 19th Century during the American Civil War and in South Africa during the Boer War and continues to this day with the Kurdish Workers Party (PKK) of Turkey reported to have poisoned wells in Turkish Kurdistan in mid-1997.

As a result, the use of chemical agents in conflicts in Europe was fairly limited through the end of the Renaissance. There was, however, considerable attention paid to poisons. The Roman Emperors, in particular the Julio-Claudian emperors, would gain a attention for poisoning members of their families and others that displeased them. Nor was the practice limited to the Emperors - Juvenal would write of it in his Satires in a way that suggested that it had become a sort of status symbol among the upper classes.

A woman named Locusta would become particularly infamous as a poisoner in Rome; she would also be one of the first to systematically investigate the use of poisons with state (or, at least, Imperial) sponsorship. Convicted for a multiplicity of crimes under Claudius, she was sentenced to death, but the sentence had not been carried out when Claudius died (the delay in the execution of her sentence is said to have been arranged by Agippina, the wife of Claudius and mother of Nero, so that Locusta might prepare a poison for Agrippina to use on Claudius). Subsequently, the new Emperor Nero is supposed to have asked Locusta to prepare a potion for use on Nero's half-brother, Britannicus. Once Brittanicus died, Nero suspended the death penalty and made Locusta his advisor on poisons. In due course, he organized a school of poisoning where she could tutor others and conduct experiments aimed at determining how to poison and how to defend the person of the Emperor against poison. Surviving accounts indicate that many tests were performed on animals and that at least some tests were performed on convicted criminals. (Nero's preferred poison is said to have been cherry laurel water, which contains cyanide.)

Poisoning would decline in popularity after the Second Century, but it would never disappear, and would occasionaly enjoy a renewed popularity. For instance, the poisoning of individuals, usually with extracts of plants such as aconite or Belladonna, would be an accepted part of statecraft in the Renaissance, especially in Italy. The meticulous records of the Council of Ten of Venice, for instance, contain considerable information on how victims were selected, poisoners contracted, prices set, and payment made for the completion of the task (indicated by the notation *factum* in the records). And in France, the use of "inheritance powders" would be widespread until the Poison Affair brought scandal to the court of King Louis XIV and the formation of the burning court (*chambre ardente*) forced, if not an elimination of poisoning, at least a greater degree of circumspection in its practice. But, for the most part, chemical poisons were employed against individuals, usually for assasination, but sometimes in battle as when poisoned arrows were used, and not in a manner calculated to produce mass casualties in groups. However, accusations of attempts at mass poisonings, especially when seen as useful to make for political ends or during times of stress (as when Jewish communities bore the brunt of attacks for "poisoning" during the plague years) were commonly heard.

The use of poisoned projectiles (arrows and, later, bullets) has been widespread:

- *arrows dipped in blood mixed with manure (Scythian archers, ca. 400 B.C., and others)*
- *arrows dipped in curare (Amazonian Indians)*
- *arrows poisoned with batrachotoxin from frogs (Hawaiian Islanders)*
- *grenade shrapnel contaminated with botulinus toxin (WW II)*
- *ricin-filled pellets (Cold War)*

In 67 B.C., Pompey was leading a campaign against Mithridates, the king of Pontus. As his troops passed along the roads in the Trebizond region (in modern Turkey), the people of the region, the Heptakometes (who were allied with Mithridates), put out honey as tribute. The honey was a local product, and it contained acetylandromedol, a grayanotoxin (as the bees visited the local rhododendron species). This toxin produced nausea and hallucinations, and perhaps some deaths, among the troops who consumed it, and three maniples of the Roman army were attacked and destroyed while intoxicated.

The Roman commanders should have studied their classics more closely - Xenophon, in his Anabasis, tells of what happened when his troops consumed some of the local honeycomb in the same area in 401 B.C. - although he was luckier than Pompey, as the Persians who were pursuing him did not attack during the four days his army took to recover.

The use of toxic materials in war was not, however, completely absent.

In 187 B.C., the inhabitants of the town of Ambracia in Epirus dealt a setback to Roman soldiers seeking to tunnel under their walls:

Filling a huge jar with feathers, they put fire in it and attached a bronze cover perforated with numerous holes. After carrying the jar into the mine and turning its mouth toward the enemy, they inserted a bellows in the bottom, and by pumping the bellows vigorously they caused a tremendous amount of disagreeable smoke, such as feathers would naturally create, to pour forth, so that none of the Romans could endure it. As a result the Romans, despairing of success, made a truce and raised the siege.

Cassius Dio, Roman History, Book XIX

Roman commanders were not always on the receiving end, however. And they could be quite inventive.

Plutarch, in his Life of Sertorius, tells us of how that worthy soldier dealt with the Characitanes, who had a redoubt formed from a series of caves that seemed impregnable. Noticing that the prevailing winds blew from the North, and that the openings of most of the caves faced the North, Sertonius had his soldiers pile up a mound of earth in front of the redoubt. As the breeze began to blow, he had his soldiers turn the earth over, and his calvary ride over it, raising a cloud of somewhat caustic dust - what might be called a particulate aerosol today - that blew into the caves, blinding and choking the Characitanes. After two days of this treatment, they surrendered, "adding, by their defeat, not so much to the power of Sertorius, as to his renown, in proving that he was able to conquer places by art, which were impregnable by the force of arms".

The Romans also practiced anticrop chemical warfare, most famously after the defeat of Carthage, when the fields were sown with salt to help prevent resettlement.

The biggest use of chemicals in war in ancient times was in the area of flame weapons. The first use of fire in war probably followed shortly after the discovery of how to make it appear on command. By the Fourth Century B.C., a number of recipes existed for producing incendiary compositions, such as that provided by Aineias in his *On the Defense of Fortified Positions*, which comprised pitch, sulfur, tow, granulated frankincense, and pine sawdust in sacks which were set alight. Aineias cites as the virtue of this mixture the difficulty of extinguishing it; while the sulfur, at least, would also have produced toxic fumes, this does not seem to have be given any particular import. Indeed, although a variety of mixtures were used containing an astonishing number of additives, the major interest in additives seems to have been related to their perceived value in producing a hotter flame (for instance, salt appears to have been added commonly because it produced a visible orange flame), rather than for the production of choking or irritating smoke.

The most famous incendiary mixture is certainly the Greek fire of the Byzantine Empire (Greek fire is a modern name - the Byzantines called it "sea fire"; their Moslem enemies "Roman fire"). The secret of this weapon is supposed to have been brought to the Byzantines by a refugee from Moslem-occupied Syria named Kallinikos (or Callinicus; the name is almost certainly a pseudonym - it means handsome winner, possibly a reference to the reward received for his invention). There was nothing particularly new about liquid fire - oil-based incendiaries had been used for some time. But this material had the astonishing property of burning on (or at least, when in) contact with water. Using it in combination with a spray device that allowed them to direct it against enemy ships, the Byzantines were able to utterly defeat the Arab fleet at the battle of Kyzikos in 678 A.D. - a remarkable achievemnt given that the Arabs had previously defeated the Byzantine fleet on an almost regular basis. The Byzantines had developed a decisive weapon, and they held it closely to keep their enemies from learning how to use or counter it. Their success with developing tactics to use the weapon, and in keeping others from using it, would serve them in good stead - Greek fire would be cred with many more victories - against the Moslems again in 717-718 A.D. and later against Russian attacks in 941 A.D. and 1043 A.D. The Moslems did not leave many commentaries about the use of this weapon against them, but the Rus, after their attack in 941 A.D., recorded the observation that "The Greeks possess something like the lightning in the heavens, and they released it and burned us. For this reason we did not conquer them."

While they didn't have Greek fire, the Moslems were adept with other oil-based incendiaries. In a siege of Mecca in 683 A.D. the Umayyads used catapaults to hurl naphtha-based incendiary projectiles against the defenders, accidentally setting the cloth covering of the Ka'bah on fire. In 813 A.D., Baghdad would be essentially destroyed by naphtha barrels thrown into the city, and in 1167 A.D. Cairo was destroyed by naphtha pots and bombs to deny it to the Crusaders.

Distillation of petroleum, to produce fractions ("white water naphtha") suited for incendiaries, was also known. A workshop for producing incendiary grenades, complete with a distilling furnace and a gasoline storage container, dating from the first half of the thirteenth century has been found in Hama, in Syria. The Book of Horsemanship and the Art of War, written by Najm al-Din Ahda in 1285, even tells how to build rockets with fire bomb warheads.

The Moslems seem to have avoided the intentional use of toxic additives in their flame weapons, perhaps because of injunctions in the Koran against poisoning the air and water.

Even without intention, disease traveled with war, both because of the poor sanitation that results and because war meant travel. The Crusades and the Arab expansion are both considered to have contributed greatly to the spread of smallpox.

Even nominally peaceful travel was a boon to the spread of disease. As Europe began to explore and colonize Africa and the New World, new diseases ravaged explorers, settlers, and natives. Venereal disease, apparently reimported from the New World and Yellow fever from Africa killed many. It was the mosquito-ridden swamps of the coastal regions of West Africa that gave rise to the term "The White Man's Grave." On the other hand, smallpox introduced by a single victim in the Cortez expion killed 90% of the Aztecs of Mexico and in the far north the Eskimos were ravaged by epidemics of measles.

Forms of biological warfare were also practiced in the Middle Ages when the catapulting of diseased or putrefying corpses into castles became a feature of siege warfare.

The earliest incidence of this which is well reported comes from the siege of Thun l'Eveque in 1340 during the Hundred Years War, where siege engines were used to (in the words of Jean Froissart, a contempory chronicler) "...cast in deed horses, and beestes stynking..." with the result that, as "...the ayre was hote as in the myddes of somer: the stynke and ayre was so abomynable," that the defenders felt they had to consider surrender. While no disease appears to have actually broken out, the defenders did subsequently withdraw.

While it may be argued that the intent of casting decomposing carcasses was simply to harass (which it certainly did) or perhaps to have something to throw during a brief shortage of the more usual stones, it seems almost certain that the aims included at least a hope on the part of the attackers that the defenders would be stricken with disease. After all, one of the prevailing theories of disease transmission of the period was that disease were caused by "bad air".

Legend has it, probably not completely correctly, that the Black Death that killed a quarter of Europe's population in the 14th Century was spread by refugees from the siege of the Genoese settlement of Kaffa in the Crimea when the Tartars used the bodies of plague victims as ammunition during the siege. Whatever the truth of this allegation, there is no question that the plague had a dramatic effect on both sides. Plague was already raging through the ranks of the Tartars when they started casting the bodies over the walls. Plague then also broke out among the defenders, leaving them too weakened and demoralized to take advantage of the situation (according to one chronicle, only one in several thousand retained health enough to flee).

Although there was no widespread interest in chemical warfare in the Renaissance, as with so many other things, the indefatigable Leonardo da Vinci seems to have done some thinking on it. He offered a proposal to throw poison in the form of powder upon galleys. Chalk, fine sulfide of arsenic, and powdered verdegris may be thrown among enemy ships by means of small mangonels, and all those who, as they breathe, inhale the powder into their lungs will become asphyxiated.

He also considered the issue of protection. In his notes we find a description of a protective mask which would serve to shield the eyes, nose, and mouth (and lungs) of the user from dust and smoke - a more effective protection against the use of his toxic powders than the damp cloth originally proposed to protect their users from retaliation in kind.

As the Middle Ages gave way to the Rennaissance, gunpowder and firearms and artillery began to play a role in warfare and they came to dominate the battlefield. They eventually reduced the utility of castle walls to the point where even the most advanced fortifications could be reduced and broken by a choreographed set of maneuvers (provided that the defenders were unable to interrupt the dance). The rise of gunpowder weapons also produced an interest in chemistry, or at least in compounding mixtures for use in war.

Gunpowder-like mixtures - mixtures containing charcoal, sulfur, and saltpeter - were known in China by 1044 A.D., primarily as incendiaries, since the proportions were not right nor were they confined for a bang to occur. By 1232, the Chinese had developed rockets and a weapon called "Heaven-shaking Thunder", an iron bomb attached to a chain which could be lowered from the walls of a city to explode among attackers.

By 1280 A.D., at least the knowledge that adding saltpeter to incendiary compositions made them work better was widespread, as a book on war engines written by a Syrian, one al-Hasan ar-Rammah, appeared which included instructions for its use and purification. At about the same time, a number of compositions which would explode, at least weakly, are described in such tomes as the Liber Ignium (Book of Fire) of Marchus Graecus. Very soon after this time the use of these materials to throw projectiles from what came to be known as guns began. Initially, the projectiles were simply stones, but as time went by, a variety of new projectiles were developed. Explosive shells, with a powder charge ignited by a fuse lit just before firing it against the enemy appeared. And so did an incendiary shell that was called, in the proper terminolgy of artillery, the carcass, also called, by those that were not artillerymen (and some few who were), the stink pot. The carcass was a hollow metal shell with perforations for the emission of flame and flaming material, and, if one wonders why that would give rise to the sobriquot of stink pot, consider that the usual fill of a carcass included sulphur, tallow, rosin, turpentine, saltpeter, and antimony.

It was quickly observed that firing carcasses at an enemy could provide, at the least, considerable distraction as a result of the action of the fumes even when the primary goal of starting fires was not achieved. While never losing their primary function as starters of fires, a variety of fills were developed for carcasses that were intended to maximize the effects of the smoke. It is said that the gunners of the Imperial Artillery were particularly prone to the use of toxic fills during the Thirty Years War. The experience with noxious smokes would lead to speculation and some experimentation in the years to come.

The use of toxic projectiles was not viewed with total equanamity. German gunners were reported in 1650 to have pledged to "not construct any poisoned globes" and to "never employ them for the ruin and destruction of men, because the first inventors of our art thought such actions as unjust among themselves as unworthy of a man of heart and a real soldier."

*The use of chemical weapons did not proceed unchecked. On the 27th of August, 1675, the French and the Germans concluded the Strasbourg Agreement, which included an article banning the use of "perfidious and odious" toxic devices (poisoned bullets).*In 1672, during his siege of the city of Groningen, Christoph Bernhard van Galen, the Bishop of Münster, acquired a nickname, "Bommen Berend" (Bomber Berend), for his profligate use of artillery. Among the explosive and incendiary devices he used were some which had a fill including belladonna, intended to produce toxic fumes. The weapons failed to prove decisive, however, at least in part because they were used without taking wind direction into account. In the end, the Bishop had to withdraw, lifting the siege on the 28th of August, an event still celebrated in the city.

While the spread of gunpowder weapons had begun to get people thinking about the use of chemical technology in warfare, there was still little or no systematic thinking about, or use of, biological weapons. The possible impact of biological weapons had always been obvious to commanders who usually found disease to kill more men in the course of a campaign than did enemy fire. But the existing theories of how disease was transmitted, coupled with the lack of knowledge about how to direct a disease only against an enemy, made the use of disease as a weapon seem little more than a fantasy.

In 1714 an article in the *Philosophical Transactions* of the Royal Society would lay the groundwork for a change in how biological warfare was viewed. The article contained a description of a technique used by a physician, one Giacomo Pylarini of Smyrna, to confer some protection against smallpox. The technique, variolation, entailed taking some of the liquid from the pustules of a victim of a mild case of smallpox and rubbing it into a small scratch made on the person to be protected. Usually, the individual variolated would suffer a mild case of the disease and then be, on recovery, immune to further infection. There were two disadvantages - usually the case was mild, but not always and the variolated patient could spread the infection during the course of the (hopefully) mild case. However, the risk of death from variolation was felt to be acceptable when held against the problems that could result from uncontrolled infection (some estimates set mortality at 2-3%, which was still less than a tenth of the mortality rates seen without variolation), and conscientious quarantine would prevent problems with variolated patients spreading disease.

The Chinese produced immunity to smallpox using a technique in which a dried powder of the material from a pustule was blown into a persons nose beginning in the Eleventh century.

The practice of variolation was introduced by Circassian traders to the Ottoman Empire, where it was practiced beginning no later than 1670.

Variolation would become especially popular in England, although not as a result of the 1714 article in the *Philosophical Transactions* (nor, for that matter, as a result of a second article that appeared in 1716). Its popularity is attributed to the actions of Lady Mary Wortley Montague, who had had been afflicted by smallpox and who had lost her brother to it. Lady Montague was married to Lord Edward Wortley Montague, who was the ambassador to the Sublime Porte of the Ottomans in Istanbul. There, Lady Montague observed the practice of variolation as practiced by the Turks and, determined not to have her family suffer as she had, directed the surgeon of the Embassy to learn the technique and, in March, 1718, to variolate her five year old son. After her return to England, she determined to promote the technique, and had Maitland variolate her four year old daughter in the presence of several physicians, including the king's physician. The royal interest was aroused, and Charles Maitland was given leave to perform what came to be known as the Royal Experiment, in which he variolated six condemned prisoners (who had been promised full pardons if they survived). When the prisoners survived (and were pardoned), further experiments were done on charity children. The safety of the procedure being established by these experiments, two of the king's grandchildren, the daughters of the Princess of Wales, were treated on April 17, 1722. After this the practice of variolation spread like wildfire, reaching even the rural areas of England by the 1740s.

Across the sea, in England's American colonies, the practice was accepted even earlier than in England. In 1721, the Reverend Cotton Mather had prevailed on Dr. Boyston to variolate some 244 people in an effort to halt a smallpox epidemic in Boston. When the deaths were tallied (six of the variolated against 844 of 5980 infected who had not been variolated) it was clear that variolation was the way to protect against the smallpox. By the 1750's, no less a personage than Benjamin Franklin was promoting the technique.

The goals of the practitioners of variolation, were, of course, benign. Smallpox was a terrible disease, killing from 20% to 60% of those afflicted (with a disproportionate effect on those younger than 5 years old - in one outbreak in Berlin, 98% of the children who caught the disease died). A significant number of the survivors of the disease were left blind as a result of corneal infection. At the least, a survivor would bear the scars of the disease.

But the popularization of variolation was a two-edged sword. Those living in the countries where variolation was popular could be presumed to know:

- that smallpox in previously unexposed population could be devastating,
- that smallpox could reliably be produced by exposing healthy individuals to materials obtained from smallpox victims,
- that individuals seemed to become infected only once, and
- that the dangers of smallpox could be significantly reduced by the practice of variolation.

In other words, if you had an army that was made up mostly of individuals who had already been exposed to smallpox, either naturally or through variolation, you would stand to gain if smallpox were to be introduced to an opposing army which was not similarly protected. And, if you had access to smallpox cases, then you could acquire materials that would allow you to be sure that you could expose an actual or potential enemy to the disease.

To Sundries got to Replace in kind those which were taken from people in the Hospital to Convey the Smallpox to the Indians

In 1763, during the Pontiac Rebellion, Captain Simon Ecuyer, the commanding officer of Fort Pitt, found himself in a difficult situation. The indians were pressing hard - three forts in the Ohio River watershed had been lost, and many settlers had come to Fort Pitt seeking safety. The Fort was crowded and uncomfortable, and smallpox had appeared among the refugees. On June the twenty-third, two Delaware indians appeared at the fort, asking for a parley with Alexander McKee, the Assistant Deputy Superintendent of Induan Affairs for the Crown. On the twenty-fourth, Captain Ecuyer, along with a delegation including Mr. McKee and also William Trent (who was the commander of a local civilian militia) met with the indians, who professed a desire to avoid conflict and called for the evacuation of Fort Pitt, indicating that, if this were done quickly, it could be done peacefully. Captain

Ecuyer declined to evacuate the fort, claiming that three large armies were coming to his aid.

The indians indicated that for their part they hoped for friendship (a hope that the British, at least, were doubtless suspicious of, since the history of wars with the American indians had been full of spurious offers of safe conduct), and at this point, as Mr. Trent records in his journal 2, "Out of our regard for them, we gave them two Blankets and a Handkerchief out of the Small Pox Hospital. I hope it will have the desired effect" In the event, the Delaware were to suffer severely from an epidemic of smallpox, although the infected materials may have been only one of several sources of infection.

The natives of the New World also used chemical and biological weapons. In South America, the smoke from burning chili peppers was used boh in local conflicts and against the Portuguese as a sort of tear gas, while in the North, there are several incidents that suggest that the Indians may also have tried to initiate smallpox outbreaks among the European soldiers and settlers.

The documentation that survives, including the ledgers (which had to be approved by British authorities up to the level of General Gage, the Commander-in-Chief of British forces in America), makes it clear that this action was not seen as something extraordinary, or an action taken under unusual circumstances by a local commander. In fact, letters survive from a correspondence in July of 1763 between General Sir Jeffery Amherst (then the British Commander-in-Chief) and Colonel Henry Bouquet, who was leading a relief force to Ft. Pitt, that the use of smallpox as a weapon against the indians was receiving general consideration. In a letter which seems to have been written shortly after he learned that smallpox had broken out at the fort, Genral Amherst suggests asks Colonel Bouqet "Could it not be contrived to send the Small Pox among those disaffected tribes of Indians?" On the thirteenth of July, Colonel Bouqet, on his way to Ft. Pitt, replies "I will try to inoculate the...with some blankets that may fall in their hands, and take care not to get the disease myself." This independent mirroring of the use of the smallpox, down to the method of delivering the infectious particles, makes it seem likely that the use of smallpox had received some attention in military circles prior to the event. Indeed, there is some evidence, although none is conclusive, that this was not the first time smallpox was employed against the indians. Certainly the inclusion of the line item noted above in his accounts makes it clear that Captain Ecuyer was not concerned that there would be any censure for his actions.

Fort Pitt was not the only time that informed attempts at biological warfare were made in the New World in the second half of the 1700s, simply the best documented one. Among the most significant would be those by the British during the American Revolution, not for their effect, but for the response they provoked.

In April of 1775, the British in Boston found themselves facing both the Continental Army and a smallpox epidemic. Reasonably enough, they began to variolate their troops. Less reasonably, they began to variolate civilians fleeing the city. While there is no documentation surviving that demonstrates the British intention in this instance, it was well known that those variolated became infectious. General Washington, the commander of the Continental Army, wrote that he believed that "...the enemy intended spreading the Small pox amongst us". He had been encouraged in this belief by the stories of British deserters, about which he was skeptical until an outbreak of the disease among the evcacuees convinced him. He delayed his attack, regarding the smallpox in Boston as "a weapon of Defence" being used by the British. When it was finally evacuated by the British, Washington advanced with great care, fearing the exposure of his troops to the disease.

Washington had himself been a victim of smallpox, and in 1776 saw his attack on Quebec fail in large part because many soldiers were affected by an outbreak of smallpox (which many believed, albeit with small evidence, to have been the work of the British, judging by the testimony given to a Congressional hearing on the attack). He knew what the disease could do, and had come to regard it as "the greatest enemy of the Continental Army". But he also knew what to do - variolate. On January 6, 1777 he issued to Dr. William Shippen, Jr., Director General of the Hospitals and Physician in Chief to the Army, an order to inoculate all the Continental troops and the new recruits, also advising him to keep "the matter as secret as possible". danger was past.

Surviving letters indicate at least the hope of causing infection among the Rebels on several other occasions. One of the most significant is that of General Alexander Leslie, who notes in a missive directed to General Cornwallis dated July 13, 1781 that more than "700 Negroes are come down the river in the Small Pox." and that he intends to "distribute them about the Rebell plantations."

The idea of speading smallpox to the rebels was discussed openly. Robert Donkin's 1777 book, "Military Collections and Remarks", published in New York, contains a footnote picturesquely suggesting that the rebellious Americans would disband in fear if the British should " Dip arrows in matter of smallpox and twang them at the American rebels, in order to inoculate them."

For the first time in history, measures had been taken to secure an army against, not only the very real risk of natural infection, but also against the risk of a deliberate biological attack. And they worked - after 1777 the Continental Army was never hampered by smallpox in its operations again.

3

Chemical Warfare in World War I

INTRODUCTION

The combat experience of World War I provided the U.S. Army with its first significant exposure to chemical warfare. The purpose of this paper is to show how the Army prepared for this kind of warfare and how soldiers in the American Expeditionary Forces (AEF), from generals to doughboys, adapted or failed to adapt to fighting a war in which chemical weapons played a prominent role. Because no one AEF division experienced every facet of gas warfare, the study will examine information pertaining to many units in order to give a more complete picture of the phenomenon.

In World War I terms, chemical warfare included not only gas, but liquid flammable material, thermite, and smoke (all of which are relevant to the modern battlefield). This study will deal only with what participants referred to as "chemicals ... gases," or "war gases."

These included real gases such as phosgene and chlorine, and also weapons that, while referred to as gases, were in fact vaporized liquids (mustard gas, for example) or finely ground solids. In this study the terms "chemical agent" and "gas" will be used interchangeably. Smoke will be discussed, but only as a ruse for gas; liquid flame and thermite will not be covered. Because most of the U.S. experience was on the Western Front, that theater of the war will receive detailed treatment.

Despite technological advances in chemical warfare since 1918, many lessons learned on the battlefields of World War I are valid for study today, if only because America's principal antagonist in world affairs, the Soviet Union, appears to be quite willing to employ chemical agents on today's battlefield. During the decade of the 1970s persistent accounts of the use of chemical agents by the Russians and their clients caused the U.S. government to pay closer attention to the problem of chemical warfare. Soviet offensive equipment captured by the Israelis in the 1973 October War contained filtration systems for survival on a chemical or biological battlefield. Reports from Laos about Vietnamese using a chemical agent called "Yellow Rain" on mountain tribesmen prompted a policy review by U.S. government officials. In December, 1979, the Soviet invasion of Afghanistan, with subsequent reports from Afghan refugees that the invaders were using gas during combat operations, again forced the U.S. Army to reassess its chemical warfare doctrine.

U.S. intelligence estimates indicate that the Russians have between 70,000 and 100,000 chemical warfare troops. Every Soviet line regiment has a Chemical Defense Company. Present Soviet chemical delivery systems include artillery, mortars, multiple rocket launchers, bombs, air spray, and land mines. The blood, blister, and nerve agents in the Russian chemical arsenal include mustard gas (a blister agent) and phosgene (a lung injurant) two of the most effective agents used in World War I.

There is an abundance of material available for a study of gas warfare during World War 1. Sources include unit reports, the published and unpublished diaries of participants, books written by chemical officers during the interwar period, and a number of secondary historical works of more recent origin. Also, I conducted several interviews with veterans of the First World War to obtain as accurate a picture as possible of what it was like for an AEF doughboy to train for, and to live, work, and fight in, a chemical environment. During the war the newly created Chemical Warfare Service (CWS)* did its best to record its activities and report on the use of chemicals. I relied extensively on these records.

A number of agencies provided a great deal of assistance to me in the preparation of this paper, and I would like to acknowledge the staffs of the following institutions: the Technical Library, Chemical Systems Laboratory, Edgewood Area, Aberdeen Proving Ground;, U.S. Army Chemical Center and School, Fort McClellan, Alabama; National Archives, Washington, D.C.; Military History Institute, Carlisle Barracks, Pennsylvania; and Combined Arms Research Library, U.S. Army Command and General Staff College, Fort Leavenworth, Kansas. I especially want to thank members of the 1st Gas Regiment Association for graciously consenting to be interviewed, and Lt. Col. Charles M. Wurm, Chemical Corps, CACDA, Fort Leavenworth, for providing me with a great amount of technical information and advice.

THE INTRODUCTION OF GAS WARFARE IN WORLD WAR I

Of all the weapons employed in World War I, none stimulated public revulsion more than poison gas. The abhorrence of chemical warfare lingered long after the Armistice of 11 November 1918. Gas victims continually reminded the general public of the effect of chemical weapons, as illustrated by the often repeated story of a veteran's coughing fit being explained by a tap on the chest and an apologetic, "Gas you know."

The employment of chemical agents in war, however, did not begin with World War I. The earliest recorded incident occurred in the fifth century B.C. during one of a series of wars between Athens and Sparta.*[1] Over the centuries that followed, combatants on several occasions engaged in rudimentary forms of chemical warfare on the battlefield. If by the end of the nineteenth century the use of poison gas was still by far the exception and not the rule in war, there were in all the great powers a number of men who foresaw its widespread use should a general conflagration engulf Europe.

A concern with poison gas manifested itself at the Hague Conference of 1899. One of the agenda items dealt with prohibiting the use of shells filled with asphyxiating gas. The proposed ban eventually passed with one dissenting vote, that of the American representative, Naval Capt. Alfred T. Mahan, who declared that "it was illogical and not demonstrably humane to be tender about asphyxiating men with gas, when all were prepared to admit that it was allowable to blow the bottom out of an ironclad at midnight, throwing four or five hundred men into the sea, to be choked by water, with scarcely the remotest chance of escape." Secretary of State John Hay, in his instructions to Mahan, argued that the inventiveness of Americans should not be restricted in the development of new weapons. For Hay it made no sense for the United States to deprive itself of the ability to use, at some later date, a weapon that might prove to be more humane and effective than anything then present in the American arsenal.

The Hague Conference declaration did not prevent some nations from discussing the use of chemical weapons, and at least one country, France, experimented publicly with gas. The French Army tested a grenade filled with ethyl bromoacetate, a nontoxic tear, or lachrymatory, agent developed for use in the suppression of small-arms fire from the concrete casements then prevalent in the permanent fortifications that dotted Western Europe. In 1912, French police used 26-mm grenades filled with this agent to capture a notorious gang of Parisian bank robbers. The Germans, unlike the French, did not experiment with chemical agents for military use as such, but at the outbreak of World War I, Germany's highly advanced dye industry gave it a sophisticated technological base from which to develop weapons of this nature.

When war erupted in August, 1914, everyone from private citizens to the leaders of the belligerent countries shared a common belief that the economies of the European nations would neither survive nor support a lengthy war. As a result, the war plans of two key protagonists, Germany and France, called for a quick, decisive offensive against one another. Kaiser Wilhelm II of Germany assured his troops that they would be "home before the leaves fall." It was not to be. By the end of 1914, the armies on the Western Front were locked in a deadly form of trench warfare (Map 1), sustained by the very industrialized economies that, because of their complexity and interdependency, had been thought unable to withstand a long war.

Unwilling to accept the indecisiveness of trench warfare, army staffs on both sides pondered ways to break the deadlock and return to open or maneuver warfare. Alternatives were proposed, some strategic, others tactical. The British, for example, sought a strategic solution by a seaborne assault against Turkey, an ally of Germany. This attack at Gallipoli in 1915 sought to open the Dardanelles as the first step toward linking up with. Russia and forcing Turkey out of the war. For a variety of reasons, the plan failed, and the deadlock on the Western Front continued.

As their attack at Gallipoli tottered to defeat, the British looked to the application of tactical innovation at Neuve-Chapelle to break the stalemate. On 10 March 1915 British artillery, instead of firing a lengthy bombardment prior to an attack, as doctrine dictated, let loose a brief but intense barrage on a relatively narrow German trench frontage. The fire was then shifted to the German rear in order to create a lethal steel curtain that would block reinforcements. To the surprise of everyone, the British infantry quickly overran the German forward positions. The attack failed, though, primarily because the high command, viewing it as an experiment, did not have sufficient reserves available to exploit a breakthrough.

Germany also searched for ways to break the deadlock and decided on a solution involving gas. Early in the war the Germans kept a wary eye out for indications that the French were using their 26-mm gas grenades. Apparently, in August, 1914, France did use this chemical weapon, but in open areas where the gas quickly dispersed with no noticeable effect on the enemy. The French soon discarded the grenades as worthless. At this same time, stories were appearing in Allied newspapers about a new French liquid explosive, turpinite. While claiming that this substance gave off lethal fumes, the articles failed to explain that the gas reached a deadly concentration only in confined spaces. Still, the Germans were apprehensive and became alarmed by the deaths of a number of soldiers asphyxiated during a French bombardment, even though a medical team rushed to the scene concluded that the men died not from poison gas, but from inhaling carbon monoxide fumes while huddled in their dugout.

In any event such newspaper stories and front-line experiences may have spurred the development of war gases by German scientists. Contributing to that effort, chemistry professor Walter Nernst suggested partially replacing the TNT in a 105-mm shrapnel shell with dianisidine chlorosulphonate, an agent known to cause irritation of the mucous membrane. The new filling would serve two purposes: it would conserve TNT and act as a chemical weapon. The German High Command accepted this new weapon, although it is uncertain which of the two purposes it initially considered more important. On 27 October 1914, 3,000 of these shells fell on British troops near Neuve-Chapelle. The soldiers suffered no ill effects and never suspected they were under chemical attack. The Germans continued to experiment with gas because they were convinced the idea had merit and because intelligence sources could not determine what effect the shells had had at Neuve-Chapelle. This lack of information on the effects of gas attacks was a common occurrence throughout the war.

The Neuve-Chapelle experiment increased the German High Command's interest in gas warfare. The German General Staff asked the Kaiser Wilhelm Institute for Physical Chemistry and Electrochemistry in Berlin to investigate the possibility of using a more effective agent. The only guideline provided by the military was that the Hague declaration of 1899, banning projectiles used exclusively for delivering poison gases, had to be circumvented. Adhering to the letter if not the spirit of the ban, the Germans devised a gas shell that also contained an explosive charge for producing a shrapnel effect. The Professor von Tappan who designed the shell also solved two technical problems related to emplacing chemicals in an artillery projectile. First, he stabilized the liquid within a shell casing in order to reduce its tumbling in flight, thereby increasing the shell's accuracy and range. Second, to ensure that two extremely reactive chemical substances did not accidently combine in the shell casing, von Tappan developed a special shell, designated the T-shell by the German Army in his honor. The T-shell was a standard 15-cm howitzer round that contained seven pounds of xylyl bromide and a burster charge for a splinter effect. A lead lining prevented contact between the burster charge and the chemical payload.

The German High Command decided to use the first T-shells on the Eastern Front. On 31 January 1915, over 18,000 shells were fired at Russian positions at Bolimov. German officers, confident that their new weapon would neutralize the enemy positions, were surprised when their attack was repulsed with severe casualties. The shelling had had little or no effect on the Russians because cold temperatures had prevented vaporization of the xylyl bromide.

To find a more effective means of employing gas on the battlefield, the German High Command turned to an assistant of von Tappan, Professor Fritz Haber. Haber, a reservist, had shown marked enthusiasm for the potential value of chemicals as weapons. Believing that T-shells did not provide a high enough concentration of chemicals to produce enemy casualties, he suggested the use of large commercial gas cylinders as a delivery system. Cylinders could deliver large amounts of gas and, like the T-shell, did not technically violate the Hague ban on projectiles. Haber also recommended the use of chlorine as an agent because it was commercially produced and readily available in large quantities. Chlorine also satisfied the requirements for military application: it was lethal immediately effective, nonpersistent, and volatile. It was also dense enough to resist dilution in a moderate wind.

Haber's gas cylinder project received the approval of the Chief of the German General Staff, General Erich von Falkenhayn, who had the professor appointed Head of the Chemical Warfare Department in the Prussian Ministry of War. The high command selected the front of the Fourth Army facing the French salient at Ypres as the location for an experimental attack. Pioneer Regiment 35 was designated to conduct the gas attack. Haber, assigned as a "chemico-technical advisor," assisted Colonel Peterson, the regimental commander, and instructed the troops on the emplacement and use of gas cylinders. By 10 March 1915 the Regiment, with the assistance of infantry labor, had emplaced 1,600 large and 4,130 small cylinders containing a total of 168 tons of chlorine. Then, for one month, the Pioneer troops sat and waited for the winds to shift westerly toward the enemy trenches in the Ypres salient. Only then could they safely unleash the chemicals by opening the cylinder valves.

Late in the afternoon of 22 April 1915, a setting sun cast long shadows over the battle-scarred terrain around the medieval Belgium city of Ypres. In the distance the faint sound of large-caliber guns could be heard. Birds fluttered and swooped, seeking places to roost on the practically treeless landscape. Suddenly, at

1724, three flares rose from an observation balloon over the German lines and burst against the darkening eastern sky. German artillery commenced a fierce bombardment that landed to the rear of the French and British lines in the Ypres sector. Then, at 1800, an eerie silence fell over the area.

Peering across the battlefield, men of two French divisions, the 87th Territorial and the 45th Algerian, saw blue-white wisps of haze rising from the German trenches. The haze swirled about, gathered in a cloud that slowly turned yellow-green and began to drift across the terrain at a height of up to six feet. As the cioud drifted, it settled into every depression in the landscape. Finally, the gentle north!.northeasterly wind brought it spilling into the French trenches, silently enveloping the occupants in a misty, deadly embrace.

To the north and southwest of the now mist-enshruded French positions, British and Canadian troops looked into the haze and, to their amazement, saw soldiers, many without weapons, emerge from the cloud, "running wildly, and in confusion" toward positions to the rear. Terror-stricken Algerians ran by the startled Dominion troops, coughing And clutching their throats. Moments later French soldiers staggered by, "blinded, coughing, chests heaving, faces an ugly purple color, lips speechless with agony." One by one, the guns of the French artillery batteries in the sector stoppedfiring, and the two French divisions collapsed. The Ypres front now had a gap over four-miles wide containing hundreds of men in a "comatose or dying condition." After half an hour, German troops, equipped with cotton wadding tied over their faces-a primitive form of protective mask-cautiously advanced into the breech created by the discharge of chlorine gas.

Following the initial shock and surprise, Allied commanders began to bring forward reserve troops and to move units from the left and right flank into the gap. The Germans advanced four and one-half miles - until they encountered the ragged edge of a hurriedly organized defensive line (Map 2). The First Canadian Division and assorted French troops manned the line in scattered, hastily prepared positions 1,000 to 3,000 yards apart. This improvised defense, together with the fact that the Germans had lost some of their combat edge during the month-long wait for favorable winds, finally slowed and then halted the attack. As for the German troops who reached their initial objective, they had only the most primitive protective equipment. When they saw the havoc their own gas had wrought, they had no wish to proceed any farther that night.

Two days later, during which time the British and French brought reinforcements into the area, the Germans discharged more gas. Although they did so again four more times throughout May, the element of surprise had been lost. The British and French troops were now equipped with their own primitive masks, and although the defenders suffered severe losses (over 5,900 casualties-nearly double the number of casualties for the attackers), the Germans could gain no more than a few hundred yards beyond the forward limit of their first attack. The German High Command, surprised as its opponents at the success of the new weapon, had no reserves to exploit a possible success. Thus, one of the war's greatest tactical surprises was dissipated on what amounted to an experimental attack with limited objectives.

With the battle front at Ypres now stabilized, the British and French had to decide whether or not retaliate in kind. Faced with the Germans' obvious technological advantage, the Allies at first hesitated to retaliate for fear of inviting the expansion of gas warfare. But when, the British Expeditionary Force commander reported that a lack of an offensive gas capability would seriously impair the morale of his troops, the British cabinet gave its approval to use chemical agents. The French government soon followed suit for basically the same reason.

On 24 September 1915, at 0550 near Loos, Belgium, the British launched the Allies' first attack supported by gas. It had taken them five frantic months to reach a point at which a large-scale gas attack was feasible. During that period, several "Special Companies" of Royal Engineers had been trained in the emplacement and discharge of gas cylinders. Unlike the Germans, the British decided to conduct their gas attack on a wide frontage. This necessitated the deployment of the cylinders clustered in batteries along the front rather than spaced far apart in one continuous line. To accomplish this, the British constructed galleries in front of the first-line trenches and positioned in them 5,500 cylinders containing 150 tons of chlorine. The frontage was too wide to saturate all of it with gas, so the British decided to utilize smoke candles to simulate gas in those areas where the agent could not be used. By alternating the discharges of gas and smoke, the gas attack could be prolonged over forty minutes. This planned smoke screen was the first used during the war.

Fortune did not favor this first British gas attack. During the evening prior to the attack, the winds died. The following morning the British commander, Gen. Sir Douglas Haig, made a controversial decision to proceed with the attack despite uncertainty as to whether or not the slight breeze that rose in the morning would continue to blow toward the German lines. On the right flank, the gentle winds brought the gas and smoke mixture into the German trench system. There, the mild wind worked to the British advantage, for the cloud lingered and did not dissipate. On the left flank, however, not only did the winds fail, but in several positions the gas wafted back into the British trenches, engulfing the troops waiting to attack.

The Germans were taken by surprise. Their troops had little awareness of the danger posed by gas and were not sufficiently trained in defensive measures. The war diary of the German Sixth Army, the unit that bore the brunt of the attack, described the results. The gas in some instances caused little but momentary confusion, while in other cases entire units lost their ability to resist the follow-up British infantry attack. The German mask, which was essentially the same one used at Ypres, broke down as the gas lingered. The chlorine also caused rifles, machine guns, and even artillery breechblocks to jam. The most effective result of the gas was that it rendered German officers and noncommissioned officers (NCOs) incapable of shouting commands loud enough to be heard through their masks. The dense clouds of smoke and gas also shrouded positions and precluded officers and NCOs from leading by example.

In spite of some British gains, the attack fell short of the desired results for three reasons. The first was the decision to proceed with the attack despite the unfavorable wind conditions. Second, the British artillery was hampered in providing support because it lacked sufficient shells. Third, there were no reserve divisions to exploit a breakthrough. In his report, the British Commander-in-Chief, Sir John French, acknowledged that, although the attack failed to penetrate the German lines, the "gas attack met with marked success, and produced a demoralizing effect in some of its opposing units." More important, the major belligerents had accepted and expanded the use of chemicals as weapons of war.

The ensuing chemical war proved to be one of experimentation with gases and with defensive add offensive equipment. As tactical doctrine and training evolved to reflect technological changes, the availability of gases and the imagination of commanders became the only limits to the employment of this new weapon.

THE EUROPEANS FACE CHEMICALS ON THE BATTLEFIELD, 1915-1918

During World War I chemists on both sides investigated over 3,000 chemical substances for potential use as weapons. Of these, only thirty agents were used in combat, and only about a dozen achieved the desired military results (Table 1). Most armies grouped war gases according to their physiological effects, that is their effects on the human body.[1]

One category, lachrymators, was composed of tear gases such as xylyl bromide, an agent that primarily affected the eyes but in large concentrations could also damage the respiratory system. Asphyxiators, such as phosgene, chloropicrin, and chlorine, were in another category. These gases caused fluid to enter the lungs, thereby preventing oxygen from reaching the blood. Toxic gases, yet another category, passed through the lungs to the blood, preventing the circulation and release of oxygen throughout the body. Hydrogen cyanide ("Vincennite" to the French) was one of the least effective toxic agents. Sternutators, such as diphenylchlorarsine, were a type of respiratory irritant composed of a very fine dust that caused sneezing, nausea, and vomiting. Some sternutators were systemic poisons that had a delayed toxic effect on the body. The final category held the greatest casualty producer-a vesicant or blister agent that, because of its peculiar odor, the British and later the Americans commonly referred to as "mustard gas."

In 1917 the Germans first used mustard against the Allies at Ypres. This was the only persistent agent used during World War I and had effects similar to those produced by a combination of lachrymatory, asphyxiator, and systemic poisons. Although called mustard gas, this chemical was not a gas, but rather a volatile liquid that, several hours after contact with the skin, would cause severe bums and blisters. The introduction of Yellow Cross caught the Allies completely by surprise. During the first attack, British infantry saw the gas shells explode, but were unable to "see, smell or taste any agent, nor feel any immediate effects." The soldiers concluded that the Germans were trying to trick them and did not put on their masks. After several hours, to the consternation of officers and medics, the troops began to complain of pain in their eyes, throats, and lungs. Later, blisters appeared on the exposed skin of the British soldiers. The German use of Yellow Cross caused British gas casualties, which had been declining, to increase markedly. Because of its ability to produce large numbers of casualties, mustard was soon being referred to as the "King" of the war gases.

The major combatants realized that the employment of gas called for specially trained troops and, accordingly, formed offensive gas units. Because of the need to emplace gas cylinders, pioneer or engineer troops usually provided the cadre of these special units. The Germans converted two pioneer regiments, the 35th and 36th, into gas units consisting of three battalions each. The regiments would deploy by companies, according to the size of the front of the attack. In addition to these units, the Germans organized a gas mortar (Minenwerfen) battalion. The Austro-Hungarians followed the German model and created their own special gas units.

As early as July, 1915, the French and British organized gas companies called "Special" by the British and "Z" for *gaz* (gas) by the French; both employed engineer troops as cadre. By 1917 the British had expanded their original four companies to twenty-one and had organized them as a Special Brigade. The French eventually created the 31st, 32nd, and 33rd gas battalions composed of three companies each. The Russians organized gas units and called them "Gas Detachments of the Chemical Department," with one detachment assigned to each Russian Army, a total of thirteen.

In addition to developing gas units and chemical agents, a constant search continued for efficient delivery systems. The cylinders used in the first gas attack at Ypres in 1915 were the major component of a cumbersome, immobile system, It usually took several days of intensive labor, with infantry providing most of the muscle, to emplace the cylinders for a cloud attack (Figure 1). One can gain an indication of the difficulty of the task by noting that as many as 12,000 cylinders, each weighing over 100 pounds, were sometimes needed for a single operation. Once emplaced, the cylinders were dangerously exposed to enemy high explosive shells and easily damaged, Cylinder discharges always depended on favorable weather conditions.

Despite these problems, the British relied on cylinders as a delivery method until the end of the war. They normally used seven to eight cylinders in a section, six sections to a Special Brigade company. Sixteen companies could produce a gas wave or cloud that covered a 24,000-meter front. Several factors influenced the British decision to continue using cylinders. First, the prevailing winds favored Allied gas clouds. Second, the British suffered from a chronic shortage of shells and were reluctant to convert the production of high explosive shells to the production of gas shells. Third, British intelligence reports indicated a dense cloud attack was effective in producing mass casualties. On 26 October 1917, Brig. Gen. Charles H. Foulkes, Commander of the British Special Brigade, reviewed intelligence reports indicating that British cloud attacks created significant German casualties as far back as thirty kilometers from, the front-line trenchm Foulkes proposed that the Special Brigade use what he termed "retired cylinder attacks," in which. a large number of cylinders would be emplaced behind British lines rather than in the front lines or forward of the trenches.

Because the Special Brigade companies could assemble a greater number of cylinders in a relatively small area without the interference of enemy small arms or shell fire, this method allowed for a significantly greater concentration of gas released at one point.

The British improved this tactic by conducting what they called "beam attacks." These attacks called for placing numerous cylinders on narrowgauge tram cars that troops pushed forward to positions just behind the front trenches. After the cylinders were opened, the resulting gas concentration became so dense that friendly troops had to be evacuated from the path of the gas "beam." On 24 May 1918 the British launched their first beam attack. This and similiar attacks, General Foulkes claimed, caused the Germans considerable anxiety, for they could not determine how and where the dense clouds originated. The beam attacks were especially deadly when launched from six or more separate railheads and when the individual clouds merged behind German lines. Prisoners taken from the German 9th Uhlan Regiment reported that one such attack caused 500 casualties in the neighboring 1st Landwehr Regiment, which, as a. result of the attack, had to be withdrawn from the line. According to the British, the effectiveness of the improved cloud attacks, with their increased density, continued to frustrate the German Army.

The Germans, for their part, arranged their cylinders so that twenty formed a battery. Fifty such batteries were required to saturate one kilometer of front line with gas. The lack of favorable prevailing winds, however, soon forced the Germans to abandon the cloud attack. On 8 August 1916, they launched their last cylinder attack at Wieltje, near the scene of the first discharge at Ypres.

Because the prevailing winds in Western Europe blew from west to east, the German Army began to place increasing reliance on gas-filled shells that detonated beyond Allied lines and whose contents could then drift back over enemy trenches. Gas shells could be fired. from standard artillery pieces with no extensive adaptation for gas employment. Although weather conditions still remained a factor, no longer did the Germans have to wait for the wind to change to a westerly direction. Now artillery could fire upward of the target, saturating it with gas and achieving the same effect as cylinders. Shells also offered an element of surprise not available with cloud attacks. Finally, gas shells proved more advantageous than high explosive rounds because the former did not have to score direct hits on a target to neutralize it. To avoid confusion and to aid artillerymen, the Germans developed a coded system of colored crosses to identify shells containing chemical agents.

The Germans were further encouraged to use gas shells by the results of an attack staged on the night of 22-23 June 1916. About 110,000 shells containing the lung irritant Green Cross fell on French forces near the fortress of Verdun. German batteries adjacent to this sector added thousands of rounds of a lachrymatory gas. The gas attack, according to French sources, had its greatest effect on French artillerymen and reserves in the rear areas, causing over 1,600 casualties. German staff officers, impressed with the results, talked of creating "special gas batteries" controlled by special gas staffs. In the interest of flexibility, however, the high command decided that all artillery units should fire gas shells. By the war's end, gas shells comprised 50 percent of a German artillery battery's basic.

The British and, French also developed gas shells with unique color codes. The French Army used these shells almost as extensively as the Germans and fired the first phosgene-filled artillery shells on 22 February 1916 at Verdun. The French also experimented with an extremely small bursting charge in order to increase the gas payload. This French innovation allowed a stable, dense cloud to form. Although the French increased the chemical payload, they erred by adding comparatively harmless (smoke producers), such as stannic chloride, thus reducing the toxic capacity of their phosgene shells by 30 to 40 percent.

The French committed another technical error in the gas war. The hydrocyanic acid (hydrogen cyanide) used in their Vincennite shell (named for the production location) was too volatile and filled only half of the shell's capacity. Unless an extremely high concentration could be built up, there were no harmful effects. All the belligerents considered the Vincennite fill practically worthless. The French, for some reason, refused to accept this conclusion and manufactured over four million shells that, when fired, caused relatively few casualties.

The British faced a constant artillery shell production shortage and supplemented their use of gas cylinders with the 4-inch Stokes mortar, introduced in July, 1916, at the Battle of the Somme, The weapon, designed specifically to fire gas and thermite shells, had a payload three times as large (six to nine pounds) as could be fired from the standard 3-inch mortar. A range of only 800 to 1,000 meters meant that effective delivery required emplacement in the front-line trenches. Members of the Special Brigade also experimented with a homemade contraption similar to a trench mortar.

Early in 1917 Capt. William H. Livens, a British officer, developed a device made from ordinary steel containers. This makeshift mortar fired oil drums packed with oil-soaked cotton waste. Captain Livens also began to experiment with firing large gas-filled shells from his homemade trench mortar. This resulted in a new delivery system known as the Livens projector. In its final form the projector consisted of a drawn steel cylinder eight inches in diameter, one and one-fourth inch thick, that came in two sizes-two feet nine inches or four feet long. Rounded at one end, the cylinders had a base plate that looked like a Mexican sombrero. The projectors were buried in a trench cut at a forty-five degree angle for maximum range. Originally buried to the muzzle, this depth was later found to be unnecessary, and the projectors were thereafter emplaced only deep enough to steady them for firing. The shells used with the projectors carried a payload of thirty to forty pounds of chemical agent and had a range, depending on the length of the barrel, of either 1,200 or 1,900 meters. The British first used this delivery system for what they called "gas shoots" at Arras on 4 April 1917. The Germans reported that the density of the gas delivered by this method equaled that of a gas cloud. Captured German documents claimed that the Livens projector was a deadly weapon because it not only developed a dense concentration of gas similar to the one created by cylinders, but like artillery, its impact came as a surprise. During the war the British fired ever 300 gas projector "shoots." On 31 March 1918 the largest of these operations took place at Lens, with the firing of 3,728 of the devices.

Increased casualties resulting from British gas projector attacks prompted the Germans to develop a similar weapon. Time constraints and the lack of industrial capacity for increased steel production forced them to retool their obsolete 18-cm heavy mortars. These tubes coal & fire a projectile containing three to four gallons of a chemical agent. In December, 1917, the Germans launched their first projector attack on the Western Front.

In August, 1918, they introduced a rifled projector, 16-cm in diameter, that increased the range of the device to 3,500 meters. The shells contained thirteen pounds of chemical agent and five and one-half pounds of pumice. The pumice kept the chemical agent from. being flung into the air upon explosion. It also made the agent, usually phosgene, more persistent. In one instance, the gas reportedly lingered for one and one-half hours. Yet, impressive as were these results, the Germans, despite their efforts, continued to lag behind the British in the tactical use of this delivery system.

Initially, the tactical employment of chemical weapons varied to some degree between the Allies and the Central Powers; however, these variations became less noticeable during the latter stages of the war. By November, 1918, the protagonists were using similiar delivery systems and chemical agents.

From 1915 to 1918 the Germans held the initiative in most areas of gas warfare. They did this through the introduction of new agents that allowed them to direct more systematic thought to the question of how the employment of gas might alter a tactical situation. They were, for example, the first to use gas as an adjunct to maneuver in support of an infantry attack. The Allies struggled to keep up with such offensive doctrine, but they had to contend first with the development of effective defensive measures to counter German initiatives.

Only after developing countermeasures could the Allies then plan their use of a new chemical agent or a new delivery system. This lag was evident in the case of the two most effective agents used in World War I, phosgene and mustard gas. The Germans introduced phosgene six months before the Allies were able to employ it and mustard a year ahead of their foe. The Allies had to adopt immediate defensive measures, such as effective mask filters and protective suits, before they could turn to the development of tactical doctrine. "As far as the tactical employment of gas was concerned," wrote Lt. Col. Pascal Lucas, a French officer, "it took us a long time to realize that the neutralization of personnel by gas could supplement the always incomplete destruction of defensive organizations" by high explosives. British gas doctrine, when circumstances did permit its development, was driven in part by a shortage of artillery shells that prohibited the British Army from mounting an artillery gas attack until the summer of 1916. In the meantime, the British, as noted, convinced themselves that chemicals released from cylinders or projectors could most effectively be used to obtain the highest possible concentration of an agent in a specific area. The consequences of this doctrine were twofold: it prevented the British from employing gas to support mobile or open warfare, and it limited the. use of chemical agents primarily to the more restricted roles of attrition and harassment.

In the case of harassment, the British High Command, relying on intelligence reports, would indicate for one reason or another what German units it wished the Special Brigade to weaken or demoralize. German divisions recently transferred from the Eastern Front were prime targets because of their ignorance of defensive measures for gas warfare. The British sought out units that they expected to be transferred to the main battle fronts, i.e., Somme or Ypres, and tried to weaken them physically and psychologically before they deployed. On at least one occasion, a gas operation was postponed to await the arrival of a particular division. Once a German unit became a target for a gas attack, the Special Brigade made a point of following that unit around the front. The 1st Bavarian Regiment, for instance, was gassed fifteen times; the 1st Guards Regiment twelve times in six months; the 10th Bavarian Regiment ten times in five months, and the 9th Bavarian Regiment fourteen times from 28 June 1916 to 1 August 1917. The effects could be devastating to the morale of the gassed units and those units around them. A captured German diary recorded, "We have again had many casualties through gas poisoning. I can't think of anything worse; wherever one goes, one must take one's gas mask with one, and it will soon be more necessary than a rifle. Things are dreadful here."

The British ultimately developed tactical doctrine for the use of gas shells. This doctrine set three methods for inflicting enemy gas casualties. The first and most favored method was by a surprise gas attack, in which British gunners attempted to establish the greatest concentration of gas in a target area by firing a "lavish expenditure of ammunition" at an extremely rapid rate. After one or two minutes of shelling, enemy soldiers who had not put on protective masks would be incapacitated by the dense gas; the remainder would be masked, rendering further bombardment uneconomical and unnecessary. The second method for using gas shells tried to exhaust the enemy by desultory fire over a period of many hours. In most instances, the British believed this attrition. method not worth the effort, because few casualties were produced. The third method was an attempt to penetrate the enemy's gas masks with new agents such as chloropicrin, which when fired in a high concentration in a specific area, seeped into the masks and created intolerable eye irritation, coughing, vomiting, and inflammation of the respiratory tract. Enemy soldiers forced to remove their fouled masks were then subjected to a shelling with lethal phosgene.

The Germans attempted to make the enemy trenches no less dreadful than their own. Having the technological advantage that gave them the ability to introduce new gases before the Allies, the Germans devoted much thought to the tactical employment of chemical weapons, and in this respect, they reached a high degree of sophistication. After abandoning cloud attacks, the Germans increased their use of gas shells. They discovered on the Eastern Front that tear gas was extremely effective in neutralizing Russian artillery. Even a few rounds would incapacitate a gun crew or, having forced it to mask, prevent it from delivering accurate fire. On the Western Front in 1916, the Germans fired some 2,000 tear gas shells at an extensive French trench system near Verdun. This massive surprise bombardment resulted in the capture of 2,400 Frenchmen who, after being temporarily blinded by the tear gas, were surrounded by German troops wearing goggles, but no masks.

The Germans introduced other agents to the battlefield for specific tactical purposes. In May, 1916, they fired their Green Cross shell filled with diphosgene, a lung irritant. Later, as an indication of the increased sophistication of gas shells, they subdivided the Green Cross shell fill, first by a mix of 75 percent phosgene and 25 percent diphosgene, which was labled Green

Cross 1. Then, in July, 1917, four different percentages of phosgene, diphosgene, and diphenylchlorosine called Green Cross 2, A, B, and C, respectively, were introduced. These were followed shortly by Blue Cross and Yellow Cross shells. The former shell was filled with an arsenic compound of finely separated dust. In field trials, this agent proved extremely effective in the penetration of all mask filters in existence. The need to encase the compound in a glass-lined shell, however, reduced its effectiveness, as the heat of the explosion failed to cause vaporization, and the force of the explosion caused only mechanical pulverization. The recipients, the French and British, considered Blue Cross a "failure and not worth the effort." The introduction of Yellow Cross (mustard gas), however, again gave the Germans the initiative in chemical warfare, which they held to the end of the war. By increasing the explosive charge in the shell, the Germans further extended the area contaminated by this blister producing agent. This shell was marked by a double (Lorraine) cross.

The Germans found gas persisted even longer when an agent and a small amount of high explosives were placed in one shell. The effect of the high explosive, when used in the proper amount, was to spread the agent over a wider area and keep it airborne longer. With this knowledge, the Germans changed their gas doctrine from attacking a, particular target to gassing large areas for extended periods of time. German staff officers began to plan operations that called for "gas barriers" and "gas pockets."

German tactical doctrine for the use of artillery gas shells offered a variety of possibilities. For the offense, it called for surprise and the concentration of as much gas as possible through the sudden and rapid placement of shells on a target area. "Cloud concentration" tactics imitated surprise tactics, but with an increase in the number of shells and an expansion of the size of a target area. Another offensive tactic was the use of gas shells that contained a high explosive charge and shrapnel. These shells, used exclusively by the Germans, had an effect "so devastating that the efficacy of a high explosive shrapnel gas shell bombardment was always increased." Once introduced, the Germans always added a percentage of these shells to any high explosive or shrapnel bombardment. The high explosive-gas shell was used extensively in German rolling barrages to support advancing infantry during the spring offenses of 1918. These shells were also used to neutralize known enemy artillery batteries and machine gun nests, thus allowing German infantry to bypass Allied strong points.

The key figure in the expansion of German gas shell tactical doctrine was Lt. Col. Georg Bruchniffiler, known as "Durchbruck" (Breakthrough) and considered an artillery genius because of his success on the battlefield. While on the Eastern Front, Bruchmiiller, a great believer in the efficiency of gas shells, developed a highly sophisticated system of gas artillery fire. His tactical ideas were incorporated in the December, 1917, edition of the German manual for employment of gas shells. Bruchmiiller's system created "Gas Squares," which were areas known to hold enemy batteries or concentrations of enemy troops. These locations would be saturated by surprise gas shell fire, and the lethal concentration would be renewed by subsequent periodic fire. Bruchmiiler's artillery tactics achieved surprise through a predicted-fire method that eliminated the usual ranging of the target by one gun of a battery. Bruchmiiller formulated advanced firing data and tables based on meteorological variables such as wind, air temperature, and barometric pressure.

When Blue Cross and Yellow Cross shells became available, Bruchmiiller devised Buntkreuz (colored cross) tactics. One of the most successful uses of this new doctrine came on the Eastern Front, in the German crossing of the Dvina River before Riga (Map 3). On 1 September 1917 a two-hour preliminary bombardment of the Russian batteries created "varicolored zones," as combinations of Blue Cross and Green Cross were used both during bombardment and then during three hours of firing for effect. For the preliminary gas fire, each German battery had a set of firing sequences every twelve minutes to counter Russian batteries, which first maintained a desultory fire and then fell silent. According to German estimates, more than 116,400 gas shells were fired, which caused at least a thousand Russian casualties, mainly because of the ineffectual respirators issued to Russian troops. The figure might have been higher had not the Russians fled. German infantry reached the opposite bank to find that the Russian artillery crews had abandoned their guns in "great haste, resembling flight." The Russian infantry, which lacked effective personal protection against chemical agents, had followed suit.

Persistent agent fire was used tactically by the Germans on both the offense and the defense. Surprise, though desirable, was not necessary for persistent agents. Yellow Cross allowed an area to be "cleared of, or rendered inaccessible to," the enemy. Fire continued for several hours, and the contamination could be renewed each day thereafter, if so desired. The areas gassed were called "Yellow Zones of Defense." In April, 1918, the Germans shelled the city of Armentieres with mustard gas. The bombardment was so heavy that witnesses claimed liquid mustard gas ran in the streets. Naturally, the British evacuated the locale; the contamination, however, prevented the Germans from entering the city for two weeks. In the spring offensives of 1918, the Germans created mustard gas zones to protect the flanks of advancing infantry, to neutralize enemy strong points, to deny the enemy key terrain, to block supply routes, and to render enemy artillery batteries ineffective. "Even in open warfare," a German officer wrote, "the troops soon were asking for gas supporting fire."

Mustard gas caused considerable consternation among the Allies. "We were outdistanced ... " a French officer noted, "the German lead on us in this respect ... was a source of real inquietude," for the units that were exposed suffered considerably and the struggle against Yperite "seemed most deceptive of solution." The Allies eventually responded in kind, but not until June, 1918, a full year after the Germans introduced the ultimate agent of World War I, did the French use Yperite, and it took the British until 26 September 1918 to retaliate with mustard. So desperate were the French to obtain the agent that British officers reported teams of French soldiers draining unexploded German Yellow Cross shells in order to reuse the gas.

Personal protection was always a problem, one neither side ever really solved in World War I. The German High Command, prior to the first attack at Ypres, made no effort to develop an efficient gas mask. Attacking German soldiers had small protective bags of mull or hemp that were soaked in a sodium bicarbonate (baking soda) solution and then tied over the mouth and nose. Not until the closing months of 1915 did the German army begin to issue a self-contained respirator. The mask had a treated leather facepiece (because of the shortage of rubber, only officer facepieces were constructed of this material, which was more efficient than leather and easier to maintain) and eyepieces of an outer glass lens and a celluloid inner lens. The first German mask had a significant drawback: the filter had to be screwed on to the facepiece each time the mask was used, which meant that more time was required to mask during a gas attack. Later, this problem was remedied by a single construction model with a replaceable filter element.

The French, British, and Russians did not coordinate their research and development of gas defenses. Although they passed information and some equipment to each other, they worked independently for the most part on their own protective masks. In England, shortly after the first gas attack in April, 1915, housewives were asked by the high command to produce what became popularly known as the Black Veil Respirator-black veiling held a pad of cotton waste soaked in a chemical solution over the nose and mouth. These makeshift masks reached the British trenches in early May. When, in the latter part of 1915, the Germans began to use tear gas, the British countered with a flour sack type mask made of flannel, called the "Hypo" or "H-Helmet" after the chemical in which it was soaked, calcium hypochlorite. This mask offered protection to the eyes as well as to the respiratory system. One British officer described it as "a smoke helmet, a greasy grey-felt bag with a tale window certainly ineffective against gas." This H-Helmet contained two celluloid eyepieces, but no apparatus to expel the carbon dioxide that built up in the mask.

In the fall of 1915 British intelligence learned of Germany's intention to use a new gas, phosgene, a delayed-action choking agent, The Russians had also learned that the Germans intended to employ phosgene and advised the British that a solution of phenate-hexamine was effective in blocking the agent. As a result, the British soaked their H-Helmet in the Russian solution and added an outlet valve to reduce the carbon dioxide buildup inside the mask. The British Army called the new device the "PH-Helmet." The troops called it a. "goggle-eyed booger with a tit."

Although the PH-Helmet successfully blocked phosgene, it had serious drawbacks: it was hot, stuffy, and emitted an unpleasant odor; it also offered little protection against dense concentrations of lachrymatory agents. To counteract both phosgene and the lachrymating agents, the British in early 1916 took an entirely different approach to protective masks by developing a two-piece device called the "Large Box" or "Tar Box Respirator." A canister worn on the back contained neutralizing chemicals and attached by a rubber hose to a facepiece covering the chin, mouth, and nose. The wearer endured an uncomfortable noseclip and a mouthpiece similar to an athlete's rubber tooth protector. Goggles protected the eyes. The advantage of the mask rested in the use of a large filter. However, this also caused difficulties because the canister was too large and clumsy to be carried for extended distances over prolonged periods. This kind of mask reached its final stage of development with the introduction of the "Small Box Respirator" (SBR), which employed a smaller filter worn on the chest and a single construction facepiece. The details of the SBR became very familiar to men of the American Expeditionary Forces.

The French wrote a different chapter to the development of the gas mask. After using the same primitive masks as the British, they set out to develop a mask that was both effective and comfortable to wear - two criteria that were, and still are, essential for the successful design of protective devices. The first significant French protective device, the M-2 mask, was similar in design to the British H-Helmet, except it did not cover the entire head, but took the form of a "snout" similar to a feedbag for a horse. Its filtration ability was limited, so French doctrine called for troops to be rotated after several hours of exposure to any gas. In 1917 the French introduced the ARS *(Appareil Respiratoire Speécial)* mask. In appearance it resembled German protective equipment. The rubber facepiece had a waxed or oiled linen lining. Inhaled air passed in front of the eyepieces to prevent clouding. A canister attached to the facepiece could not be removed.

In September, 1917, these French masks were followed by another, the *Tissot,* which became one of the most effective masks of the war. As one postwar American observer noted, "the French deserve great credit" for the introduction of this defensive piece of equipment. In design, the *Tissot* was similar to the British Small Box Respirator except that the former's filter canister was carried on the soldier's back, not chest. This meant that infantrymen could carry only the *Tissot* and no other equipment. It covered the entire face, but without the uncomfortable nose clip and mouthpiece.

The design allowed air to enter the mouth across the eyepieces, thus removing the normal phenomenon of condensation. The circulation of fresh air also diluted any lachrymatory gases that might enter the mask. Finally, the entire facepiece was of thin rubber. The French thought the filter location, the same as for the Large Tar Box Respirator, clumsy and difficult to adjust and, therefore, judged it unsuitable for infantry. Troops, such as artillery gun crews and stretcher bearers, who were not loaded with personal equipment and who had to continue to fight or function during a gas attack, did receive the mask. These soldiers found, in addition to comfort, that one could breathe easier and that the filtration system was superior to the ARS and M-2 mask.

Unlike the British and French, the Russians devoted few resources to the development of chemical protective equipment. Consequently, they suffered the greatest number of chemically inflicted casualties in World War I. On 2 May 1915, not quite a month after the second Battle of Ypres during which French Colonial and Territorial troops collapsed under the first German gas attack, the Russians were subjected to a similar experience. German pioneer troops directed by Fritz Haber released 263 tons of chlorine gas from 12,000 cylinders against Russian troops at Bolimov.

The first cylinder attack on the Eastern Front killed 6,000 Russian soldiers. Two more gas cloud attacks were made on the same position, and upward of 25,000 Russian casualties resulted. According to German sources, in June, 1915, at Bzura, two Russian regiments, the 55th and 56th Siberian, suffered approximately 9,000 gas casualties, or about 90 percent of their total strength. On 7 September 1916 a German cloud attack killed 600 Russian officers and men. The following month Transbaikal Cossacks suffered 4,000 casualties. A gas attack in 1917 cost the Russians 12 officers,

1,089 men killed, and 53 officers, 7,738 men incapacitated. Despite these casualties, the Tzarist Army developed only one mask in addition to the basic chemical-soaked gauze respirator. The fabric facepiece of this mask covered the head and attached directly to a canister containing a charcoal filter.

It looked similar to the bill on a duck. Although the mask had no noseclip or mouthpiece, soldiers still found it extremely uncomfortable because the weight of the filter placed a great strain on the muscles of the neck. To make matters worse, the filter of this mask was of questionable effectiveness. By 1917 different types of British and French masks were being sent to Russia and used, to some limited extent, by Russian troops.

By the summer of 1917, when U.S. troops began to arrive at French ports, chemical warfare had become commonplace and, in practice, had reached a high degree of sophistication compared to the first significant gas attack at Ypres a little over two years earlier. By July the most effective chemical agent of the war, mustard or Yellow Cross, had made its appearance.

Gas shells now might contain two or even three different agents. All of the delivery systems for chemical war were in operation and efforts were being made by the combatants to improve on these weapons. The British had, for example, devised electronically detonated cylinders on tram cars for beam attacks. Also, the British had finally begun to overcome their shell production problems and had used gas shells in large quantities at the Battle of Arras in April, 1917.

Tactical doctrine for chemical warfare had reached a high level of sophistication, especially in artillery employment. In this area, the Germans, thanks to Lt. Col. Georg Bruchmüller, led the way. German artillery firing instructions became increasingly complex in regard to the selection of the gas or combination of gases to be used in a variety of tactical situations.

Given the advantage of viewing the development of chemical warfare from afar, the United States Army, upon entering the war, should have been in a position to operate in a chemical environment without repeating the costly experiences of the French, British, and Germans. Unfortunately, this was not to be the case.

THE U.S. ARMY'S RESPONSE TO CHEMICAL WARFARE, 1915-1917

Most of the information Americans received concerning the war and chemical warfare in Europe came from the news media. Because the Royal Navy had cut the German trans-Atlantic cable early in the war, almost all news from the Continent flowed through British and French censors.

According to one author of a study on chemical warfare, Frederick Brown, Allied control of chemical warfare information to the United States can be divided into four distinct phases. During the first phase the Germans were portrayed as violators of the Hague Convention. Reports indicated that the German Army had introduced a barbaric and inhumane weapon. This line, of course, was geared to gaining, support and perhaps intervention by the United States on the side of the Allies in the European war. When the French and British decided to retaliate with gas, the message changed, with Allied releases indicating that the German's first use of gas justified retaliation and the reluctant employment of similar weapons by the Allies. A note of righteous indignation pervaded these reports, although the reports were toned down considerably when discussing the effects of gas. In the third stage, which occurred during the spring and summer of 1917, there was a total news blackout on information concerning the gas war. Assistant Secretary of War Benedict Crowell speculated on the cause. He acknowledged an increased use of chemical agents on both sides and believed the Allies "feared and perhaps with reason" that a picture of gas warfare, if presented to the Americans, would result in a "unreasonable dread of gases on the part of the American nation and its soldiers." The fourth and final phase, which came after U.S. entry into the war, was ushered in with a burst of information with virtually no censorship. The use of chemicals in this phase was depicted as a triumph of Allied technology, an example of good overcoming evil.

Restricted Allied propaganda during the first three phases mentioned above impeded U.S. preparedness in chemical warfare in two ways. First, it gave U.S. officers the impression that the belligerents were making minimal use of gas and that chemical weapons, when employed, had little or no impact on the battlefield. Second, it created the perception among Army officers that chemical warfare, introduced by the barbaric Hun, was inhuman and somehow sullied the honor of the professional soldier.

There were other reasons for the military's lack of appreciation of this new weapon. President Wilson's efforts to maintain strict neutrality during the first two years of the war hampered the Army's planning for defense. When, at one point, Wilson discovered that the General Staffs War College Division had prepared contingency plans for a war with Germany, he reprimanded Secretary of War Lindley Garrison. When the Army did tackle the problem of preparedness, chemical warfare, because it was an unfamiliar subject to most planners, received little attention. Other matters seemed more pressing. There were, for example, significant shortages of all kinds of war materiel. In 1915, the U.S. Army had only twenty-one aircraft, as compared to Britain's 250 and France's 500. The United States had fewer than 700 3inch guns, while the French alone had 4,800 of a similar caliber prior to the outbreak of war. Based on Western Front usage, the U.S. Army had only a two-day supply of artillery shells. Similarly, four days of trench warfare would exhaust the U.S. inventory of small arms ammunition. In the assignment of priorities to overcome these and other deficiencies, chemical warfare came nowhere near the top of the list.

During the summer of 1915, the U.S. Army War College published studies on the impact of the war on each belligerent's industrial base. In this report, the implications of chemical weapons and gas warfare received no notice. In November, 1915, two months after the British retaliated with gas at the Battle of Loos, the War College published a supplement to the earlier studies. This report included a survey of developments in weapons, equipment, and force structuring, but interestingly, still did not mention gas warfare.

Even the preparedness movement and the passage of the 1916 National Defense Act did nothing to spur an American assessment of the chemical war being waged in Europe. In fact, during Congressional hearings over preparedness for national defense, poison gas was mentioned only once when Col. Charles G. Treat of the U.S. Army's General Staff testified on the subject of changing artillery doctrine in Europe. Following a discussion of shrapnel shells, one Senator asked Treat, "Are they still using the poisonous gas over there, Colonel?" Treat replied, "The papers say so, but we have not had any actual reports from our observers that they are using them." In November, 1916, the same month that Treat testified, the War Department's Board of Ordnance and Fortifications noted that "certain practices" with poison gas in the European war made necessary the procurement of appropriate defensive equipment, such as gas masks for the Army. The board observed that no branch of the U.S. Army then handled anything remotely connected with chemical warfare.

The board, in its final report, recommended that responsibility for the design, but not the supply, of gas masks be given to the Army's Medical Department. In reviewing the records of the board, the Adjutant General sent extracts of the comments that pertained to gas defense equipment to the Surgeon General, who concurred with the board's findings. The Chief of Staff also concurred, after which the Secretary of War gave the Surgeon General responsibility for the development and design of gas masks. No decision was made as to which branch of the Army would supply troops with protective gas equipment.

The Surgeon General had detailed a number of medical officers to serve as observers with the French and British armies. Reports on the medical aspects of the European conflict, including the diagnosis and treatment of gas victims, were received by the Surgeon General from 1916 on. Unfortunately, for unexplained reasons, the Surgeon General took no action to initiate the development of protective gas devices. The Adjutant General, for his part, shelved the entire matter. Thus, on the eve of American intervention, the Army acted as if it had barely heard of chemical warfare.

The Secretary of War's *Annual Report* for 1917 reflected this neglect. The report pompously declared that the "councils of prudence and forethought" should prepare the Army to surprise the enemy rather than lag "defensively behind the surprises which he prepares for us." The Secretary went on to acknowledge the tremendous impact of science on the war in Europe and referred specifically to the introduction of the airplane and the submarine. As for chemicals, he merely noted that there were other "scientific novelties" that had surfaced in the European conflict.

In February, 1917, the question the "scientific novelty" called poison gas was finally raised by an anxious Quartermaster General who pointedly asked the Adjutant General exactly which bureau of the War Department would furnish the Army with gas masks if the need arose. The question prompted the Adjutant General to initiate correspondence with the'Chief of Ordnance, the Quartermaster General, and the Surgeon General to decide on the responsibility for gas mask production. At the time of the correspondence, the Surgeon General had yet to begin a program of gas mask development.

That same month the Department of Interior's Bureau of Mines took the first positive steps toward preparing the Army for chemical warfare. The director, Van H. Manning, displayed a great deal more vision and foresight than did his military colleagues in Washington. At a bureau meeting, Manning asked his department chiefs what they could do to be useful if the nation should become involved in the European war. Since its founding in 1908, the bureau had investigated poison gases found in mines, conducted research on breathing devices, and examined ways to treat miners who had succumbed to noxious fumes. Obviously, this work had a direct application to chemical warfare. The day following the meeting, the Secretary of the Interior authorized Manning to contact another civilian organization,. the Military Committee of the National Research Council. In a letter to C. D. Walcott, the chairman of the committee, Manning pointed out that the bureau could adapt for military application a self-contained breathing apparatus then in use for mine rescues. Also, the bureau had a test chamber at the Pittsburgh, Pennsylvania, experimental station that could be used to conduct tests on military gas masks then in use by the Europeans. The bureau hoped that the information obtained from this research could be given to the Army, allowing it to adopt the best gas mask, should the need arise.

Upon receipt of this letter, Walcott arranged a meeting between representatives of the General Staffs War College Division and the

Bureau of Mines. The meeting proved productive: at the end of February, 1917, the War Department accepted the bureau's offer of assistance and agreed to furnish the support, exclusive of funding, necessary to move the work along. Still, no immediate action. was taken by either the Army or the Bureau of Mines to begin a defensive gas equipment research program.

On 6 April 1917, when the U.S. declared war on Germany, the Army not only lacked defensive equipment for chemical warfare, but also had no concrete plans to develop or manufacture gas masks or any other defensive equipment. Even if gas masks had been available, the Army would have had no idea how to conduct defensive gas training. Moreover, no one in the nation seemed to have any practical knowledge concerning offensive chemical warfare equipment or the doctrine then used by the Allies and the Germans for its employment.

Even after the declaration of war by Congress and the decision to ship an American division overseas, preparations for chemical warfare lacked a sense of urgency. The same day war was declared, the Council of National Defense formed a Committee on Noxious Gases. The group met in Washington and immediately adjourned to study British and French gas warfare literature. At later meetings the committee established definite guidelines for Bureau of Mines research to follow in the development of masks. Only then did the chemists at the bureau's Pittsburgh experimental station begin in earnest to develop an American gas mask. The committee also recommended that gas mask production be kept separate and distinct from research.

In May, 1917, the General Staff awoke to the fact that the division requested by the French and British as a token force might well be in combat in a matter of months without any defensive gas equipment L. P. Williamson, liaison officer between the Bureau of Mines and the War Department, received a directive from the General Staff telling him to seek the bureau's assistance in the manufacture of 25,000 gas masks. George A. Burrell, a civilian chemist in the bureau's Research Laboratory, "readily and willingly accepted" the task, but not, as he later noted, "fully appreciating all the conditions which a war mask had to encounter." Burrell should not have been so hard on himself. No one in the United States really understood or even knew much about the employment of chemical defensive equipment on the battlefield.

Working day and night, employees of four different civilian companies fabricated 20,088 masks and filters, using a British Small Box Respirator (SBR) as a model. The masks were shipped overseas to be examined and tested by British experts. They were quickly rejected. The British cabled back that the masks were unacceptable for combat because the mouthpiece was too large and stiff. They also found the rubberized cloth facepiece did not filter out the agent chloropicrin, which was then being used by the Germans in increasing quantities. The filter, which was worn on the chest in a container, had soda-lime granules that were too soft. With repeated jolting, the granules would clog the canister and increase resistance to breathing.

While this was going on, the acting Chief of Staff, Maj. Gen. Tasker Bliss, after a lengthy round of memoranda initiated by the Adjutant General, informed the Surgeon General on 16 May 1917 that, in addition to research and development, the Medical Department would be responsible for supplying the U.S. Army with gas masks and other defensive equipment. During the next fiscal year the Medical Department would be responsible for supplying 1,000,000 gas masks, 8,500 decontamination sprayers for use in trench warfare, and 1,000 oxygen resuscitators for the treatment of chemical casualties. Unfortunately, neither the Chief of Staff nor the Surgeon General created an office to procure the equipment. The Surgeon General did, however, assign an officer to the National Research Council's Committee on Noxious Gases.

The Committee on Noxious Gases soon met with representatives from the Army and Navy and with members of a French scientific mission. After several sessions, the committee sent a memorandum to the Secretary of War on 2 July 1917, informing him that it had worked out a partial organization plan for a "gas service." Unfortunately, the use of the term "gas service" was misleading, because what the committee recommended turned out to be a cumbersome decentralized system for preparing the Army for chemical warfare. The offensive aspects of gas warfare, the committee explained, should be handled by the Ordnance

Department, the defensive measures by the Medical Department. The Bureau of Mines would continue to direct research, and the Corps of Engineers would receive responsibility for handling all chemical warfare material on the battlefield. The General Staff immediately put this decentralized system into effect.

On 24 July 1917 the Chief of Staff ordered the Medical Department to provide nine officers as instructors for a Gas Defense School to be organized at the Infantry School of Musketry, Fort Sill, Oklahoma. As a result of this order, the Medical Department received the additional responsibility for the conduct of defensive gas training. Medical officers with absolutely no experience in gas warfare were now expected to train other medical officers for duty as instructors for an Army that would eventually be expanded to over three million men.

After an interminable delay, the Surgeon General on 31 August 1917 finally created a Gas Defense Service composed of three sections: Field Supply, Overseas Repair, and Training. He placed a Medical Corps officer in command and filled his staff with members of the Medical Department's Sanitary Corps. The officers had no chemical warfare doctrine to guide them. Only two War Department publications existed in the United States to assist these gas officers: a hurriedly compiled *Notes on Gas as a Weapon in Modern War and a Memorandum on Gas Poisoning in Warfare*. Both publications appear to have borrowed extensively from French and British gas warfare doctrine, some of it outdated.

The creation of a Training Section, even with its limited expertise, came none too soon. In September, 1917, draftees, volunteers, and National Guardsmen began to arrive at the thirty-six training cantonments scattered across the country. Sanitary Corps and division medical officers, with only several thousand masks at their disposal (including the 20,088 rejected by the British), faced the overwhelming task of training hundreds of thousands of troops in gas warfare and gas defense. Shortages of equipment, manuals, and knowledge were not the only problems facing the new gas officers. Gas was such a new weapon that division commanders and their staff officers were unwilling to give up training time for chemical defense at the expense of more traditional military skills such as close order drill and marksmanship. It was a wonder that any defensive training in gas warfare took place. Many times it did not. Initially, there were at best one or two hours of gas defense lectures, sometimes accompanied by a demonstration of how to wear the gas mask.

The lack of knowledge and experience with gas bred "ignorance and superstition" among recruits and veterans alike. Rumors swept through the camps that Germany had "a gas that would make soldiers' eyes drop out of their sockets or their fingers and toes drop off." To the unsophisticated youths who filled the training camps, "gas was mysterious enough, but add to it the word chemical, and it became hopelessly beyond ... their conception." Gas was such an "intangible thing," a division commander noted, that a level of understanding adequate to guard against the dangers it posed was difficult to reach. Reaching such a level continued to be a hopeless task because no coherent U.S. gas warfare doctrine existed. As a consequence, a majority of World War I doughboys found themselves in a chemical combat environment with only a minimal amount of defensive gas training and with "no idea of what this training really meant."

Confronted with this unfortunate situation, the War College of the General Staff examined the evolving gas defense program in the fall of 1917. Defensive training in gas warfare - regardless of how rudimentary - had to be given to men going to Europe. Ypres had proved what chemical warfare could do to unprepared soldiers. Severe casualties and battlefield defeat might well occur if immediate steps were not taken to train men in the defensive aspects of chemical warfare. As a result, the War College requested and received a British gas officer and a gas NCO for each of the thirty-six training cantonments.

In late October, 1917, the British gas experts arrived in the United States. Their activities were coordinated and directed by Maj. S.J.M. Auld, Special Brigade, Royal Engineers. Auld quickly made his presence felt. Impressed by the British gas officer's knowledge and practical experience, the War College and the Field Training Section asked him to prepare "a working textbook on gas" in order to fill the U.S. Army's doctrinal void in chemical warfare. Working with Sanitary Corps Capt. James H. Walton, Auld wrote four pamphlets that were later combined as Adjutant

General Document 705, *Gas Warfare.* They were initially published individually in the following order:

Part Three: *Methods of Training in Defensive Methods*

Part Two: *Methods of Defense Against Attack*

Part One: *German Methods of Offense*

Part Four: *The Offensive in Gas Warfare -Cloud and Projector*

Thus, British gas warfare doctrine edited by the War College Division of the General Staff became U.S. Army doctrine.

Auld strongly influenced the organization of the U.S. Army for chemical warfare in one other way. When he and other British officers discovered that the General Staff had placed defensive training under the Medical Department, they were appalled. The British officers insisted that gas defense was "purely a military affair"; in their opinion, proper defensive measures were "largely a question of discipline."

Based on the experience of the British Army, such procedures were so closely connected with the soldier's "fighting activities" that preparation for chemical warfare could not be carried out by a noncombat branch of the'Army. The British were so emphatic that, in January, 1918, by order of the General Staff, the Field Training Section of the Sanitary Corps passed to the Corps of Engineers.

Major Auld also suggested the establishment of a Central Army Gas School to train "Divisional, Brigade and Regimental Gas officers and other personnel whom it might be desirable to educate in Gas Warfare." This idea was already under consideration by the General Staff. The result was the establishment of an Army Gas School at Camp A. A. Humphreys, Virginia, where in May, 1918, two initial courses began. The first, a four-day course for officers and noncommissioned officers, provided general information on gas warfare.

The second, a twelve-day course, was for Chief Gas Officers who would be assigned to division and higher echelon staffs. Although there were similarities between the two courses, the Chief Gas Officers' instruction went into greater detail on most matters. The shortage of trained gas officers in the AEF prevented students from being held for longer periods of field training on subjects such as gas detection, construction of gas-proof dugouts, and the proper wearing of respirators.

Auld assisted in training the first U.S. gas officers, forty-five first lieutenants, all chemists, who were assigned to the Field Training Section of the Sanitary Corps. The instruction took place at the American University in Washington, DC. In January, 1918, after three months of training in gas warfare and general military subjects, thirty-three of the forty-five officers, together with their British instructors, departed for duty at division training camps. The other twelve went directly to France. Unfortunately, by January, 1918, six of the thirty U.S. divisions destined to see combat in France had either left the States or had completed training. The men in these units had received no chemical warfare training before embarking for Europe. As for the divisions that did receive some training before shipping overseas, their division gas officers were afterwards assigned to the 473d Engineer Regiment, a stateside administrative holding unit. Thus, the first trained gas officers did not deploy with the men they had trained. Although necessary for the training of subsequent divisions, this decision had, in the words of one gas officer, a "discouraging effect upon the men and upon gas training and discipline in general" in the unit deployed overseas. The confidence of the embarking troops was hardly bolstered when the "experts" on chemical warfare stayed home.

As the war progressed, the training in the division camps improved. In January, 1918, the 29th Division's gas training at Camp McClellan consisted of a brief lecture and gas mask drill for one hour daily, five days a week, under the close supervision of British instructors. This compared favorably to the weekly one-hour "anti-gas instruction" in October, 1917. As training became more sophisticated, men underwent tests at the end of their division's training cycle. They masked and entered a chamber filled with chlorine gas. Next, they went through a chamber filled with a tear agent, where they unmasked. Although by the summer of 1918, recruits received standardized chemical warfare training, reports filed by division gas officers in Europe indicated the key to successful preparation had yet to be found. Still more training was needed, and it had to be integrated with other subjects.

In the summer of 1918, with news reaching America of Germany's increased use of gas, an Army regulation was promulgated, requiring every doughboy who left the country to have a certificate indicating he had completed gas training. No other military skill required such validation.

Unfortunately, the requirement was usually ignored, and most men continued to arrive in France without the benefit of adequate instruction in gas defense. Gas officers realized that sufficient time for training in the camps did not exist. To make up for the deficiency, units attempted to use the time aboard transports for defensive gas training. The 80th Division, for example, ordered that shipboard activities would include physical training, manual of arms, guard duty, and "anti-gas instruction."

Although the U.S. Army's first efforts in chemical warfare were directed toward "anti-gas" or defensive measures, the development of the means to retaliate in kind soon followed.

On 15 August 1917, with the approval of the General Staff in Washington, AEF General Order 108 authorized the organization of special and technical engineer troops that would be assigned to each army as a "Gas and Flame" Regiment.

The War Department ordered recruits for the newly formed 30th Engineers to report to the American University campus in Washington, DC, where they were transformed into the 1st Gas Regiment.

Unfortunately, with no one to instruct them in offensive or even defensive gas warfare, the only training the first companies of the gas regiment received in the United States involved close order drill. The unit underwent no special training in gas warfare. Beginning in December, 1917, the companies of the 1st Gas Regiment left the United States without gas masks.

The gas mask problem continued to plague the Army as a whole. An effective American mask was eventually developed using the British Small Box Respirator as a model. However, production of American gas masks peaked just one month prior to the end of the war. Late delivery and the initial small number of masks produced were offset only by the AEF's decision to purchase several million British and French gas masks.

The same unpreparedness and production lag applied to offensive chemical weapons. The Army attempted to contract out the production of war gases to a number of civilian chemical companies, but these firms objected immediately to the contracts because of the inherent dangers in the production of large quantities of war gases and because the demand for the product would not extend beyond the conflict. Besides that, the firms had already overcommitted their plants and personnel for the production of other war-related chemical products.

The Army thus found itself with no alternative but to construct its own production facilities. In December, 1917, construction of plants to produce chemical agents began at Gunpowder Neck, Maryland. By the summer of 1918, the Edgewood Arsenal there had plants in operation producing phosgene, chloropicrin, mustard, chlorine, and sulfur trichloride.

The arsenal also had a capability for filling artillery shells, although most of the agents produced were shipped overseas to the Allies in fifty-five gallon drums. Because of insufficient time, not one single gas shell manufactured at the arsenal ever reached an American artillery piece in France. When production of chemicals finally peaked one month prior to the Armistice, the plants had to stop production for lack of shell casings. artillery units and special gas troops fired American produced war gas, but in French and British shells.[26]

As the emphasis on chemical warfare increased, there arose a need to coordinate the various agencies assigned responsibility for gas warfare. Accordingly, on 28 June 1918 President Wilson, using the authority given to him by the Overman Act, ordered the establishment of the Chemical Warfare Service (CWS) as a separate branch of the National Army.

Immediately, all activities pertaining to chemical warfare were placed under Maj. Gen. William L. Sibert, formerly Commanding General of the First Infantry Division. The creation of a branch of the Army dedicated to chemical warfare was significant because it acknowledged, albeit belatedly, the tremendous impact the new weapon was having on the AEF The CWS, with the concurrence of the General Staff, established ten subordinate divisions:

Administration	Proving
Research	Medical
Gas Offense	Training
Gas Offense(Edgewood Arsenal)	Overseas(Gas Service, AEF)
Development	1st Gas Regiment

With the exception of the Overseas Division and the 1st Gas Regiment, the division chiefs were located in Washington, DC, and the operations of their divisions were scattered throughout the United States. The Administration Division facilitated routine matters and coordinated the activities of the other CWS divisions. A Research Division, as the name implied, handled all basic research, from the discovery of new chemicals to the development of protective masks and offensive equipment. Another division, Gas Defense, conducted research, but primarily administered the manufacturing, testing, and inspecting of gas masks for men and animals. This division also had the responsibility for manufacturing gas-proof dugout blankets, protective suits and gloves, antigas ointment, and "gas warning" signals. The Gas Defense Division administered Edgewood Arsenal. A Development Division experimented with charcoal suitable for gas mask filters, a manufacturing process for mustard, and a means of producing casings and adapters for 75-min shells of similar design to the French glass-lined gas projectiles. A Proving Division tested prototype gas shells before production and spottested shells prior to shipment overseas. The Medical Division coordinated work on the therapy, pharmacology, physiology, and pathology of war gases on the body. This division's primary emphasis was on the prevention and treatment of casualties from mustard gas.

The agency that had its most direct impact on the AEF was the Chemical Warfare Service's Training Division. The division's responsibilities included the organization and training of gas troops, the training of "casual detachments for overseas duty," the maintenance of a Chemical Warfare Training Camp detachment, and the procurement and training of chemical officers for overseas duty. In recognition of the division's importance, the Assistant Director of the Chemical Warfare Service, Brig. Gen. H. C. Newcomer, assumed operational command. This was the only division, other than Administration, headed by a general officer.

The structure of the CWS in the United States was determined by the personnel and equipment requirements of the AEF. Stateside training and preparations for chemical warfare had to be curtailed in order to rush American troops to France. Initially, expertise in chemical warfare was lacking. As a consequence, combat divisions deployed without proper training, equipment, and leadership. Until late 1917, there was no chemical warfare doctrine to rely upon. Nevertheless, American troops had to fight on a chemical battlefield against an opponent highly skilled in the use of chemicals in combat. Out of necessity it fell to the Overseas Division, CWS, to bear the brunt of the responsibility for preparing American soldiers for chemical warfare.

The majority of the thirty AEF divisions to see combat in World War I entered the line during and after the five German spring offensives of 1918. These offensives saw chemical warfare at the highest level since its introduction three years before. Regardless of the emphasis eventually placed on gas warfare by GHQ, AEF, and the Army General Staff, new doctrine'for gas weapons could not be fully absorbed or mastered by the inexperienced Americans. Prewar neglect of gas warfare equipment and accompanying doctrine had a significant impact on the ability of the AEF to defend against, and to successfully employ, chemical agents in World War I.

THE AEF ORGANIZES FOR CHEMICAL WARFARE

On 13 June 1917, while the General Staff in the United States struggled to organize, man, and equip an army, General John J. Pershing, Commander of the American Expeditionary Forces (AEF), arrived in France with a staff of fifty-three officers and 146 enlisted men. After a continuous round of official visits and ceremonies, Pershing and his staff settled into temporary headquarters in Paris. Two weeks later the first American troops arrived in France. General Order 8, published on 5 July 1917, established the organization of the AEF General Headquarters (GHQ). This order also created on paper the GHQ position of "Chief of the Gas Service," whose responsibilities included procurement of gas personnel and supplies, the "conduct of the entire Gas and Flame Service both offense and defense," the supervision of training for gas officers and troops, and experimentation with new gases, delivery systems, and protective devices.

Ordering the creation of a Gas Service was a simple matter. The actual organizing of a new branch of the Army, however, would take a tremendous amount of effort and time. Time was precious. By mid-July, over 12,000 doughboys were within thirty miles of the front, all without gas masks or training in chemical warfare. Yet, because of more pressing problems, it was not until 17 August 1917 that General Pershing sent a cable to Washington requesting the organization of a Gas Service and the authority to appoint Lt. Col. Amos A. Fries, Corps of Engineers, as its chief.

Lieutenant Colonel Fries had arrived in France three days earlier. As an engineer officer he was assigned responsibility for organizing a road network to support the AEF Services of Supply (SOS). Several days later Col. Hugh A. Drum and Col. Alvin B. Barber of the GHQ, AEF, approached Fries. As Fries recalled after the war, the staff officers asked what "I should think if my orders were changed so as to make me Chief of the newly proposed gas service." Given overnight to decide, Fries accepted. On 22 August 1917 he began to build an organization based on information Barber and Drum had compiled about the British Special Brigade and French "Z" units. In addition, the staff officers gave Fries a draft of a proposed General Order 31 that would establish a Gas Service.

General Order 31 assigned the Gas Service responsibility for both offensive and defensive operations, including the organization of gas personnel, gas warfare supplies, and gas warfare training in the AEF.

Appended to the order was a draft chart of the Gas Service Organization. In reviewing the chart with Fries, Pershing noted that the offensive arm included Stokes mortar companies. This prompted him to ask why existing trench mortar companies could not be utilized to fire gas rounds. Barber and Drum, who were also present, explained that gas operations were too technical and dangerous for untrained personnel to conduct and, therefore, required special troops. They also told Pershing that in the British Army the Special Brigade used 4-inch Stokes mortars.

Acting on Pershing's instructions, Fries, with Colonel Church and Captain Boothby of the Medical Department, visited the British Special Brigade headquarters at St.Omer. Church had served as an observer with the French Army for a year and a half and, during that time, had collected information on chemical warfare defense. Boothby did the same while observing British chemical warfare procedures and also took a course at the British defense school. At St. Omer the medical officers discussed British defensive gas doctrine, while Fries obtained information on the offensive aspects of chemical warfare. Fries elicited information on gases in use, special troops, chemical ammunition, and delivery systems. He also visited the large chemical material depot for the British Fifth Army.

After returning to AEF headquarters, the three officers reviewed both the draft General Order and the organizational chart. They modified the original proposals to provide general rather than specific guidelines, anticipating that only actual combat experience would glean the information necessary to build a truly effective organization. Fries criticized the British system that divided responsibility for offensive and defensive gas warfare. Paradoxically, the British liaison officer in the United States, Maj. S. M. J. Auld, warned the Americans against just such a practice. Thus, the AEF Gas Service made it the responsibility of all gas officers to be knowledgeable in both areas, a point driven home in subsequent general orders detailing the duties of army, corps, and division gas officers. On 3 September 1917, almost five months after the United States entered the war, the final version of General Order 31 was published.

Not until 27 May 1918, as U.S. divisions were coming on-line in increasing numbers and experiencing heavy gas casualties, did GHQ, AEF, issue General Order 79 for the establishment of unit gas officers. Only then did Fries have the authority to appoint chief gas officers for armies and corps and gas officers and assistants for divisions. Until this time, division commanders had been appointing gas officers as they saw fit. Under the new arrangements, chief gas officers of armies and corps and division gas officers would be staff officers responsible to the commander. Parallel reporting procedures were established in order to ensure that accurate information reached the proper authorities. In addition to reports through official channels, the order authorized these officers to send required reports directly to the Chief of the Gas Service. The Chief, with GHQ approval, could also order these unit staff officers to attend meetings necessary for the coordination of defensive gas measures.

The division and higher echelon gas officers had specific duties assigned. By direction of their commanding officers, they were to instruct and supervise the gas officers and NCOs within their command, supervise all defensive training and drill, collect enemy chemical warfare material for submission to AEF laboratories, inspect defensive measures, and advise the commander and staff regarding all aspects of chemical warfare. The division gas officer had the responsibility of reporting to the commander all gas casualties and actions taken to prevent recurrences. The division commander forwarded this report, together with a list of the actions he had taken to correct the deficiencies, to the Chief of the Gas Service.

Regimental and battalion commanders assigned duties to their gas officers. At this level, gas officer and gas NCO responsibilities were considered additional, not primary duties. A gas officer and NCO assistant were required for regiment, battalion, and separate units, and two NCOs were appointed for each company. Selected on the basis of undefined "special qualifications," the men were trained at the AEF Gas Defense School or corps gas schools. Among their duties, they supervised training in the use of gas masks, gas proof shelters, alarm systems, and related defensive measures. When the division entered combat, the gas NCOs were required to inspect all defensive equipment and antigas procedures at least twice a week. They reported weather, terrain conditions, all new enemy gas tactics and material, and any noted deficiencies. This information was reported officially to the company commander and informally to the battalion commander.

General Order 79 established an AEF Gas Defense School with a course of instruction "adequate for the training in gas defense of gas officers and noncommissioned officers." The school director received specific instructions, to coordinate his activities with those of officers engaged in offensive gas instruction and with those at the AEF's new chemical experimental station at Hanlon Field near Chaumont. Instructors at the Gas Defense School kept abreast of the latest changes in gas warfare by personally reviewing files of Allied and American gas officer reports and by reading translated copies of captured German and Austrian documents.

General Order 79 dealt primarily with the Gas Corps and the training of its officers, but it also called the attention of "all ranks" to the "increasing importance of gas warfare." Although the Gas Corps would do every thing that was possible to prepare individuals and units to avoid casualties from gas, the "ultimate responsibility" for defense against gas, the order concluded, "devolves upon commanding officers" who must provide for the training of their men and the maintenance of gas discipline. In order to maintain gas discipline and provide adequate training, the order urged commanders to cooperate with Gas Corps officers.

The extensive use of gas by the Germans in their spring 1918 offensives caused the AEF General Staff to expand the duties of gas officers. As of 2 July 1918, gas officers were to be consulted and their technical knowledge utilized in the preparation of all plans involving the extensive use of gas, whether by artillery or other means. Thus, the duties and responsibilities of gas officers grew with the increasing awareness of the impact chemical agents were having on the offensive and defensive capabilities of AEF units. Fries, however, faced a chronic problem of locating competent men to serve in a branch of service that lacked precedent and had an unknown future. was further complicated by an Armywide shortage of personnel. The Corps of Engineers, originally the primary source of gas officers, became reluctant, as its own demand for officers grew, to have men reassigned to another branch.

The AEF Gas Service had other problems with which to contend. There was, for example, a severe shortage of gas warfare supplies. The lack of protective masks for members of the AEF caused the greatest concern. On 2 August 1917, GHQ, AEF decided to utilize the British Small Box Respirator (SBR) as its primary mask and the French M-2 mask as an "emergency" protective device.

The SBR consisted of a canister-type filter of absorbent charcoal with alternating layers of oxidized soda lime granules. A flexible rubber tube connected the canister to a rubberized facepiece that was held to the face by elastic bands in order to provide an airtight fit. Inside the facepiece was a rubber nose clip. A hard rubber mouthpiece that the wearer grasped by his teeth was connected to the flexible hose attached to the filtration canister. A soldier exhaled air through a rubber flutter valve at the front of the mask. The wearer viewed the world through two lenses made of celluloid or specially prepared glass. Each soldier had a tube of "antidimming" or defogging paste that could be used to prevent condensation from forming on the lenses. Lacking an American mask, the AEF placed an initial order for 600,000 SBRs and 100,000 French M-2 masks. Additional orders followed, as it would take the United States a year from its entry into the war to begin providing its troops in the field with an acceptable American-made version of the SBR.

The shortage of respirators notwithstanding, no individual could enter the combat zone unless equipped with a mask. Commanders and staff officers went to considerable lengths to ensure that all members of their units had respirators. In late December, 1917, the newly arrived 42nd "Rainbow" Division was moved by rail to a training site in France. On the train were masks for the unit, which the division's Chief of Staff planned to issue on its arrival. The 1st Division, however, was due to go "on the line shortly" and submitted an urgent request for respirators. The Chief of the Gas Service responded by ordering the 42nd's Chief of Staff to transfer his masks to the 1st Division. To circumvent the order, the 42nd's Chief of Staff immediately stopped the train and ordered the masks issued to his men. He then reported to Fries that it was impossible to comply with the order because the masks had already been issued.

Several thousand men of the 1st Division lacked masks, and its 1st Brigade was scheduled to move to the front line in January.* Fries finally obtained a "priority of shipment" and detailed several gas officers to accompany the masks from Le Havre, the major British supply base, to ensure their safe delivery to the 1st Division. Despite these precautions, one carload of 4,000 masks disappeared in transit. Fries finally had to order the 2nd Brigade of the 1st Division to turn in their SBRs. These were cleaned and reissued to the Division's 1st Brigade. This episode was not an isolated one.

Gas equipment and supplies in the United States and France were initially the responsibility of the nearest related branch of the Army. The AEF Gas Service found this procedure "exceedingly embarrassing, cumbersome and inefficient." Despite initial resistance, the General Staff in Washington approved AEF requisition submitted on 10 September 1917 for 50,000 cylinders, 50,000 Livens projector shells, and a large quantity of Stokes mortars and ammunition. None of these weapons or ammunition reached the AEF in time to be used in combat. To avoid duplication of effort and to save time, Fries, in February, 1918, received permission to make direct purchases of equipment from the Allies. At that time almost all of the gas warfare material used by the AEF came from the British. Not until April, 1918, did any material manufactured in the United States begin to reach the AEF. As noted in the preceding chapter, a number of war gases were manufactured in the United States during the war, and more than 3,600 tons of these did reach the French and British.

Because of a shortage of artillery pieces, artillery units of the AEF were equipped primarily with the French 75-mm light field gun, the 155-mm medium howitzer, and the 240-mm heavy howitzer, as well as with British 8-inch and 9.2-inch heavy howitzers. The U.S. Army also adopted, with minor modifications, the French gas shell. The AEF Services of Supply purchased French shells and painted them according to an American color code.

Originally, the SOS defensive gas equipment fell into Class I with clothing, leather goods, and optical instruments. In February, 1918, when the Gas Service was given authority to requisition its own supplies, all items of gas warfare equipment were placed into a new category, Class V. In September, 1918, the Army created four subclasses within the general Class V classification. Subclass A material included offensive gas supplies, such as gas shells and grenades, that were not used by gas troops but by the combat arms. Subclass B material included those gas supplies issued exclusively to gas troops. Subclass C supplies encompassed aviation, smoke, and incendiary material. Subclass D items included all defensive gas material. The Ordnance Corps transported and issued subclasses A and C, while the Gas Service did the same for B and D items. The Gas Service distributed all "anti-gas supplies." Fries ordered a 10 percent reserve of all equipment at the division gas dumps, and each company or regiment maintained a 5 percent reserve supply. The division gas officer issued the required masks to the regimental supply officers, who distributed them to battalions. Gas officers also issued gas alarm devices, Strombo horns, Klaxon horns, and gongs directly to company commanders in each sector. Later, army and corps gas officers were given similar responsibility for the issue of gas supplies to corps artillerymen and all rear echelon troops.

Another branch heavily involved in chemical warfare was the Army's Medical Department. The General Staff anticipated that medical officers would require some knowledge of the actual symptoms brought on by chemical agents and the various methods of treatment for gas poisoning. Consequently, in May, 1917, the War Department issued a "Memorandum on Gas Poisoning in Warfare with Notes on Its Pathology and Treatment," based on British sources. Still, despite this assistance from Washington, most of the planning and organization for the treatment of gas casualties was done by the AEF in France.

Maj. J. R. Church, Medical Department, was the first Medical Director of the Gas Service in France. While on the General Staff, he had assisted in the initial planning for an AEF Gas Service. As Medical Director he devoted most of his time to organizational matters. The increase in gas casualties, however, resulted in a personnel change in the position, with Lt. Col. Harry L. Gilchrist, M.D., the former commander of Number 9, General Hospital, replacing Church. Gilchrist prepared for his new assignment by attending the British Gas School at Rouen, France.

When Gilchrist reported for duty as Medical Director, he found no records or guidelines detailing the responsibilities of his position. His first priority, and one agreed to by Fries, was to launch a gas instruction campaign directed specifically at AEF medical officers. On 9 February 1918, Gilchrist published a pamphlet, "Symptomology, Pathology and General Treatment of Gas Cases," which provided medical officers basic information on the treatment of chemical casualties. Following this publication, the Medical Director's office issued a constant stream of bulletins aimed at keeping AEF medical officers up-to-date on the latest medical developments in gas warfare. Gilchrist visited most AEF divisions and hospitals, where he lectured to officers and men on chemical warfare from a medical point of view, emphasizing prevention and treatment of gas casualties.

As the chemical war escalated with the introduction of mustard gas, the Medical Director's responsibilities and, indeed, his department's tasks became increasingly crucial to the AER Gilchrist inspected troops at the front and visited medical personnel in hospitals, hospital trains, and other locations. He also served as the liaison officer between the Gas Service and the Medical Department, advising both the AEF's Chief of the Gas Service and the Chief Surgeon on gas-related medical matters. In addition to these general duties, he collected all medical information relating to gas warfare and relayed it to the AEF's Chief Surgeon. Gilchrist focused his attention on such matters as new treatment for gas casualties and "combating-the effects of the enemy gases not only from a therapeutic, but also from a prophylactic point of view." To obtain information, he visited the sites of battles where large numbers of gas casualties had occurred.

Because armies and corps of the AEF were formed after the arrival of a number of divisions, the medical structure to treat gas casualties evolved first within the division. On 1 March 1918, the 42nd Division became the second American division to occupy a sector on the Western Front. Although initially the division had few gas casualties, the medical officers prepared for a large influx of gas victims.

All four of the division's field hospitals were set up to accept gas victims, and orders were given that a total of 500 beds be put aside for such cases. On 20 March the Germans launched an artillery bombardment of mustard and high explosive shells that hit the 42nd Division's 165th Infantry at 1730 hours. In thespace of a few minutes, the mustard caused 270 casualties, including one death. The first-aid station through which the casualties passed also received a drenching with. gas, so medical personnel wore masks as they treated the patients.

As a result of this attack and others that followed, the 42nd Division took several steps to improve the treatment of gas casualties. These later became standard for AEF divisions in the line. The first measure was to dedicate one of the four division field hospitals to gas cases. The position of division Gas Medical Officer was also created. Memorandum 148, HQ, 42nd Division, published on 23 April 1918, listed the duties of this officer as the instruction of medical personnel in gas defense; the supervision of gas protection of medical dugouts, aid stations, and field hospitals; the early diagnosis of symptoms; and the treatment of all types of gas casualties.

The AEF adopted the 42nd Division's practices when it instituted the position of division Gas Medical Officer in AEF General Order 144, dated 29 August 1918. GHQ took this measure in the face of mounting gas casualties and a high incident of gas malingering. As a consequence, in addition to the duties indicated in the 42nd Division's memorandum, the AEF order added duties such as the instruction of all division personnel on the early symptoms and treatments of gas poisoning and the instruction of line officers in practical medical matters connected with gas warfare. The orders stated that any officers selected must be "live, wide-awake, energetic men, and must show a keen appreciation of the work." By the first week in October, 1918, each AEF division had a Gas Medical Officer. These men were sent to the School of Pharmacy's School of Gas (Ecole de Gaz) at the University of Paris for a four-day course to prepare them for their division duties.

Beyond the division field hospitals, each army established its own gas hospitals. The first such installation began operation on 29 August 1918. Army-level hospital personnel were casuals, or officers and men loaned from base or evacuation hospitals or anywhere else medical personnel could be found. To meet the demands of the Meuse-Argonne offensive, the Chief Surgeon, AEF, in September, 1918, established five gas hospitals with a total of 1,650 beds. Colonel Gilchrist suggested three mobile 1,500-bed gas hospitals be established, one for each U.S. corps. This plan, however, was never implemented because of insufficient personnel. Another plan called for the creation of two "emergency gas teams" to be assigned to each base hospital. Their mission was to "relieve the strain" that sudden gas attacks put on division field hospitals. The GHQ, AEF, organized several "emergency gas teams," each consisting of a medical officer, two nurses, and two orderlies. The Chief Surgeon of the 1st U.S. Army, Col. A. N. Stark, however, objected to these teams on the grounds that base hospitals were too far removed from the fighting. He also believed that the division field hospitals set aside forgassed soldiers were effective and needed no further assistance. HeedingStark's objections, the Chief Surgeon disbanded the teams.

Another problem with which Fries and his staff had to contend was training in gas defense. When the 1st Division arrived in France, Pershing thought it best to have the Americans train by serving with a French divi sion. This proved to be unsatisfactory because the training varied from unit to unit within the French division. When the Training Section of the AEF's GHQ became operational, it prepared a standardized division training schedule. Initially, the period of time a division spent preparing to enter the line was supposed to be three months. Only two days of the schedule were allocated to Gas Service instructors. Later, as the demand for combat units increased, the gas instruction decreased to a mere six hours. This was vigorously protested by the Gas Service. In the spring of 1918, when the German offensives required a shortening of the division training cycle to bring new units on line, gas instruction was cut further.

Formal defensive training was supplemented by wearing the masks during other training activities. Pvt. Norman A. Dunham of the 40th Division remembered wearing the SBR and full pack during two and three hour marches. He thought the mask "the worst thing a soldier has to contend with" and the "most torturous thing" a person can wear. Lt. Edgar D. Gilman remarked that when he wore the mask he found that it was not only disagreeable, painful, and smothering, but also that his saliva flowed profusely from his mouth, through the flutter valves, and down the front of his shirt. Personal protection was survival on the battlefield,however, and command emphasis had to be placed on defensive gas training, to include the wearing of the mask.

It became obvious to GHQ, AEF that many commanders were not supporting the training activities of their gas officers and

NCOs. To remedy this problem, officers in brigades that were rotated off the line received a comprehensive lecture course on gas defensive measures. However, continued reports of over 25 percent gas casualties indicated to General Staff that, after basic training, comparatively little was to be gained by instructing individuals in units on the line. The consensus among gas officers was that training had to instill an interest and awareness of gas defensive measures throughout an entire unit to give the best results in combat. Gas officers also believed more realistic training was needed. One result of this conviction was that artillery batteries, when they trained, received a minimum of three surprise gas attacks as part of the training schedule. To test the alertness of sentries and to correct such carelessness as leaving masks out of reach, attacks were often scheduled at night, while the troops were sleeping at their position. Men firing on the ranges were subjected to simulated surprise gas attacks in order to familiarize them with laying artillery pieces during an attack and to acquaint them with the difficulty of transmitting firing data while masked. During night marches, men were subjected to gas attacks as a means of teaching them to overcome confusion.

During the first year of American participation in the war, men arriving as individual replacements had little or no formal instruction in defensive measures until they reached their units in the forward areas. In the summer of 1918, the Army acted to rectify this haphazard method. Training stations were established at the AEF debarkation ports of Brest and St. Nazaire. Each center had five Gas Service instructors: one officer and four NCOS. Three enlisted men acted as gas mask fitters and helpers. When troops arrived at the stations, they marched single file into a warehouse to be fitted and issued. masks. After an inspection, the troops moved to a large lecture hall where instructors did everything possible to impress on the men the importance of defensive gas measures. To complete the training, seventy-five to 100 men at a time entered a gas chamber filled with a tear agent for five to ten minutes. At peak times more than 2,000 men a day were put through this initiation into gas warfare.

In Army rear areas, depot divisions, such as the one at La Querche, handled three categories of personnel: newly arrived line replacements, special units such as engineer troops, and casuals who were recently released from hospitals and scheduled to rejoin their units. During the normal three-week course, the replacements received a minimum of eighteen hours of gas defense training. Their training consisted of lectures, mask drills, games with the mask worn, and firing weapons while wearing the The troops also went through simulated tactical operations, with the instructors lighting smoke candles and throwing tear gas grenades to provide added realism.

Special troops such as pioneer infantry, engineer, and medical service units first received basic infantry training and then were given three days' intensive instruction in gas defense. During the three days, the men practiced their specialty while wearing masks. For example, medics with SBRs in place applied bandages and carried stretchers through woods and over rough terrain. Engineers constructed roads and pioneer troops dug ditches while wearing masks. After duty hours, trainees played baseball in their SBRs.

Hospital convalescents, the last category of men run through the divisions, numbered anywhere from a handful to 2,000 a day. These men were reequipped with masks, and those with prior gas training - Class "A" men - were excused from formal instruction until August, 1918, when the mounting number of mustard gas casualties compelled the Gas Service staff to give all personnel short classes on ways to avoid being contaminated by this persistent agent.

The increased German employment of chemical agents-especially mustard gas - for counterbattery fire forced American artillery training camps to place special emphasis on defensive gas instruction. During a gas attack, a poorly trained artillery man would be totally incapable of serving his weapon or delivering accurate fire. Initially, artillery officers and NCOs attended a week-long course of lectures, drills, and practical exercises. Later NCOs received an additional week of training. If the artillerymen failed to score 70 percent or better on the final examination, they had to repeat the course. Just before returning to the front, the graduates had to visit.a base hospital to see gas casualties. The experience, according to instructors, "furnished a great stimulus to general gas training." Still, despite these efforts to train every doughboy arriving in France, many received no training in gas warfare because of the pressing need for troops,on the front lines.[24]

In conjunction with the emphasis on gas defensive training, the AEF paid increasing attention to the offensive gas capabilities of the American Army in France. On 10 January 1918 the first two companies of the 1st Gas Regiment (30th Engineers) arrived in France. The companies reported to the British Special Brigade training area at Helfaut, where Brigadier General Foulkes personally directed the training of the unit. Eventually, four of the six companies of the regiment passed through Helfaut.

The training of the 1st Gas Regiment in offensive gas operations began in February, 1918, and employed the delivery systems used by the British. The American troops spent five days learning to use Livens projectors, seven days for Stokes mortars, and two days for cylinder operations. The men first attended classes and then conducted practical field exercises in which they applied their newly acquired knowledge. Projector operations called for the emplacement of the guns at night and their detonation the following day. Stokes mortar drill required the men to conduct rapid fire with gas rounds, thermite, and smoke, both day and night. Officers of the regiment opened cylinders of chlorine, and the men walked through the gas cloud to instill confidence in their training and equipment. The American officers were then detailed to a sector of the British front and assigned to Special Brigade companies, where they observed projector, mortar, and cylinder operations. The overall result was that these men better understood offensive gas operations and could assist in training the other companies of the American Gas Regiment.

On 6 June 1918 these trained officers and men held a practice shoot for the AEF General Staff at Hanlon Field, the home of the AEF's Gas School and experimental station in France. Twelve Stokes mortars and 100 Livens projectors were fired. On 22 June, after several more exercises, companies of the 1st Gas Regiment moved to the U.S. sector to conduct offensive gas operations.

Artillery was the other branch of the Army capable of conducting offensive gas operations. In the first gas warfare manuals prepared by the U.S. Army War College, artillery employment was not included because of the continual changes in gas tactical doctrine on the Western Front. Therefore, almost all artillery training in gas warfare was conducted in France, where the AEF adopted British and French doctrine for gas shell fire. The U.S. 1st Army, for example, published its own "Provisional Instruction for Artillery Officers on the Use of Gas Shell," based on French field manuals. At artillery camps, gas officers lectured on the problems involved in the use of gas shells, but no evidence exists to indicate that gas shells were ever fired in training. Yet, by 1 November 1918, 20 percent of all shells delivered to the AEF were gas filled, and a 25 percent ratio was planned for 1919.

No other preparations or plans were instituted in AEF rear areas to prepare and sustain the American armies in chemical warfare. The burden of the gas war fell to the combat divisions of the AEF. How well they fought and how well they adapted to this new experience is the subject of the next chapter.

"THE QUICK AND THE DEAD": THE AEF ON THE CHEMICAL BATTLEFIELD

Between 18 and 21 January 1918, units of the U.S. 1st Infantry Division relieved the French 1st Moroccan Division manning the front lines in the Ansauville sector. In doing so, the "Big Red One" became the first American division to occupy a portion of the Western Front. The movement of American troops into the lines was uneventful except for one incident, "As we take our positions in the trenches," Maj. Gen. Robert Bullard, the division commander, noted, "from the French position on our right some two hundred gas casualties are evacuated-our first object lesson."

This grim "object lesson" reinforced French warnings that the Ansauville sector was a highly active gas front with both sides constantly employing large amounts of chemical agents. The German use of Yellow Cross especially concerned the French. The XXII Corps commander, prior to the arrival of the ist Division, had his troops post in every dugout instructions in English on the correct procedures to follow during and after a Yellow Cross attack. The French warning advised the Americans to mask when the first gas shell exploded and remain masked for four hours following a gas bombardment. The instructions also called for anyone in a gassed area to beat and shake his clothing prior to entering a dugout and to use soapy water to decontaminate skin exposed to mustard. Further instructions from the French corps commander followed, emphasizing the gas-proofing of dugouts and the maintenance of gas mask discipline.

Based on the 1st Division's experience over the previous months, these instructions should not have been necessary. Although the unit arrived overseas without the slightest bit of gas training, it received in France the most complete chemical warfare preparation of any AEF division during the war. Gas training pamphlets, directives, and orders were showered on the 1st Division by an anxious and apprehensive GHQ, AEF. The 1st Division became the only American division to undergo the complete GHQ, AEF, training schedule, which included defensive and offensive gas training.

Instruction in chemical warfare began for the 1st Division in December with nine hours devoted to defensive training. Proper masking was a key element of this training. With troops in the practice trenches, instructors sounded gas alarms and lit smoke pots to simulate gas clouds, thereby increasing the troops' "skill in putting on and wearing the gas masks." During the drill, gas instructors reminded their students that "in case of gas attack, there are only two classes of soldiers, the quick and the dead."

The British had decided for reasons now obscure that SBR masking should take no longer than six seconds, to be accomplished in five steps. In step one, the doughboy had to hold his breath, knock off his headgear, grip his rifle between the legs, and reach into the case on his chest to grasp the mask by the "breathing joint" and nose clip.

At step two, the soldier thrust his chin out, held the mask in front of the face with both thumbs inside and under the elastic headband. In step three, the chin was placed into the facepiece while the headband was pulled over the head to secure the mask. Next, at step four, the soldier grasped the mouthpiece with his teeth. The last step, five, required the soldier to reach through the facepiece to secure the nose clip and then run his hands around the mask to ensure a snug fit. Division gas officers complained that when it came to defensive gas training, many commanders were satisfied when their men simply achieved the six-second requirement. Proper adjustment, the gas officers believed., was more important than speed.

When finally issued, each mask came with a small log book tied to the canvas case. Soldiers received instructions to record the length of time they wore the mask, both for drill and in combat. They were also required to identify each type of gas encountered. The purpose of this log was to ensure that the filter in the canister was replaced at the proper intervaL Filters for an SBR had a life of fifty to 100 hours of exposure, depending on the chemical agents. As might be expected, the log system did not work. As one gas officer remarked, "any man who in the hell of battle can keep such a record completely should be at once awarded a Distinguished Service Medal." Gas officers in some divisions came up with an alternative: they painted the number of the month of issue on the case. If and when filters became available, the officers replaced them based on their own estimate of exposure time. There were three types of AEF filter canisters. Those painted black were for training only and offered no protection against smoke or gas. Canisters colored yellow protected against smoke, offered greater gas protection, and had a high resistance to breathing. The green canister offered protection against smoke, had "sufficient" gas protection, and had a low resistance to breathing.

While the British SBR was initially worn by the 1st and other divisions, the American version was in ready supply by the late summer of 1918. The American mask had both advantages and disadvantages. Although its fuller facepiece permitted easy cleaning of the eyepieces, these eyepieces had a tendency to fall out; also, the larger facepiece with an increase in dead space made it more difficult to clear. The larger canister gave greater protection, but was heavier and clumsy.

There is no question but that the SBR, whether British or American, was extremely uncomfortable. General Bullard admitted that he could never "fulfill the qualification of a successful wearer" because as much as he tried he could not wear the mask longer than three minutes without feeling smothered. Since the SBR was difficult to wear, division gas officers reported troops would change from the SBR to the more comfortable M-2 in the midst of a gas attack, in the process inhaling the poisonous air. The M-2 did not offer the filtration protection of the SBR. Its flimsy construction and susceptibility to water damage also reduced. its effectiveness, as did the fact that it did not block mustard gas. The widespread problem with the M-2 prompted AEF, GHQ General Order 78 on 25 May 1918. This order forbid anyone who entered the alert zone to use the M-2. As noted previously it was retained and attached to stretchers for men with head wounds or for those unable to grasp the mouthpiece. Labor troops in rear areas were authorized to wear the M-2.

A number of U.S. officers apparently procured, on their own, another French mask, the ARS (described earlier). This created morale problems since it gave American enlisted men the "impression that our protective equipment is defective." A Gas Service report demanded that these officers "be taught" that only the material issued by the Gas Service was authorized for use, and that they had no authority to secure equipment from the French.

Another mask, the *Tissot*, was officially procured from the French, although it was for issue only in "small numbers" to artillerymen, Signal Corps troops, and front-line medical units whose personnel had to be active during gas attacks. Not only did this mask's filter offer less resistance to breathing and have the same quality filtration of the American SBR, but the problem of fogged vision associated with the SBR did not exist.

The *Tissot* design allowed air to flow between the two lenses of each eyepiece, eliminating condensation. Most important, the *Tissot* design did away with a nose clip and mouthpiece, making it a comfortable yet safe mask. Unfortunately, as noted earlier, the filter location on the back, together with the flimsy rubber facepiece, made it unsuitable for infantry.

If soldiers wearing gas masks in defensive positions experienced a variety of problems, they encountered even more difficulties when they shifted to the offensive. The standard issue American or British SBR made normal breathing difficult, it made obtaining sufficient oxygen during heavy exertion, such as in infantry attacks across No Man's Land, impossible. Additionally, exertion caused perspiration to form on the lens, limiting vision even more than what was normal. "Standing Orders for Defense Against Gas" published in November, 1911, stated that within two mile& of the front lines and within areas specially exposed to gas shelling, the gas mask case would be carried in the alert position, which was on the chest.

At Ville Savoye, for example, Pvt. Moses King, 305th Infantry, 77th Division, had difficulty seeing through his mask and received an order from his company commander - whose own vision was obscured - to remove his facepiece, but to keep the nose clip and mouthpiece in place. This "pernicious habit," the Chief, Chemical Warfare Service, AEF, noted in September 1918, "has been the cause of many casualties"; the practice has been "condemned at every opportunity." Despite the condemnation, the practice never ceased, and the increased use of mustard gas by the Germans resulted in a significant number of Allied casualties suffering from eye damage.

As a consequence of these and other problems, standing orders did not call for troops to mask during the attack. Doughboys did, however, wear the mask on the chest in the alert position with the helmet chin strap on the tip of the chin, rather than under it, to facilitate quick placement of the mask if gas were encountered.

In addition to the problems associated with gas masks, the persistency of chemical agents combined with the methods of AEF commanders to produce a significant number of gas casualties. Under normal attacking conditions, an area in which phosgene was used would clear in ten minutes. Diphosgene would take longer to dispel, perhaps fifteen to twenty minutes. Mustard gas would linger for several days. A problem arose, however, when AEF commanders intent on taking an objective regardless of the cost often launched an attack before a gassed area had cleared. The reason for this disregard lay in the fact that the AEF, from General Pershing down to division commanders, never hesitated to relieve an officer considered lacking in an aggressive spirit.

Of the chemical agents employed by the Germans against the Allies, mustard gas was responsible for 39 percent of AEF gas casualties. Once mustard gas made contact with the skin, it destroyed tissue as long as it remained, doing damage several hours before the first symptoms appeared. To combat this persistent blister agent, the Gas Service made available to line units an ointment called Sag paste to protect exposed flesh. Sag paste came in a 3.5-cm by 16-cm collapsible tube and became a standard-issue item for the prevention and treatment of mustard burns. According to one veteran, it looked like and had the consistency of "carbolated vaseline." Doughboys who entered a mustard-contaminated area or who anticipated a shelling of Yellow Cross smeared their bodies with the ointment. It proved very effective, a medic in the 35th Division noted, if used in time. However, it was uncomfortable because it caked when the men perspired and rubbed off on clothing when a soldier engaged in any physical activity. The paste also presented a danger: if not removed after exposure to gas it eventually absorbed the mustard agent without neutralizing it, which meant that the agent ultimately came into contact with the skin. There were other uses for the paste: medics, for example, found it to be effective in soothing mustard burns by blocking the oxygen to the contaminated area. Enterprising men in the trenches found it extremely effective in exterminating "cooties," the doughboy slang for body lice.

The Defense Division, CWS, sought other ways besides masks and Sag paste to protect troops from mustard gas. The division designed and had manufactured a protective suit for artillery gun crews, medics, and decontaminating teams. The suit consisted of cotton sheeting impregnated with linseed or "vegetable drying oil." The coveralls had elastic ties at the ankles and wrists. A zipper down the center from neck to crotch provided an airtight fit. The hood was worn under the headgear. Mittens had been provided prior to the development of the suit and were "highly valuable ... but somewhat stiff and clumsy." Special boots were also provided to complete the uniform. Unfortunately, the suit trapped body heat and moisture so it could rarely be worn longer than fifteen to thirty minutes. A gas officer reported men tearing off the suit "while working in an area reeking with mustard gas because they couldn't stand the discomfort any longer."

The effects of mustard gas could be lessened or even avoided by removing it with hot soapy water shortly after exposure. To this end, GHQ, AEF, on 29 August 1918, ordered the Medical Department to activate a number of "mobile degassing units." Each division in the "line of battle" would have two such units attached, commanded by a Sanitary Corps captain or first lieutenant. To each eleven-man unit a specially trained medical gas officer would be detailed from the supported division, This individual's duties included the supervision of the unit's operation, instruction of the medical personnel on the treatment of gas casualties, and responsibility for the maintenance of the proper equipment for the treatment of gas casualties at the battalion advance aid station. The degassing units remained in the division rear. When a unit became contaminated and could be withdrawn from the line, the degassing station rushed to treat the men as close to the front as possible. The units equipment consisted of a five-ton tank truck with a 1,200 gallon capacity and an "instantaneous heater" mounted on the rear of the vehicle to provide hot water. The heated water flowed to portable shower baths similar to modern field showers. Another vehicle carried fuel, underwear, uniforms, and medical supplies. These supplies included bicarbonate of soda to Rush the patient's eyes, ears, mouth, and nasal passages. Unfortunately for the thousands of mustard casualties, very few degassing units saw service, as evidenced by the late date of the order creating them.

While methods were being sought to "degas" men, efforts were also undertaken to decontaminate the ground they held in the static trench warfare. General orders created decontamination squads at regiment and battalion level. These units decontaminated shell holes with lime and new earth, buried gas shell duds, reported to gas officers the location of dud shells that could not be buried, and removed contaminated equipment and clothing in special oiled bags. Each man in the squad was issued a new SBR, a reserve M-2 mask, a suit of protective coveralls, and two pairs of oiled mittens. The decontamination equipment consisted of shovels, buckets, and long-handled tongs for handling dud mustard shells.

In the trenches, mustard gas and other agents were counteracted in a variety of ways. During a gas attack, standing orders called for as little moving about and talking as possible, because gas poisoning was sometimes intensified by exertion. Once an attack ceased, trenches were cleared of low lying gas. One method required the use of an Ayrton or trench fan. This device consisted of a two-foot-long handle attached to a rigid piece of canvas hinged to a fifteen-inch section that moved in one direction. In effect the fan was used like a shovel, with the moveable flap creating an upward air current, thus removing the gas. Americans adopted these fans as called for by British defensive gas doctrine. Unfortunately, the fans, according to British General Foulkes, were "worse than worthless." Not only did they not remove the vapor, but the exertion of masked users led to exhaustion and increased susceptibility to gassing. The fans were eventually discarded and burned to create an updraft, soon recognized as a better method of clearing trenches and dugouts of gas.

Another method of decontamination used in the trenches consisted of placing boxes of chloride of lime outside of dugouts. Prior to entering, men stepped in the substance, neutralizing any mustard agent clinging to the shoes. The Vermoral sprayer, which was a hand-pumped fire extinguisher filled with a sodium thiosulfate solution, could neutralize chlorine, but little else. The sprayers were used, however, to moisten the blankets at the entrances of the gas-proof dugouts.

The prolongation of German gas attacks, the increased quantity of chemical agents fired in an attack, the extensive use of the persistent agent mustard, plus the fact that 80 percent to 90 percent of all gas attacks experienced by the AEF took place during the hours of darkness, made the construction of gas-proof dugouts essential for survival in the trenches. Basically, the gas-proofing of dugouts required a wood frame entrance and a snug fitting blanket, usually soaked with glycerine and kept damp with a diluted solution of sodium thiosulfate. If space allowed, "complete protection" could, be obtained by hanging two blankets over the entrance in such a way as to leave an air space between the two. Such measures made it difficult for men in front-line trenches to get out of a dugout rapidly in the event of an infantry attack, and for this reason early U.S. manuals advised against protection of front-line dugouts. But this advice was generally ignored because of the need to have a gas-free environment in which to sleep and occasionally remove the SBR. The same Army manual stated that "Medical aid-posts and advanced dressing stations; Company, Regiment, and Brigade Headquarters; at least one dugout per battery position; Signal Shelters and any other place where work has to be carried out during a gas attack should *always* be protected."

Oftentimes, casualties occurred when a gas shell or projector shell fell at the entrance of a dugout and the force of the explosion threw open the blankets and drove the gas inside. On 27 May 1918, at the beginning of one of the German 1918 spring offensives, a concentration of 983 phosgene projector bombs caught doughboys of the 168th Infantry, 42nd Division, asleep in dugouts on the side of a ravine. The Germans, in order to keep the U.S. troops pinned in the gassed position, shelled the area in the rear of the ravine for an hour with shrapnel and Yellow Cross. The division G-3 reported one soldier killed and six wounded by shrapnel, 236 gassed, and thirty-seven gas deaths resulting from the attack.

It was the duty of the gas sentry to sound the warning of a gas attack to the other troops. Usually the sentry received general instructions to alert his unit as soon as he heard the hissing sound of gas leaving cylinders, saw a cloud moving along the ground, observed a distant flash, heard a muffled explosion of projectors, saw a shell burst with a small pop, or sniffed a suspicious odor. In addition to shouting, "Gas!" he would, after masking, sound a mechanical alarm. Such alarms ranged from air horns, known as Strombos, to metal shell casings, steel triangles, or even church bells. When, in the fall of 1918, the AEF went on the offensive, the Gas Service decided that Klaxon horns and European police rattles produced the most audible warning of gas to troops on the move.

Whether on the move in open warfare or manning the trenches in static warfare, the most critical individuals in chemical combat were the unit gas officers. On 27 May 1918, AEF General Order 79 formalized and standardized defensive duties for gas officers, the positions having been created by individual divisions on their own initiative after arrival in France. Two months later, General Order 107 expanded the functions of gas officers: in addition to their previous duties, they would be advisers whose technical knowledge would be solicited "in the preparations of all plans involving the extensive use of gas, whether by artillery or by other means." Despite the order, staff officers too often told gas officers that their advice for offensive planning was not required and that they should concern themselves only with defensive duties. The success of division gas officers in integrating plans for the use of gas in offensive operations eventually depended on, in the words of the Gas Service's Chief, their ability to "go out and sell gas to the army." Despite such promotional efforts, resistance by staff officers continued. During the Meuse-Argonne campaign in the fall of 1918, an unidentified division gas officer reportedly recommended to a division operations officer (G-3) that gas be used during a particular phase of the engagement. The staff officer replied that he would employ the artillery firing gas shells only if the gas officer stated in writing that the gas would not cause a single American casualty. This request was unrealistic in that a thorough staff planner in World War I "usually included an allowance for casualties due to a friendly barrage." Another objection raised to the use of gas was that commanders feared its employment would subject their men to unnecessary retaliatory gas attacks.

Even if a division commander and his staff were reluctant to employ chemicals, they could not afford to be careless about the protection of their troops from chemical agents. A unit's effectiveness depended on proper gas defensive measures. GHQ, AEF, delegated significant responsibility for gas defense to division, regiment, battalion, and company gas officers and NCOs. These dedicated and harried men attempted to insure that their respective organizations could cope with gas attacks while sustaining minimal casualties. Once in the trenches, exposed to a chemical warfare environment, most commanders soon realized the need for competent gas officers.

After selection and training, gas officers had to prove themselves to the commander, staff, and the troops in the trenches. The most effective way to gain the respect and confidence of the troops, one gas officer discovered, was to join a unit under an attack. This practice offered a number of advantages. First, the gas officer learned the immediate effects of a gas attack and what individuals endured during such an attack. He could suggest corrections and give guidance during the attack, as opposed to afterwards, when men were already casualties. The confidence of the men in the gas officer's instruction grew when they observed him "take what they did." Infantry officers proved more willing to accept the advice of such a gas officer because they knew he spoke from "actual and not book knowledge."

This knowledge afforded the gas officer the credibility to obtain a "hearing and accomplish results" when he called to the attention of unit officers and staff both "good results of proper gas discipline and the bad results of bad discipline."

While division gas officers worked with the staff, the regimental and battalion gas officers had the greatest impact on the doughboys, At these lower echelons, gas officers assumed a variety of responsibilities that ranged from instruction to inspection of defensive equipment and selection of alternate positions during an attack. It fell to these officers to assure that gas alarms were installed, gas sentries posted, gas alert signs displayed, and dugouts selected for gas-proofing, In addition these officers took wind readings twice a day. When required, gas officers became bomb disposal experts who located and removed all unexploded enemy gas shells. As the Table of Organization for AEF units, did not include gas officers, General Order 79 of 27 May 1918, which ordered the appointment of gas officers down to battalion level, caused some grumbling in recently arrived divisions. Plagued by a shortage of line officers, commanders assigned men to gas duties grudgingly., When the need arose, the men chosen were subjected to double duty as infantry officers.

With the absence of sophisticated detection and warning systems, one of the most important functions of a gas officer became the determination of when to give the order to mask and when to unmask. At gas schools, trainees were taught to "taste" gas, sniffing just enough air to identify a chemical agent by its own peculiar odor. They had to know the persistency and the properties of each gas and then be able to determine how soon after an attack the air would clear. Most of the officers became very proficient at identification. At times, though, some gas officers were "too conscientious" in "tasting" for gas and became casualties themselves.

When night settled in, gas officers in the trenches slept fitfully, waiting for the cry of "Gas!" One such officer described an evening that was shattered, after the troops had gone to sleep, by the sound of artillery followed by gas alarms. Everyone, he recalled, "came out of their holes" with masks in place, the "fine fruit" of constant training. The officer lifted his mask, sniffed, and determined the fumes to be from high explosive shells. After taking his mask off, the gas officer gave the all clear and the men unmasked. Toward dawn the men again awoke to the sound of gas alarms and cries of "Gas!" This time the officer raised his mask and detected the "mild pungent breath" of a chemical agent. He masked and told the others to do the same. A gas shell exploded upwind with a "light pop and puff of vapor." After the shells ceased dropping he checked up and down the line for casualties and found none. Several minutes passed, and he took another taste only to detect a lingering odor. Five minutes later a light wind drove the gas away, and the all-clear sounded.

The Americans were not always so fortunate in responding to gas attacks. On 26 February 1918, at 1330 in the Ansauville sector, men of the 1st Division received the first German projector attack directed against U.S. forces. The estimated 150 to 250 bombs contained phosgene and chloropicrin. Conditions were ideal for such an attack: the heavy evening air kept the gas low to the ground, and what wind there was soon became calm. The bombs fell over a 600-meter front, where heavy underbrush held the gas in place. Of the 225 men exposed, 33 percent (eighty-five men) became casualties. Two men died soon after the attack, and six soldiers succumbed after they reached the division field hospital.

Col. Campbell King, 1st Division Chief of Staff, believed that there were several causes for the casualties. The sudden attack caught men unprepared on sentry duty or in their dugouts; they did not have adequate warning to adjust their masks or lower the gas curtains. After the attack, men removed their masks on their own initLtive, or changed to the M-2, although the gas lingered in a dangerous concentration. Furthermore, the unmasked doughboys remained or worked in the dugouts and in low places in the woods, where gas stagnated. A captain who witnessed the attack amplified the Chief of Staffs observation. He reiterated that the premature removal of the mask, a breach of discipline, caused casualties and that the men failed to mask in time and to lower the gas-proof curtains.

At the same time, the soldiers neglected to put out fires in the dugouts, thereby drawing gas from the trenches into the sealed shelters. Men who were only slightly gassed exerted themselves, contrary to standing orders, thus complicating their symptoms. The captain attributed the donning of the M-2 to the discomfort involved in wearing the SBR. A field hospital report mentioned that one man had had his mask disarranged in. an attempt to force a mask on a comrade who had gone berserk and torn off his own mask.

In another commonplace incident, an entire platoon of infantry in the 28th Division became gas casualties before they reached the front. While moving forward one night toward Châuteau Thierry, the men stopped to rest in shallow shell holes near the road. A recent rain had diluted the usual smell of mustard, and no one advised the green troops that the holes were craters from Yellow Cross shells. Unwittingly, they slept through the night in fresh mustard contamination. The following morning the men awoke with backs and buttocks so badly burned that the skin appeared to be flayed. The battalion gas officer could only try to relieve their agony with generous applications of Sag paste. That same day the 28th Division's gas officer noted his dwindling supplies of paste and masks. Since German gas seemed to be "coming over in increasing quantities with the resulting casualties," he ordered. one of the battalion gas officers back to the SOS depot at Gievres on a foraging expedition to secure antigas supplies for the division.

There were times when division, regimental, and battalion gas officers, in their more zealous attempts to prevent gas casualties, ran afoul of line officers. A battalion commander in the 23d Infantry, 2d Division, complained to his superior that the requests, orders, and reports required by the regimental gas officer were "absurd, ludicrous, and, in many cases, impossible" to carry out. For instance, the gas officer had ordered that all men within 1,200 yards of the front line must sleep in gas-proof dugouts with sentry posted over each. If this order were respected, the commander complained, no one in the unit would get any rest because the facilities for compliance did not exist. Another directive informed the infantry officer that men exposed to mustard should take a warm bath and change uniforms. To this he replied, with frustration, "We don't get enough water to wash regularly." The battalion commander closed his letter by explaining how tired he was of receiving directives "doped out of a book." Staff officers, he believed, must become more aware of the conditions at the front.

To View: Infantrymen of the 28th Division masking during a gas attack, 23 August 1918.

Likewise a division commander complained that new gas officers were "almost hysterical" in their attempts to educate the troops in gas defense. "Knowledge and real efficient training," he observed, "came after hard experience" and the "hysteria" of gas officers passed. When the 1st Division suffered 800 gas casualties at Villers-Tournelle, General Bullard complained of a report filed by a GHQ gas officer who, he believed, "spoke without knowledge or consideration" in a tone of "superior criticism" that comes from "abstract study." After Bullard complained, the officer's superiors ordered all gas officers to abstain from such criticism. Fortunately, incidents such as these were the exception rather than the rule, and line officers eventually realized that the gas officers were there to help them, not to harass them.

Still, the job of gas officer continued to be a demanding one, especially in regard to defensive training for replacements. The "square" World War I division had a Table of Organization strength of approximately 28,000 officers and men. In this war of attrition with high casualties (referred to as "wastage"), these large square divisions had a constant flow of new men into the ranks. The 1st Division, for example, after 223 days in the line, received over 30,000 replacements, The 2nd Division's statistics were even more striking: following 139 days in the trenches, it took in over 35,000 new men. Six other divisions received over half their strength in replacements, and another five received over a third. The rapid mobilization and rush to send men overseas led to a situation in which men had little overall training. The 42nd Division, after some time in the trenches, withdrew to train for the St. Mihiel offensive. During this time the division received replacements, "cannon fodder if there ever was any." One, company obtained forty-three new men of whom "one man had had but one week of training; four had had two weeks; twenty had had three weeks;

six had had four weeks"; and the balance had had between one and three months. Gas officers were therefore faced with a continual personnel training problem, having to instill a proper respect for gas defense in green officers and men.

Protecting officers and men of the AEF required more than training. Contamination of food, water, tobacco, and equipment by chemical agents emerged as a significant problem for gas officers. On an interim basis the Gas Service issued tar paper and oil cloth to cover food and tobacco. Water contamination was always a problem, because the scarcity of water often compelled men like a 79th Division doughboy at Montfaucon to risk drinking from a suspicious source. Driven by thirst, this American ignored the warning of French soldiers and drank stagnant water from a shell hole. He later suffered chest pains from the gas contaminated water. After being evacuated he eventually returned to his unit, but only after twenty-three days in a base hospital. No one ever devised an effective means to stop troops from drinking contaminated water. Late in the war, the Quartermaster Corps packaged foodstuffs destined for France in gas-proof, airtight trench ration containers.

As for equipment, the corrosive properties of most war gases created problems of contaminated artillery shells not being able to be chambered, breechblocks jamming, gun surfaces rusting, and contaminated small arms cartridges not chambering properly. AEF regulations required weapons and shells be cleaned with oil immediately after a gas attack, but the metal continued to corrode unless small arms were disassembled and boiled in a solution of sodium bicarbonate and water. The difficulty of applying decontamination method in the trenches, not to mention in No Man's Land during a prolonged assatilt lasting several days, can be well imagined, Protection of animals was also a problem, and they, too, were fitted with protective masks.

When doughboys went "over the top," they, their commanders, and their gas officers alike faced increased challenges and "many difficulties not met with in trench warfare." At times, good gas discipline had little or no impact on casualties in the maelstrom of battle. The reports of gas officers constantly referred to gas casualties caused by men being "knocked down, or shocked and stunned" by German high explosive shell fire. The concussion of the exploding shells slowed the men's reaction or worse, knocked them unconscious, and they never had a chance to put their mask on. Many times the blast tore off a mask or flying shrapnel cut the facepiece or damaged the hose from the filter to the mouthpiece. The extensive use of gas both at day and night often meant prolonged use of the mask. Lt. Robert A. Hall, for example, blamed a significant number of the 1st Division's gas casualties at Villers-Toumelle on the fact that after seventeen to eighteen hours of good gas discipline wearing the SBR, perspiration impregnated with gas seeped under the elastic head band. Perspiration also caused the nose clip to slip, and as a result, men inhaled poisonous vapor or had their eyes affected and, as a consequence, became gas casualties.

Troops caught in the open by enemy gunners often sought cover in shell holes, ravines, and patches of wood, the very places where gas lingered the longest. Even if men maintained strict gas discipline, casualties were inevitable when the enemy concentration of gas shells became too dense. From 0600, 12 October to 1600, 13 October 1918, the 114th Infantry, 29th Division, attacked German positions at Bois Ormout. The Germans fired an estimated 2,000 gas shells at the regiment in bursts of about 300. Yellow, Green, and Blue Cross 77-mm and 105-mm shells landed around the 1,500 men of the 114th Infantry while they deployed in ravines, shell holes, and wooded areas. As a consequence, 500 men became gas casualties, mostly with lung injuries. The commander requested permission to evacuate the contaminated area. The French 66th Regiment commander, who had operational control of the attack, told him to remain in place. The Frenchman believed the withdrawal of the regiment was not tactically sound, for the Germans would counterattack if they detected any sign of an Allied retreat. Maj. James H. Walton, the division gas officer, remarked that this incident, in which high gas casualties were inflicted despite good gas discipline, was one of the "best examples of the deadly effects of gas shell" he had seen in combat.

Combat decisions that had little reference to gas warfare often resulted in incurring or aggravating gas casualties. For example, although AEF tactical doctrine called for the preselection of alternate positions, many requests to relocate infantry units during combat were denied even though the tactical situation and the enemy's use of chemical agents called for relocation. In the determination to show the AEF's battle prowess, many of its senior commanders were loath to give up an inch of occupied or captured ground. In one such case, on 15 July 1918, the commander of the 30th Infantry, 3d Division, filed a graphic report of the unit's plight after repelling a German attempt to cross the Marne. His men, after being shelled with various chemicals for ten hours, were "absolutely worn out." They had not had "even a drink of water" during that time. The shells landing in their sector contained mustard, chloropicrin, and "chocolate" (diphosgene has the odor of candy) gases. If the men remained in their contaminated uniforms, he noted, they were certain to become gas casualties, because the mustard gas would eventually reach their flesh. It was "absolutely impossible" to feed the regiment. because the rations had been contaminated by the gas. He reported to division that "they are still there in the line and they will hold the line, but they ought to be relieved...." They were not. Such decisions exhibited a crucial lack of understanding of the nature of gas warfare.

Like the infantry, AEF artillerymen and animals suffered under the fury of German gas shell bombardments. While nonpersistent gas caused artillerymen problems in their attempt to deliver accurate fire, "mustard yellow cross gas," remarked a cannoneer with the 91st Division, "seems to be about the only Boche weapon of which the men are really afraid." Efforts were made to displace batteries subjected to counterbattery gas attacks, but this was difficult and time consuming. To assist the artillerymen who had to remain in a gassed area, the French *Tissot* mask was issued when available.

As previously noted, not only did this mask's filter offer less resistance to breathing, but the problem of fogged vision associated with the SBR did not exist. Most important, without a nose clip and mouthpiece it was a very comfortable mask to wear. In addition to the *Tissot* mask, gas gloves made of oil cloth were issued together with "impervious clothing." However, because the antigas suits were not ventilated, men would tear them off in warm weather even while working in an area reeking with. mustard.

As an alternative to the protective coveralls, artillerymen used Sag paste. Many artillerymen shaved off all their body hair prior to an application of the ointment. "Every man in the firing battery," noted a gunner, "is now denuded of hair on top of his poll, under his arm pits, between his legs, and his underwear is soldered to him with 'sag paste.'"

The German use of chemical agents during World War I also placed a tremendous burden on a noncombat branch, the AEF Medical Department. Initially, no actions were taken at division level to provide medics with special expertise in the treatment of chemical casualties. As a result, division medical personnel were unprepared initially to handle the influx of gas victims. In the confusion of organizing and placing an American army in combat, it took GHQ, AEF, until October, 1918, to establish a uniform procedure to handle casualties.

The 42d Division, the second most experienced American combat division of the AEF, appointed a gas medical officer a position that eventually all divisions of the AEF were ordered to establish. The 42d's decision to appoint a gas medical officer came in the wake of several disastrous contacts with chemical agents in the division's early combat. One such incident occurred on the evening of 20 March 1917, when approximately 400 German mustard rounds and 7,000 high explosive and shrapnel shells landed on a position manned by the division's 165th Infantry. The weather conditions were excellent for the persistent mustard agent. It had rained earlier, and there was no breeze to dissipate the gas as it hung in the air. At midnight, men began to suffer the delayed effects of the gas. Company K lost two-thirds of its effectives. A week later Lt. Col. H. L. Gilchrist, Medical Director of the AEF, reported observing at a base hospital 417 gas casualties from the 165th Infantry.

As the intensity of fighting increased, so did the number of men who claimed they were gassed, further burdening the Medical Department. Many shell-shocked soldiers or men who suffered from exhaustion and hunger believed themselves to be victims of gas poisoning. Others panicked after smelling shell fumes and reported themselves gassed. Then there were the shirkers who feigned being gassed. "The symptomology of gas poisoning is so complex," observed Maj. William V. Sommervell, 3d Division Gas Officer, "and at the same time so indefinite" that anyone who claimed to be gassed was immediately sent to the rear.

As a consequence GHQ, AEF, expanded the number of medical personnel available to diagnose gas victims and weed out malingerers. At the hospital to the rear, division medical personnel devised several traps to detect suspected malingerers. One trap involved offering the gas casualty a large meal. Men on the front line were always hungry; they rarely had enough to eat. But a gas victim's symptoms would include a loss of appetite, so anyone who devoured the food found himself promptly returned to the line. Medical personnel also offered suspected malingerers a cigarette laced with diphosgene. If the soldier gagged he was feigning gas poisoning. Some idea of the magnitude of the problem may be derived from one division field hospital commander's establishment, of a board to review the 251 gas cases in his wards. The board's report indicated that only ninety of the men actually suffered from gas poisoning. The problem, though, was never satisfactorily resolved in the AEF.

The Medical Department processed gas casualties in combat divisions, using procedures similar to those used for sick and wounded. Medics at the battalion aid stations did what they could for the gas wounded. This consisted of plastering Sag paste on mustard burns, often having to cut a uniform open to expose the swollen flesh. A wet compress applied over the eyes eased the pain of those blinded. Men who inhaled mustard gas could only be comforted with. words, for no treatment could ease their pain. Medics could do nothing "but try to put the mask back on and get them to a Field Hospital." From the battalion aid station, men moved to the "Ambulance Head," the closest point to the line safely out of reach of German artillery fire. When possible, all gas casualties rode to avoid exertion. Men blinded by chemical agents were usually led to the ambulance head by comrades who could see, although in some instances, large numbers of blinded soldiers groped their way to the rear by holding on to a cord set up by the medics.

When possible, division field hospitals were located in the same general area, with one hospital designated to handle gas victims. At this hospital the division medical officer supervised triage. Soldiers were placed into one of the following categories: fit for duty, immediate return to unit; fit for duty in twenty-four hours, return to unit; severely gassed, evacuate to an Army hospital. Exhausted men who complained of gas symptoms but who showed no outward signs of having been gassed were held in the division rear for rest, food, and observation. If medics verified their claims to gas poisoning, they too were evacuated.

Division gas hospitals had to be located near a source of water because persistent and even nonpersistent agents clung to clothing, hair, and skin. After admission to a hospital, doughboys stripped off all their clothing and showered. Those casualties with serious symptoms were bathed while still on their stretchers. The bath house of the 2d Division gas hospital had a portable heater and six shower heads. When a doughboy left the showers, medics sprayed his eyes, nose, and throat with bicarbonate of soda. Depending on the diagnosis, the patient might be given a special treatment. of alkaline, oxygen, and, if necessary, venesection (bleeding) to counteract the effects of inhaled gas. For those soldiers who had eaten food or drunk water contaminated by gas, doctors prescribed olive or castor oil to coat the irritated stomach linings. When treatment failed to allow free breathing, or when the patient developed additional symptoms, medics immediately evacuated him to a base gas hospital. By November, 1918, the Medical. Department was well on its way to developing procedures to handle gas Victims.

If American defensive doctrine and procedures for dealing with gas warfare were rudimentary or nonexistent to begin with and evolved during the war, the same was true of offensive gas doctrine and procedures. The American Army's Artillery Corps had not determined its own doctrine for gas warfare prior to entering combat. Instead, U.S. artillerymen borrowed from both the French and British, as well as from the Germans. The first U.S. field manual for the use of chemical artillery shells was a translation of a current French manual. The AEF, emulating the French, classified chemical shell fire into two types of bombardment. The first type, destructive fire, consisted of two minutes of rapid fire with rounds landing in close proximity, so as to create a dense gas cloud that, given surprise, could inflict heavy casualties. The second type, a neutralizing bombardment, was fired over a longer period and was used to lower the enemy's physical resistance and morale. It also interfered with the enemy's activities by forcing him to wear a mask for extended periods of time. Mustard gas best accomplished neutralization according to the AEF field manuals.

AEF manuals identified several kinds of missions that utilized surprise or neutralizing bombardment. For purpose of harassment, a neutralizing fire was used to exhaust and hinder the movement of enemy personnel. Interdiction fire was a kind of neutralizing fire that rendered positions untenable. Barrages in support of an infantry attack were to consist of 25 percent gas, or one gun per battery. The balance of high explosive fire disrupted enemy reinforcements and prevented counterattacks. AEF manuals duplicated German doctrine by ordering the inclusion of gas in all barrages; this would, it was hoped, deceive the enemy into believing a great concentration of gas was being fired at all times and cause him to mask frequently, thus wearing him down physically and mentally and limiting his ability to defend his position.

Artillery counterbattery fire with gas came to be an extremely effective tactic. Before gas shells came into use, the attempt to neutralize enemy batteries on the Western Front required large amounts of high explosive shell. Regardless of the length of time or the number of rounds fired, complete destruction of the enemy's batteries was never accomplished. Between 1914 and 1916 the average length of time required for artillery counterbattery fire to be effective was estimated at over six days. By 1917, gas made it possible to neutralize a known artillery battery in as little as fifteen minutes. Effective counterbattery fire over a wide front could neutralize enemy artillery in only two to four hours. By the spring of 1918, artillery commanders called for gas shells constantly, and the number of rounds fired was limited only by the availability of such shells.

Of special demand was mustard, the agent that had become the king of the chemical war. The effect of mustard shells was so striking that there was a "constant unfilled demand" for them.

One division commander remarked that when his cannoneers were at last issued the agent their morale soared. The arrival of mustard from French gas ammunition points in July, 1918, "caused a great jubilee" among AEF division artillerymen. That same month, on 2 July 1918, AEF General Order 107 allowed division gas officers to take an active role in the preparation of all plans involving the extensive use of gas by artillery and special gas troops.

AEF tactical employment of mustard and other chemical agents improved somewhat as artillerymen became more experienced. If, for instance, the exact location of an enemy battery in a wooded area was unknown, an AEF battery would shell the access roads with mustard, rather than waste limited gas shells by dowsing the entire woods. The artillerymen would then fire high explosive shells to damage the access roads and make it difficult for resupply trains trying to reach the battery to avoid contamination. The enemy battery would soon have to move. This tactic was also used to block reinforcements passing through defiles or over bridges. It proved to be an extremely efficient and economical method of counterbattery fire.

Unfortunately, many senior U.S. Army officers remained oblivious to the potential use of chemicals by artillery or special gastroops in the offense. When it came time for the AEF to launch its first major offensives at St. Mihiel and the Meuse-Argonne, the use of gas was minimal. In preparing for the Meuse-Argonne campaign, for example, the U.S. First Army Headquarters studied the spring offensives of 1918, where the Germans literally smothered the Allies with hundreds of thousands of gas shells in a relatively short space of time. To its credit, First Army HQ disseminated this information to its units and, in field orders during the campaign, urged subordinate corps and divisions to use gas. Gas was made available by the French to the Americans in a sufficient quantity to neutralize enemy batteries, strong points, and installations, and to produce casualties. The final decision to utilize gas, however, rested with the corps and division commanders. With little or no doctrine, training, or experience they were reluctant to employ gas. The offensive use of chemical weapons, according to one First Army general, "does not seem to be understood." Army-level operational planning for the campaign included extensive use of gas, but its use by corps and divisions was halting. While the First Army's divisions did gain some confidence in the use of gas towards the end of the campaign, they never really mastered its employment.

After training with the British Special Brigade, the other gas offensive arm of the AEF, the 1st Gas Regiment, went into action on 22 May 1918. The Ist Battalion, 1st Gas Regiment, which consisted of Companies A and B, reported for duty attached to the 26th Division. On 18 June, Company B, temporarily attached to the XXXII French Corps, conducted the regiment's first independent operation. At 2230, seven hundred 8-inch Livens projectors, emplaced the night before and loaded with sixty-pound drums of phosgene, were fired at two targets located 1,500 meters away. The first target was a company of infantry with one *Minenwerfer* (mortar) company and the second a reserve battalion of infantry. Artillery fired shrapnel and high explosive shells in conjunction with the projector attack. A month later prisoners revealed that this attack caused at least fifty casualties, including ten enemy deaths.

The AEF tactical doctrine for the employment of special gas troops cited the advantages of using gas in terms of accuracy, the extended casualty producing area, and. lasting results. The doctrine noted the effectiveness of gas for the elimination of well-entrenched targets that high explosive fire could not destroy. The amount and type of chemical agent employed depended on the tactical situation, as well as wind and terrain features. Projectors, the primary weapon of U.S. gas troops, provided "the means for producing casualties and demoralization second to none." When used aggressively, Livens projectors could keep enemy forces off balance; when employed on a quiet front, they could lessen considerably the likelihood of that front being used as a place to rest battle weary troops.

In the offense, special gas troops could be utilized, according to AEF manuals, in five tactical situations. In the first, they would precede an offensive operation, keeping enemy positions in a gas environment until attacking troops arrived. This tactic would cause casualties and demoralize and reduce the "fighting efficiency and morale" of the enemy. Second, gas employed by special troops could eliminate machine gun nests just prior to an attack. AEF 4-inch Stokes mortars offered the best means of eliminating a machine gun position: two to ten Stokes mortars firing phosgene could form a localized concentration, either creating casualties or forcing the masking or the abandonment of the gun. Third, gas was ideal for sustained operations. Each night, gas could be placed on enemy machine gun nests, strongpoints, and troop concentrations, thereby weakening future resistance. Fourth, after friendly forces had taken an objective, reorganized, and consolidated their positions, gas employment acted as a temporary check or block to potential enemy counterattack formations. Fifth, the doctrine stipulated that in a stabilized situation frequent surprise fire with projectors could create the high concentrations of gas on suitable enemy targets from one end of the line to the other needed to harass enemy troops. In addition, local concentrations of gas, fired from Stokes mortars on machine gun nests, mortar positions, strongpoints, trench intersections, and other sensitive points further reduced enemy morale and strength.

In the brief time it was deployed, the 1st Gas Regiment never matched the sophistication of the British Special Brigade. With the return to open warfare, the 1st Gas Regiment made superhuman efforts to meet AEF needs and moved their Stokes mortars with advancing infantry rather than remain in the trenches, as the British did. The regiment mortar men became very proficient in using thermite shells against machine gun positions and in covering advancing infantry with smoke. The regiment did not, however, employ gas during the attack as extensively as it did thermite and smoke. Gas was used, though, in conjunction with smoke, in order to cause enemy troops to expect gas whenever they received smoke. This tactic forced the enemy to mask, further limiting his vision.

Many commanders resisted the employment of special gas troops. The use of gas was new to American commanders, so it came as no surprise to officers of the Gas Regiment that trouble occasionally arose with the unit they were to support. The 1st Gas Regiment company commanders, lieutenants and captains attached to infantry divisions, tried as best they could to explain what results gas would achieve. During the Saint Mihiel operation in the fall of 1918, infantry officers quickly took advantage of the close support furnished by the Gas Regiment, whose mortar crews knocked out German machine gun nests with thermite and created smoke to screen the U.S. infantry. Still, the infantry appeared reluctant to use gas consistently. When the American First Army launched its first attack, the 1st Gas Regiment did not support the offensive with gas.

During the Meuse-Argonne offensive, the 1st Gas Regiment did support Anierican troops with gas. Company E, 1st Gas Regiment, attached to the 28th Infantry Division, bombarded enemy hilltop positions with Stokes mortar rounds of smoke, thermite, and "deceptive gas." Covered by this suppressive fire, doughboys executed a flanking movement and took the hill with very little difficulty. On 2 October 1918, Company F, while in support of the 33d Infantry Division, received authorization to fire fifty-six projectors loaded with phosgene bombs at German units near Bois La Ville. Results of the gas mission were unknown. Soon after, however, German artillery retaliated by firing a number of Yellow Cross rounds at the 33d Infantry Division. As a result, the infantry regiment being supported by the gas company refused to allow it to fire its scheduled second projector attack. The official history of the Gas Regiment indignantly reported that American troops near Bois La Ville constituted a "normal mustard target" for German gunners and that, "irrespective of our gas operations," the locale normally experienced such attacks.

Company F fired one of the largest American gas bombardments of the Meuse-Argonne campaign in support of the French XVII Corps. The men of Company F installed 230 Livens projectors in two nights. To assist in the operation, 100 French soldiers with forty-seven horses pulled narrowgauge rail cars containing projectors and shells to the front. At exactly 0330 on 16 October 1918, drums of phosgene, fired in a dense fog and rain, fell on a known enemy troop position. Corps artillery fired high explosive shells in conjunction with the attack.

As the Meuse-Argonne operation continued infantry commanders gained confidence in the effectiveness of chemicals and increasingly called upon gas troops to exercise their skills. By the latter stages of the offensive, some division commanders actively sought out gas company commanders to support their operations. The 2d Division staff consulted the supporting gas company in planning an attack and, as a result, projectors were used for the first time preceding a significant American advance. The results confirmed the claims of the gas unit in that a large number of enemy troops became casualties; the gas cloud itself had a demoralizing effect on other German troops as the wind pushed it to the enemy rear.

The initial hesitancy by the AEF to employ gas was judged understandable by an officer of the 1st Gas Regiment. The American Army was unprepared to engage in gas warfare when President Wilson committed it to battle. As a result, the use of chemical weapons and the defense against them became a deadly learning process for all branches of the Army under the stress of battle. Many commanders were simply unwilling to employ a weapon with which they had had no prior experience and which, if used, could invite German retaliation in kind. For those commanders who did allow the use of gas, some became enthusiastic supporters of offensive gas operations; some did not. The American experience with the offensive use of gas remained uneven to the end of the war.

"WE CAN NEVER AFFORD TO NEGLECT THE QUESTION"

General John J. Pershing, in his *Final Report*, made specific reference to three weapons introduced in World War I and the impact each had on the conduct of the war. The three weapons Pershing listed were the tank, aircraft, and poison gas. Only one, gas, caused him to reflect on its use in any future war. He declared, "Whether or not gas will be employed in future wars is a matter of conjecture, but the effect is so deadly to the unprepared that we can never afford to neglect the question." Pershing, with the experience of the war behind him, pointed out that gas was a significant weapon, but not as a producer of battle deaths.

The AEF suffered 34,249 immediate deaths on the battlefield. Of these, an estimated 200 were caused by gas. The number of men wounded and evacuated to medical facilities numbered 224,089. Medical Department reports indicate 70,552 of these hospital patients suffered from gas wounds. Of these gas victims, 1,221 died in AEF hospital wards. When, looking at the total figures, 27.3 percent of all AEF casualties, dead and wounded, were caused by gas. With respect to the burden gas casualties placed on medical facilities, not to mention the replacement system, a significant 31.4 percent of all AEF wounded were treated in hospitals for gas wounds.

Gas in World War I did not have to cause large numbers of casualties to be an effective and versatile weapon. Gas warfare placed additional strain on every aspect of combat. According to British Maj. Gen. Charles H. Foulkes, Commander of the Special Brigade, the "appearance of gas on the battlefield ... changed. the whole *character* of warfare." In World War I, gas was everywhere, in clothing, food, and water. It corroded human skin, internal organs, and even steel weapons. The smell of gas hung in the air, and the chemical environment became a reality of everyday life. Not only did men have to train constantly, but an entire logistical network had to be established for offensive and defensive gas equipment. A new branch of the U.S. Army came into existence, and new units, such as decontamination squads, mobile degassing units, and special gas troops, were created. These organizations, in turn, took manpower away from the combat arms, as combat arms officers became gas officers in divisions, regiments, and battalions. Also, the impact of gas on the Medical Department posed tremendous problems in the treatment of casualties. The number of gas wounded became so great that one field hospital out of four per division was dedicated to the treatment of gas victims.

Despite the pervasive impact of chemical agents on the battlefield, commanders and staffs had difficulty adjusting their thinking and planning in such a way as to make effective use of these new weapons - weapons totally different from anything they had ever been trained to use. Not only did commanders and staffs have difficulty determining how they would employ the new weapon to their tactical advantage, but they also had to consider the effects of enemy gas on their own troops. By entering the conflict without preparation for chemical warfare, AEF commanders never fully comprehended the potential of gas on the battlefield. The experience of the United States Army before and during World War I suggests several shortcomings in the military's preparation for, and later employment of, chemical warfare.

Prior to American entry into the war, the War Department and General Staff virtually ignored the deployment of chemical weapons in Europe and did, little or nothing to prepare the Army to fight and survive in a chemical environment. This pervasive neglect had an adverse impact on the capability of the AEF to fight effectively on a chemical battlefield. American troops entering front-line trenches were usually poorly trained and ill equipped to engage in gas warfare.

Proper defensive equipment is a minimal requirement for the successful engagement of forces in chemical warfare. The indispensable item for the World War I doughboy was his protective mask.

Besides the filtration of all harmful agents, the mask had to fulfill a number of other requirements to be efficient. It had to be comfortable and allow for freedom of movement, full vision, easy breathing, communication, and durability.

The American failure to develop a mask that could meet these requirements limited the combat effectiveness of the soldiers of the AEF. The decision to purchase the British SBR and, later, to manufacture an American version of it rather than to adopt and modify the more efficient and comfortable French Tissot was a serious error in judgment brought about by a lack of foresight and preparation.

The prewar failure to develop and experiment with new gases was also a serious shortcoming. If attention had been paid to the rapidly changing technology of chemical warfare, the United States, with its untapped industrial capacity, might have been able to overcome the German advantage. American technology might have produced the "king" of war gases, the persistent mustard agent, in a timely fashion. Instead, the Germans introduced this agent a year before the Allies.

After entry into the conflict, the United States geared up for production of war gases currently in use. Eventually mustard and other agents were shipped from the United States, but only in fifty-five-gallon containers. Production of chemical shells, based on French designs, was belatedly undertaken, and not a single American gas shell ever left the muzzle of an AEF artillery piece in combat.

The unfortunate shortage of gas shells restricted the AEF's capability to retaliate in kind against the Germans; this, in turn, had a demoralizing effect on troops whose own positions had been liberally drenched with gas from German shells.

The AEF never found the key to effective education and training for the offensive and defensive aspects of chemical warfare. A significant advantage could have been obtained if both offensive and defensive training had been integrated into all aspects of instruction.

Once a soldier understood the overall nature of gas warfare and acquired confidence in his equipment and gas officers, he more easily accepted and adjusted to chemicals in actual combat. Unfortunately, U.S. training in chemical warfare never reached the sophistication needed to achieve the desired results. Equipment shortages and the lack of trained, instructors hampered the AEF's preparation to engage in chemical warfare. The Army suffered needless casualties as a consequence.

Good gas discipline was also essential to the conduct of chemical warfare. Very few soldiers reached the level of the 1st Infantry Division doughboy who, when asked by a staff officer if the gas alarm signified a drill, replied through his mask in muffled tones, "Put on your mask, put on your mask, you damn fool and don't ask questions."

"Here," said the division commander who learned of the incident, "was the real thing in discipline." Discipline and training were required if men were to be expected to remain in a contaminated area. The soldier's determination to fight on would certainly have been enhanced if he had had faith in his equipment and the knowledge that provisions had been made for the decontamination of himself and his gear.

Had the U.S. Army's leaders; prior to America's entry into the war, prepared themselves intellectually by studying German gas doctrine or by reviewing observer reports, gas officers would not have had to overcome such strong resistance to the tactical employment of chemicals.

Because the U.S. Army failed to develop gas warfare doctrine, the average AEF officer never really understood the potential value of chemicals. Nor could he put aside his preconceived, if perhaps erroneous notion, that chemicals were unusually inhumane weapons whose development should not be pursued. For America the real inhumanity of chemical warfare in World War I lay in the blindness of U.S. civilian and military leaders who, having ignored the real and present threat posed by gas, deployed the doughboys of the AEF to fight unprepared in a chemical environment. Ignorance, shortsightedness, and unpreparedness extracted a high toll at the front, a toll that the United States with its intellectual and technological resources should not have had to pay.

4

Types of Chemical Weapons

NERVE AGENTS

Nerve agents attack the bodies nervous system. Nerve agents causse breathing difficulties, convulsions, paralysis, and death. Nerve agents can be inhaled or absorbed through the skin. Symptoms of nerve agent poisoning include runny nose, tightness of chest, difficulty breathing, excessive sweating, nausea, vomiting dimness of vision, pinpointing of the pupils, convulsion, and death.

Blister Agents: Blister agents attack the lungs, eyes, and skin. They blister both skin and mucous membranes.

Blood Agents: Blood agents interfere with the bodies ability to absorb oxygen. The victim dies because the body tissues are starved of oxygen. Blood agents cause headaches, vertigo, and nausea before death.

Choking Agents: Choking agents attack the lungs, causing them to fill with fluid. Choking agents are detected by their smell and their irritancy. The victim suffocates by drowning in his own body fluid. Choking agents cause coughing, choking, tightness of the chest, nasea, headache, and watering of the eyes.

MASS CASUALTY CARE STRATEGY FOR A CHEMICAL TERRORISM INCIDENT

The United States Domestic Preparedness Program, instituted by the FY97 Defense Authorization Bill (PL 104-301, September 23, 1996) was established to increase America's domestic response capabilities to a nuclear, biological, or chemical (NBC) attack. In an effort to successfully identify issues related to weapons of mass destruction (WMD), the Department of Defense (Dodd) delegated responsibility for executing this legislation to the U.S. Army Soldier and Biological Chemical Command (SBCCOM). In combination with the DoD's expertise in WMD, SBCCOM created the Chemical Weapons Improved Response Program (CWIRP) that would network with civilian responders to identify key response issues.

One of the most prevalent issues identified by the CWIRP, was a community's inability to care for an overwhelming number of chemically contaminated patients. Even when emergency responders successfully decontaminate and triage large numbers of patients at the scene, it is unlikely that area hospitals are prepared to receive these patients and treat them within the boundaries of the existing health care system. Jurisdictions need a plan to carryout victim triage, decontamination, treatment, transportation, and hospitalization in a time critical manner that improves patient outcome. Thus, planners must avoid intentionally overwhelming the health care system and may need to redistribute existing resources to positively influence patient outcome. In response to this issue, the CWIRP developed an alternative health care facility, herein referred to as the Off-site Triage, Treatment, and Transportation Center (OST3C or Center). This facility will supplement a community's existing health care system in managing the overwhelming number of casualties, both actual and psychosomatic, following a terrorist incident. Specifically the OST3C is meant to care for those patients who have been triaged "Minimal" at the scene, those patients who are worried that they might have been exposed, and those who self-refer to the Center.

The intention of this document is to provide jurisdictions with a basic understanding of the OST3C so that they can customize the concept to fit their specific needs and incorporate their version of the Center into the larger response effort. The *Concept of Operations for the Off-Site Triage, Treatment, and Transportation Center* was written to assist planners, administrators, responders, medical professionals, public health, and emergency management personnel better prepare for and provide mass casualty care. This document presents the philosophy of care for the OST3C as well as operational planning considerations. The OST3C Concept of

Operations is meant to be flexible and modular. The intention of this document is to provide jurisdictions with a basic understanding of the OST3C so that they can customize the concept to fit their specific needs and incorporate their version of the Center into the larger response effort. Emergency planners must undergo a certain amount of preplanning to execute the OST3C concept, practice that plan with supporting agencies, and evaluate and refine the plan before implementing it in an actual disaster. Some jurisdictions may not enact the OST3C concept but will recognize the need to provide for and plan for some or all of the critical aspects identified within this document.

AN ALTERNATIVE HEALTH CARE FACILITY: OFF-SITE TRIAGE, TREATMENT AND TRANSPORTATION CENTER (OST3C)

Given the potential for acts of terrorism it is now imperative that health care systems be prepared to respond to a chemical weapons attack on a civilian community. An alternative temporary medical care facility, herein referred to as the Off-Site Triage, Treatment, and Transportation Center (OST3C or the Center) is envisioned to supplement the existing health care system in managing the overwhelming number of casualties, both actual and perceived, following a terrorist incident. It has been designed by the Improved Response Program (IRP) under the auspices of the Department of Defense's Domestic Preparedness Program via a series of exercises called Baltimore Exercises (BALTEX).

The OST3C will be capable of handling approximately 80-125 non-critical patients per hour (or 400 to 750 patients during a six-hour period). In addition to triage and treatment, patients will also undergo a detailed decontamination meant to remove chemical contaminants. The patient care endpoint is either transport to a higher level of care facility or discharge to home with selfcare instructions.

The goal of the OST3C is to provide care for a specific patient population and thereby improve overall patient outcome for the community. By re-directing those who are triaged Minimal at the scene, the psychophysiologic casualties who have no physical injury (anticipated ratio of psychophysiologic casualty to actual casualties is expected to be at least 5:1), the non-critical patients that show up at over-crowded hospitals, and the citizens who self-refer directly to the Center, hospitals can focus on patients who require in-hospital services and the OST3C can focus on patients who need basic symptomatic and supportive care.

The OST3C is an interim patient clearinghouse that will be disassembled once the flow of new patients has diminished to the point that they can be handled by the existing health care system.

INTRODUCTION

Purpose

The purpose of this document is to describe an alternative health care facility concept developed by the Improved Response Program (IRP). The information herein may be used as the basis from which governmental jurisdictions, agencies, or health care systems can develop an alternative health care facility as part of their own emergency response plan.

Mission

The mission of the OST3C is to supplement the existing health care infrastructure by providing triage, decontamination, treatment, and if necessary transportation to a higher level of care, for victims of a chemical weapons attack or similar emergency.

Background

The threat of chemical or biological terrorist attacks against U.S. citizens is of national concern. The Tokyo subway attack in March 1995 illustrated the likelihood of a chemical weapons attack against a civilian population and the overwhelming impact 5,500 patients had on the existing health care system. This occurrence, together with other more recent national and international terrorist incidents, heightens concerns about the United States' ability to effectively manage incidents involving chemical agents. It is the intent of terrorists to cause damage and confusion in an attempt to throw society into a state of chaos. They are more tempted then ever to use weapons of mass destruction (WMD) for an attack because of their effectiveness in creating mass casualties and hysteria. It is impossible to predict exactly which agents will be used, how they will be disseminated, where they will be employed, and which population will be targeted. The best way to effectively mitigate the effects of a chemical WMD incident is through comprehensive planning, training, and preparation.

The Tokyo Sarin attack exemplified how even an educated civilized society responds to an act of terrorism. The ratio of those who thought they were injured to actual casualties was 5:1. Twelve people died as a result of the incident, less than 200 patients were treated as hospital inpatients and approximately 1,000 others needed to be evaluated and treated in the emergency department; yet more than 4,500 additional people sought medical care.

The Off-Site Triage, Treatment, and Transportation Center (OST3C) supplements the existing health care system in managing the overwhelming number of casualties, both actual and psychophysiologic, following a terrorist incident.

The overwhelming number of casualties from a WMD incident will put a tremendous strain on a community's health care system. Victims might leave the scene contaminated and attempt to seek medical care on their own. They may arrive at their private physicians' offices, managed care organizations, and local emergency departments without the benefits of decontamination or triage. They could contaminate their own homes, their loved ones, and anywhere they may go from the incident site. Most hospitals will have difficulty coping with the sudden onslaught of patients and the need to decontaminate those victims arriving from the scene. In order to cope with these large numbers of patients, communities should be prepared to activate pre-planned mass casualty plans.

The IRP, under the auspices of the Domestic Preparedness Program, through a series of exercises entitled Baltimore Exercises (BALTEX), identified key response issues unique to a chemical weapon of mass destruction incident. These exercises identified the need for jurisdictions to formulate response plans that optimize their existing resources by coordinating them differently during a disaster. One recommendation was to re-direct less serious, potentially contaminated, and possibly psychophysiologic casualties to an interim medical facility to avoid purposefully overwhelming the health care system. In an attempt to manage a large number of casualties, the IRP developed an alternative health care facility concept.

This facility, referred to as the Off-Site Triage, Treatment, and Transportation Center or OST3C, is a casualty clearinghouse that is capable of handling between 80-125 non-critical patients per hour, or 400-750 victims during a sixhour period. The OST3C facility can be replicated to meet the need to handle a larger patient population. The duration of the OST3C is short-lived, as most chemical agent casualties will not require extended patient observation or in-hospital patient care.

Assumptions

- The citizens of the United States are subject to an act of chemical terrorism.
- A well-planned chemical agent release is likely to produce a significant number of casualties that will overwhelm the current health care system.
- Some chemical agents (e.g., mustard agent) produce delayed signs and symptoms of contamination. Patients exposed to theses types of agents are more likely to cross-contaminate those with whom they come in contact.
- Most chemical agent liquid exposures (e.g., nerve agent) will produce immediate signs and symptoms. Those patients who have been exposed to nerve agent and only present with mild signs and symptoms will likely not die from agent exposure.
- A terrorist attack involving a chemical WMD will have instantaneous effects on the community's emergency response system.
- Local hospitals can expect to receive contaminated victims directly from the scene.

An Alternative Health Care Facility

- Potentially contaminated victims will self-refer to the closest medical facilities and private medical care providers.
- There will be a large number of ambulatory psychophysiologic casualties.

- A mass casualty management system that rapidly integrates existing medical resources will be needed to care for victims.
- People will be reluctant to go to an alternative health care facility and will still attempt to enter traditional hospital emergency departments.
- During a large-scale chemical terrorist incident the standard of care may temporarily change to provide the most effective care to the greatest number of people affected.
- The local health department will play a role in assisting hospitals by supporting the activities of alternative health care facilities.
- Most health departments have medical staff trained to a minimum of the first responder level.

ASPECTS INFLUENCING OPERATIONAL METHODOLOGY

Similar To A HAZMAT Response

Responding to a terrorist attack, which involves the use of chemical agents, is similar to a hazardous materials (HAZMAT) response, with the exception of the following:

- There exists the potential for an extremely large number of casualties because of the deliberate nature of a terrorist incident.
- Since the incident is a deliberate attack, there is a concern that secondary devices will be employed targeting responders.
- The entire incident is a crime scene requiring the collection of criminal evidence and suspicious victim belongings. The preservation of a proper chain of custody must be maintained for all evidence.

Managing a chemical weapons (CW) incident requires addressing all these concerns; therefore those providing patient care at the OST3C need to be aware that patients could be suspects and their belongings may be evidence.

As with a large HAZMAT incident or any multiple casualty incident, it is imperative for the emergency response community to ascertain whether or not the hospitals in the area will be able to cope with the sudden surge of patients. With appropriate training and forethought these responders will be in a better position to evaluate the impact that will be placed on the health care system.

Hospitals Will not be Able to Handle the Patient Surge

Traditionally in any type of HAZMAT incident, hospitals provide the bulk of decontamination and treatment for victims. In a CW incident however, it is questionable if hospitals will be able to handle the patient surge, as HAZMAT incidents produce only a few casualties and CW incidents can produce a multitude of patients. Most hospitals are not prepared to decontaminate a large number of potentially contaminated patients. Such an influx of patients may threaten the integrity of the hospitals and the safety of their personnel. If a few hospitals shut down in a particular health care system, due to internal contamination, then the system may no longer be in a position to care for the remaining casualties.

Maintaining the current or routine patient load for a community is an important consideration during a mass casualty incident. For example, there will still be people who will suffer from heart attacks (possibly even more than normal, which occurred in the 1996 Centennial Park bombing in Atlanta, (Nordberg, 1996)), medical emergencies, motor vehicle collisions, traumatic incidents, etc. The health care system must continue to accommodate the so-called "unaffected community."

In addition to the patients transported from the incident scene, the health care system will be inundated with the following populations:

- Large numbers of psychophysiologic patients.
- Victims who have left the scene and seek treatment on their own.
- Friends and family members seeking information regarding casualties.

In order to accommodate the patient surge, hospitals should look to initiate their own disaster plans. Those disaster plans may include discharging patients that can be moved to outlying facilities or to their respective homes. Other options may include relocating some of the in-patient populations, who are stable enough, to a ward unit or unused portion of the hospital. Further options may include transferring patients to an alternate location outside the hospital to make room for patients arriving from the incident. Hospitals will not be able to accommodate the patient surge from a terrorist incident involving chemical weapons of mass destruction. This was evident in the 1995 Tokyo Sarin incident that resulted in over 5500 patients trying to enter the health care system.

Re-Distributing Resources During a Disaster

Ideally, hospitals should continue to provide care for those patients who need a level of treatment that only a hospital is most suited to provide. Hospital resources even under disaster conditions cannot be easily replicated, supplied, or staffed. The traditional mission of a hospital may shift during a disaster from rendering care for the community at large to rendering care for acute patients.

A more generally accepted premise in disaster management is to provide treatment for triaged Minimal patients outside traditional emergency departments. Minimal casualties require considerably less resources thereby making it easier to provide appropriate care in non-traditional settings. Minimal casualties generally do not require in-patient services, or extensive medical tests, nor do they demand acute care treatment.

Well before hospitals are taxed beyond their capability or when the health care system is forced to handle a patient load beyond its designed ability, a jurisdiction should establish a means to treat casualties outside the boundaries of the traditional hospital realm. One example of an alternative health care facility is the OST3C.

Emergency managers must determine when opening one or more alternative health care facilities is beneficial. Several factors influence when a community should set-up an OST3C or when treating casualties outside the normal hospital setting is beneficial. Such factors include but are not limited to:

- The size/magnitude of the incident.
- The geographic distance from the incident site to a planned alternative health care facility site.
- The need to care for patients within a reasonable period of time.

- The expected surge of patients will likely occur within the first six hours of the incident.
- The length of time needed to stand-up an OST3C.
- The optimal number of patients that can be treated per hour in proportion to the number of staff available to operate each Center.

FACILITY REQUIREMENTS

An ideal OST3C has the following resources. It can be established however, with considerably fewer resources and adapted to fit a jurisdiction's assets and disaster plans.

- Separate male and female locker rooms and showers.
- Large open areas to support helicopter delivery of state and federal resources.
- Spacious parking facilities.
- Good internal access roads, allowing for emergency vehicle ingress and egress.
- Electricity, preferably with generator backup.
- Internal and external water supply (e.g., fire hydrant).
- Access to sanitary sewer system.
- Easily identifiable to the public.
- Large enough facility to co-locate multiple services within one campus, (e.g., patient decontamination/treatment, crisis intervention, law enforcement investigation, animal decontamination).
- Gymnasium or large room.
- Bathrooms.
- Heating/Air Conditioning/Ventilating System that can be sectored off to avoid cross contamination.
- Securable internal and external rooms.
- Chairs.
- Tables.
- Areas to post information (e.g., chalk and bulletin boards).
- Public announcement systems.
- Cafeteria/food service facility.

- Auditorium.
- Copy machine.
- Fax machine.
- Hard-wired phone lines.

Examples of buildings that may have much of the recommended items or buildings that can be modified to facilitate an OST3C include fitness centers, medical buildings, hotels, college dormitories and campus facilities, motels, high schools, and middle schools. Even warehouses and tents can be converted into an OST3C, providing a jurisdiction is prepared to allocate extensive resources to set up such a facility. Of the aforementioned facilities, high schools and middle schools contain much of the needed equipment and may be an optimal choice for many jurisdictions.

For any building to be readily available as an OST3C, there should be a specific memorandum of understanding (MOU) in place between the lead agency, which would be designated by a jurisdiction's emergency management agency, and the superintendent of the facility. A jurisdiction may need a separate memorandum for each building that is designated as a possible OST3C.

Facilities that have the following items are optimal: male shower/locker room, female shower/locker room, large parking areas, good access roads, easily identifiable by the public, large gymnasium or similar area, electricity, heating, securable internal and external rooms for storage, and internal and external water supply.

Planners may want to identify possible alternate health care facility sites based on the locations of suspected terrorist targets or based on pre-existing resources that would supply staff and equipment to the OST3C, such as a hospital. Planners should be careful to outline buildings that have not been previously committed as disaster assets (e.g. Red Cross Shelters, National Guard Armories). An OST3C should be easily recognized and its location should be accessible by the general public. Ideally, it should be located close to the population it would serve although outside of the affected or contaminated area. It should be close to public transportation for those individuals who self-refer.

If the initial incident is an alleged terrorist attack, then building security is a major facility requirement. Planners must choose a building that can be secured and its access roads easily controlled. Officers should consider that terrorists might employ secondary devices targeting patients and staff, thus they should routinely perform sweeps of the facility and the surrounding grounds as part of their perimeter security effort.

Memorandums of understanding (MOU) should address how the point of contact for each building will be notified, how the building will be evacuated if necessary, and if any specific personnel from the building are needed to staff the OST3C such as the building maintenance engineer.

Once buildings have been identified as potential OST3Cs, the lead agency should review those buildings and determine how patients will move in and through the building/campus. The jurisdiction should make notes regarding the particular needs for each building, specifically for buildings that do not have the aforementioned resources.

The potential exists that the facility may become contaminated during its use. Wooden floors for example, are specifically subject to irreversible contamination, as they are porous. Jurisdictions may choose to use older buildings first so that new facilities are not razed or closed down if the building cannot be fully decontaminated. Even if a building is fully decontaminated, the jurisdiction may need to temporarily close down a building due to the initial stigma that may be associated with a supposed "contaminated" building.

ORGANIZATION AND STAFFING

The command and control for the OST3C is modeled after the Medical Aid Station Incident Command System (MASICS). MASICS is a medical management plan based on the nationally recognized Incident Command System/Incident Management System (ICS/IMS) intended for use during medical crises.

It is important to note however, that the MASICS management plan must be altered to prevent cross-contamination at the OST3C. Those who staff the Warm Zone (contaminated portion) of the Center must remain in the Warm Zone and those who staff the

Cold Zone (uncontaminated portion) of the Center must remain in the Cold Zone. Annex A delineates a proposed organizational chart, but jurisdictions may revise the chart to suit their resources and terminology. Each jurisdiction should determine necessary key positions to accomplish each function.

COMMAND: MANAGEMENT PERSONNEL

OST3C Commander

Overall command and control falls under the auspices of OST3C Commander. A jurisdiction's emergency management agency (EMA) must designate a lead agency for the OST3C. Agencies that may be best suited as the lead agency include a community's emergency management agency, fire department, EMS department, third party EMS service, or health department. The lead agency will assign the role of the OST3C Commander.

Critical functions of the OST3C Commander include:

- Manage and control the overall operation of the facility.
- Coordinate the operation of the Center so it can function at the highest level of efficiency possible, given available staff and equipment.
- Report staffing and resource needs to the lead agency.
- Appoint officers for the other command functions.

Safety Officer

The Incident Command System requires the use of a Safety Officer. The critical function of the Safety Officer is to monitor safe practice at the Center and mitigate any safety issue before undo harm is posed to personnel or patients. Like other operations involving contaminated zones, the lead agency may determine to staff additional safety officers in specific zones to avoid cross-contamination. The IRP also recommends there be a Safety Officer in the Cold Zone and the Warm Zone of the Center.

Information Officer

The critical functions of the Information Officer are to release information to patients and the media in accordance with the jurisdiction's protocols. This officer will be responsible for both internal briefings for patients and external briefings for the public as a part of the Incident Commander's public affairs plan. The OST3C Information Officer must be linked to the Joint Information Center (JIC) so that all information regarding the incident is consistent, accurate, and released to the public in a controlled manner. The Information Officer generally disperses information regarding the incident, hotline/help-line numbers, and information regarding the location of those transferred from the Center. Public confidence is strengthened when the same individual makes these announcements at regular intervals.

Operations Chief

Critical functions under the Operations Chief include security, triage, decontamination, treatment, and patient out-processing. Jurisdictions may use sectors or zone operation chiefs to accommodate the Warm and Cold Zones of the Center and divide critical functions accordingly. The Warm Zone Sector Chief should oversee the following critical functions of the OST3C operation:

- Perimeter security.
- Traffic control.
- Initial triage.
- Gross decontamination.

The Cold Zone Sector Chief should oversee the following critical functions of the OST3C operation:

- Internal security/detention.
- Detailed decontamination/redress.
- Re-triage.
- Treatment.
- Out-processing.
- General assistance.

Logistics Chief

Critical functions within logistics include transportation, facility maintenance, communications, and supply. Transportation must be coordinated as patients will arrive from the scene by bus or will self-refer. They may arrive by private vehicle, bicycle, commercial transportation, or foot. Transportation also includes coordinating patients requiring transfer to outlying hospitals. Transferring patients to area hospitals requires coordination with the on-scene Transportation Officer as to which hospitals are available to receive patients. Additionally the transportation component must organize transport for citizens to a Reunification Center or home.

Another logistics critical function includes developing and maintaining an internal and external communications system at the Center. The system may include 2-way radios, cell phones, laptops, computer network, palm pilots, runners, or whatever technology the jurisdiction presently uses. The facility must also be maintained. Logistics must coordinate for the mundane needs of staff and patients such as bathrooms, water supply, chairs, tables, food service, and securable rooms. The IRP recommends that a person who is familiar with the facility provide maintenance support for the OST3C. Logistics must also organize and coordinate pharmaceutical and supply acquisition and distribute such items throughout the Center, both in the Warm and Cold Zones. Staff must create an approach to deliver equipment in the Warm Zone of the Center without perpetuating cross-contamination. The Incident Command System helps jurisdictions organize the OST3C and divides tasks within each respective officer's span of control.

Planning Chief

Critical functions within the planning section include maintaining a liaison role between the multiple agencies that support the Center and the OST3C Commander. Agencies need one point of contact to discuss personnel and supply support. Often the OST3C Commander will be engaged in coordinating the efforts of the Center and will not be immediately available for this function. Another critical function of planning is organizing the staff and assigning them to appropriate positions. Medical licenses and credentials must be verified before staff are assigned. Furthermore, those assigned within the Warm Zone must be given personal protective equipment (PPE).

Since the Planning Chief is directly involved with each agency and with assigning staff, he/she will know the current capability of the Center. Once the Center is fully staffed and the maximum number of patients is being treated per hour, the Planning Chief may request that other Centers open to handle additional patients if necessary.

Lastly, the Planning Chief must develop a means to track patients through the Center. This task can be delegated to others assigned within this division, but such information regarding how many patients are entering the system, is necessary to planning the overall needs of the Center.

Finance Administration

The finance section has the responsibility for accounting for the costs associated with the operation of the OST3C. It is important that all personnel at the OST3C document employee hours and associated costs to include supplies, pharmaceuticals, transportation, food, etc., to facilitate disaster relief money reimbursement. Additional functions will include:

- Staff time keeping.
- Filing compensation claims.
- Authorizing the purchase of supplies.

Medical Director

The medical director has the responsibility for overseeing all medical aspects associated with patient care at the OST3C. The medical director should be located specifically in the treatment area, assisting other providers with patient treatment, and should be in direct radio contact with triage personnel stationed in the Warm Zone of the Center. The medical director reports directly to the Operations Chief but can provide the OST3C Commander input and should be considered part of the command staff.

Inter-Agency Command Post

Establishing an OST3C requires coordinating several agencies from one jurisdiction. The OST3C Commander must establish an Inter-Agency Command Post. The Commander must brief all chiefs and officers regarding their primary objective and to whom they directly report. Each agency should present their current capability and their ability to accomplish their designated objective. Such briefings should be held on a regular basis.

Following the briefing, chiefs/officers should meet with those who will support their designated objective. Officers should hand out written job descriptions, relay if staff need to wear PPE, specify to whom they report, confirm from whence patients originate, and where patients need to go, before the Center is ready to receive patients. The IRP recommends that officers provide staff, in writing, any specific information that is different from what they are accustomed to performing on a daily basis (e.g., administering antidote treatment therapy).

General Staffing

There are many critical factors jurisdictions must consider when composing a compliment of staff to work at the OST3C. Each jurisdiction will have different resources from which to draw, therefore the specifics for staffing the OST3C should be planned by the jurisdiction.

One factor that directly affects the number of staff needed is the number of OST3Cs a jurisdiction may establish at one time. The IRP identified that a community must be able to process the majority of casualties within the first six hours following an incident. Thus a jurisdiction may need to open more than one OST3C. The decision to open multiple Centers will be based on an estimated number of patients and the availability of personnel and supplies. Moreover, the geographic location of the incident or location of assets may influence the decision to open several Centers to accommodate the patient surge. The maximum number of patients that can be evaluated and treated within the first six hours is directly proportional to the number of personnel who staff a Center. Other variables that strongly influence the number of patients that can be decontaminated and treated include ambulance transportation availability, the maximum capability of gender specific showers, and how quickly patients can be transferred from the Center to home or a Reunification Center.

All OST3C staff should receive Domestic Preparedness (DP) Awareness and Operations training and be familiar with the OST3C Concept of Operation. Annex B outlines training performance requirements, based on the 120 City Domestic Preparedness Training Program, called the Performance Objective Matrix,

(Supporting Information Section, of the CWIRP Playbook, May 2001). In exigent situations, when jurisdictions are unable to staff the Center with people who have received this training, the general staff should be assigned positions that are closely related to their regular job function. (For more information regarding the type of staff an OST3C requires, see Annex C. Annex C correlates the required skill set staff needs to perform each critical function.) Another critical factor when selecting staff is their ability to perform assigned tasks while wearing Personal Protective Equipment (PPE). There are specific safety requirements associated with PPE that individuals must meet, especially with respirators (29 Code of Federal Regulation 1910.120, 1910.134). Again, the jurisdiction may need to assign staff that are already accustomed to wearing PPE to specific roles in the Warm Zone of the Center, whereas others can be assigned within the Cold Zone.

Sources that may be able to allocate medical providers include volunteer fire and EMS departments, private ambulance companies, allied health agencies, and health professional education institutes (e.g., physician/medical school, nursing, nurse practitioner, physician assistant, and paramedic schooling programs). Veteran's Administration hospitals, home-health agencies, and temporary nursing agencies may also be able to medically support the efforts of the OST3C. Laboratories, epidemiologists, and health departments may have staff that could support data collection and tracking functions.

Some jurisdictions may not have the capability to support an alternative care facility due to a lack of staff. Under disaster circumstances, jurisdictions may request specific institutions (i.e., hospitals and clinics), to allocate a certain number or percentage of staff to disaster relief functions.

For example, Florida State Sheriff's Department has a Statewide Emergency Mobilization Plan that mandates in the event of a Level I Disaster, each law enforcement agency will assign a voluntary number of their work force to the disaster relief effort; in a Level II Disaster, 5% of the work force is required, and in a Level III Disaster, 10% of the work force is required to support disaster relief efforts (Florida Sheriff's Association Statewide Task Force, 1999). The magnitude of the disaster will determine the level of disaster and thereby the number of staff to mobilize. Jurisdictions should consider applying the Florida mobilization concept to staff alternative health care facilities. Though it may appear that a hospital's capability is decreased as its in-house staff is assigned to a disaster effort that will only be the case, preliminarily. Overall, the larger incident will be better managed and consequently fewer patients will flood the hospitals, thereby creating less strain on the health care system. Under disaster circumstances, jurisdictions may need to initiate MOUs with specific institutions to allocate a certain number or percentage of staff to the disaster relief effort.

VOLUNTEER STAFFING

Volunteer organizations can be a good source for additional staff. Some jurisdictions may already have established a disaster volunteer compliment of personnel. The more prepared this pool of personnel are, the easier it will be to assign them to an alternative health care facility or any disaster relief function. Jurisdictions may need to offer volunteer workman's compensation coverage, train them on Domestic Preparedness Awareness and Operations, and pre-credential them to facilitate overall placement at the OST3C. A recommended list of training performance requirements is listed in Annex B called the Performance Objective Matrix. This matrix is based on the 120 City Domestic Preparedness Training Program (Supporting Information Section, CWIRP Playbook, May 2001).

When a jurisdiction must depend on a large contingent of volunteer support, the IRP recommends that the lead agency assign key personnel to leadership positions and place volunteers in support roles.

Should citizens arrive at the OST3C attempting to volunteer their services, the OST3C Commander or Planning Chief should direct them to the larger part of the Incident Command structure that supports assigning volunteers. Those in charge of logistics for the entire incident will be better prepared to assign personnel to areas that have the greatest need. Moreover, jurisdictions must verify medical credentials/license, training and suitability before assigning persons to medical positions.

Control: Communications

The OST3C must have a communication system. The form of communication, e.g., 2- way radios, cell phones, runners, or networked computers, will depend on the jurisdiction's available resources. Like any disaster, communications is vital to the overall operation at the OST3C. The lead agency is responsible to provide a communication system that works and that their people know how to use. As in any disaster the lead agency should prepare a backup communication system. If that system entails the use of runners, the logistics chief must educate staff how to effectively use them.

Implementing a communication system, which is already in place or a type of technology that personnel are already accustomed to using, is the most helpful. Some jurisdictions may have elaborate communication systems with palm pilots, barcode readers, networked computer laptops, etc. Other jurisdictions may still use paper systems. Whatever technology is used, the OST3C should staff the appropriate level of technological support.

SCOPE OF PRACTICE

General

General care provided at the OST3C will be performed at the basic life support (BLS) level. Jurisdictions can determine additional aspects to providing general supportive care based on their assets. If a jurisdiction has the capability to provide a contingent of advanced life support (ALS), the medical director for the OST3C should allocate these resources to the treatment area to stabilize patients who become critical. The OST3C is not intended to be a definitive care site nor is it intended to operate at the level of a traditional emergency department. Staff should conservatively assess a patient's chief complaint, vital signs, and pre-disposing medical history when determining if a patient should be sent to a higher level of care facility. Although the OST3C operates at the basic life support level, jurisdictions may want to broaden its scope of practice to include administering chemical agent antidote. Ultimately jurisdictions must determine how much antidote to allocate to the OST3C effort and if the antidote is for patients or staff. If jurisdictions do allocate a small cache of antidote, the IRP recommends that jurisdictions place it where patients are initially triaged to help stabilize those who arrive in critical condition.

General care at the OST3C will be performed at the basic life support level. The OST3C is not intended to provide definitive care.

Ethics and Liability

Depending on the magnitude of such an event, the level of care that American citizens are accustomed to will temporarily change to effectively care for the greatest number of victims. Medical decisions at every level will be made swiftly and will be based on limited information and can only be enacted based on limited resources. In response to a chemical mass casualty incident, planning should clearly indicate the level of care that will be provided at specific treatment facilities.

Jurisdictions should develop guidelines regarding the scope of practice and document them as part of their jurisdiction's plan for responding to chemical terrorism. These guidelines should be formulated with state licensing and public health agencies and approved prior to use.

Jurisdictions should consider developing guidelines pertaining to the OST3C with ethics professionals and the state's attorney general. Aspects that affect a citizen's basic expectations regarding level of care, patient confidentiality, and patient privacy, may concern citizens to the point of pursuing litigious outcomes in the aftermath of the disaster. Although the community would not directly dispute that the enormity of the disaster will likely affect the availability of resources, they will grow concerned when there is a change from the medical norm. Plans developed with input from the aforementioned officers will minimize litigation resulting from implementing the OST3C concept.

NOTIFICATION, ACTIVATION, AND DEPLOYMENT OF PERSONNEL

Notification

Jurisdictions must determine the lead agency to manage and coordinate OST3C efforts. A representative of the lead agency should be assigned the task of maintaining the plan so that it does not become antiquated. Though it need not be a full time duty, appointing a responsible lead agency will help the community's readiness posture.

The lead agency should establish a notification process to activate those other agencies that will support the OST3C. The notification process should follow pre-established protocols and call-down lists. Automated emergency phone calls, reverse 911 systems and/or automated fax notifications are methods to notify supporting agencies of an OST3C activation.

Part of the notification process includes informing hospitals where the incident occurred, the chemical agent, the impact of the incident, the level of personal protective equipment hospital personnel should wear, signs and symptoms that warrant treatment, treatment modalities, as well as specific information regarding the OST3Cs. Regarding the OST3C, the notifications should specify the following:

- The location of the OST3Cs.
- The purpose of the OST3C.
- Its anticipated duration of operation.
- What kinds of patients should be re-directed to the OST3C.

The lead agency should also notify mass transportation assets and inform them of the aforementioned information, if they will be used in conjunction with establishing the OST3C.

The public must also be informed of the OST3C. The media should be briefed and their help enlisted in disseminating accurate information to the public.

The lead agency should request that the Public Information Officer at the Emergency Operations Center (EOC) announce the OST3C's purpose, location, and duration of operation. Involving the media early will help inform the community that they can obtain care quickly and it will instill the public's confidence that an alternative health care facility will be able to help them. Jurisdictions must determine the lead agency to manage and coordinate OST3C efforts. A representative of the lead agency should be assigned the task of maintaining the plan so that it does not become antiquated.

Activation

The amount of time a jurisdiction needs to establish an OST3C can greatly influence its effectiveness in mitigating a mass casualty incident. If it takes an extensive period of time to establish an OST3C, it may not be a valuable tool. The OST3C should be operational within approximately one hour of notification. Activation procedures will entail the lead agency deploying specific pre-packaged resources/equipment that can be automatically delivered to or stored at an OST3C site, or requiring supporting agencies to deploy pre-packaged disaster items.

To decrease the amount of time needed to open an OST3C, the IRP recommends that staff and resources should not be mobilized at one central location but rather at each agency's headquarters or other pre-determined location.

Each supporting agency should mobilize their own required staff and resources and be responsible to check their personnel's credentials/identification and deployment readiness.

Each agency should maintain their own personnel rosters and staff assignments at the OST3C and share the information with the OST3C Commander. Once agencies are mobilized they should report directly to the OST3C and send an agency representative to the OST3C Command Post.

Deployment of Personnel

Assigned personnel should report directly to the OST3C. An agency representative should report to the Planning Chief and brief the chief of their present capability. The Planning Chief should remind the agency of their primary mission, hand out written objectives/tasks, request that they assign personnel to specific jobs, obtain a staff roster from the agency and request that those assigned to leadership roles report to the command post at a specific location and time.

Patient Population

General

The intent of the OST3C is to care for the following types of patient populations:

- Triaged Minimal patients from the scene that have been transported by EMS.
- The self-referring patient population upon hearing a public announcement.
- The psychophysiological patient.
- The non-critical patients that arrive at area hospitals but would be more appropriately cared for at the OST3C.

For the purposes of this concept, Minimal will be defined as a known casualty that was at the incident site and falls within the triage parameters of Minimal versus Immediate or Delayed. In general, patients who fall within the Minimal category can breathe spontaneously, are oriented to their surroundings and have adequate circulatory/tissue perfusion.

Psychophysiological patient is defined as persons who present at health care facilities with the intent of receiving a medical evaluation and treatment. Often these patients may not have been part of the initial incident nor have they sustained a physical injury. The psychophysiological patient generally does not have any physical ailments but do believe that they may have some physical injury and are concerned that they have been harmed. These patients do need a medical evaluation and emotional support.

The OST3C is intended to care for patients that were triaged Minimal at the scene, the psychophysiological patient, the non-critical patients who show up at over-crowed hospitals and those who self-refer.

Non-critical patients fit the same description as Minimal, however, hospital personnel do not always triage patients in the same manner as EMS providers. Patients generally fall into other sub-categories such as acute/critical, monitored, and non-critical/fast track. Non-critical patients do not require in-patient hospitalization.

Based on the assumption that many patients will leave the scene and arrive at area hospitals seeking care, those patients that hospital personnel deem non-critical may be more appropriately cared for at the OST3C. This is especially true when an excessive number of patients are waiting for care at a hospital.

Patients transported from the incident scene to the OST3C may have received at best an initial triage evaluation but no treatment. Self-referring patients will not have been evaluated at all. It is possible that even though the Center is not intended to receive critical patients, Immediate or Delayed self-referring patients may arrive. Most of the patients who arrive at the OST3C may not have been decontaminated. Some patients, especially the elderly, may have refused to remove their clothes or to be wet down at the incident scene. Parents with young children may not have wanted them exposed to environmental elements especially in inclement weather. Therefore, providers will not know if patients are contaminated.

Unaccompanied Children

It is likely that the OST3C, as well as all health care facilities, will receive unaccompanied children during a disaster. Children may have been separated from their parents at the scene and arrive at the OST3C without them; or families who arrive at the Center may be separated from their children when directed to the detailed decontamination area; or critical patients requiring immediate transfer to a higher level of care may result in unaccompanied children.

Jurisdictions must plan to manage unaccompanied children. One suggestion is to buddy mental health providers with those children that show up unaccompanied. In situations when children may become separated from their parents after they arrive at the Center, jurisdictions may choose to process families according to the family member having the highest triage category to prevent separation. In either case, staff will need to make provisions for managing unaccompanied children, which may include contacting extended family members that can care for the child and watching the children until they are taken home.

Special Needs Population

Elderly and handicapped patients may also arrive at the OST3C seeking care. These patients can fall into the Minimal or non-critical triage category but have difficulty ambulating at the Center, (e.g., the blind). Staff must take into consideration that the OST3C demands a lot of walking and navigating through the building.

Additionally, decontamination areas will be slippery and staff may be needed to physically assist patients. Moreover, jurisdictions may purposefully choose older buildings, which may not be handicapped accessible.

Options may include:

- Staffing the OST3C with additional patient assistant volunteers.
- Re-directing all physically challenged persons to traditional emergency departments.
- Setting up OST3Cs in handicapped accessible buildings.
- Making existing buildings more handicapped accessible with portable wheelchair ramps and portable outside showers.

TRACKING

Patient Tracking

Most factors that influence patient tracking at the OST3C are similar to what a jurisdiction would confront for other mass casualty incidents (MCI). There are a few issues, however, that may likely present during a chemical terrorist incident (as well as at the OST3C) that would not necessarily present during other MCIs. One critical factor to consider when tracking patients is that a terrorist incident can create an excessive number of patients. To triage 500 patients in the same manner that EMS would triage 50 patients may be too time consuming and ill effective. If it takes approximately 30-60 seconds to triage each patient (using the START Triage method) and track them by a roster, it would take over four hours to triage 500 patients.

Jurisdictions may need to use other methods of collecting triage data. Howard County Fire and Rescue Services in Maryland is experimenting using a tape recorder to expedite the process. Minimal casualties speak and spell their name into a tape recorder which cuts the time spent per person down to approximately 15 seconds. Patients that are processed at the OST3C must be tracked and their medical status/evaluation documented. Some jurisdictions may choose to begin patient tracking after patients have undergone decontamination and treatment, leaving all data collection until the end of the process. Other jurisdictions may determine that they must capture only a name and a triage tag number/identifier, at the beginning of the process (e.g., during initial triage).

If patients leave the Center before they have completed the process, then a more accurate list of who arrived at the OST3C is available. Overall, patients that arrive at the OST3C may have been waiting and thus will want to be treated right away. Patients may no longer tolerate the "system" when paperwork hinders their ability to obtain treatment.

Tracking methods may include the use of a triage tag or medical chart number. Jurisdictions should implement tracking systems that they are accustomed to using or systems that can compile large quantities of data. If jurisdictions use triage tags and triage tag numbers as unique patient identifiers, then these tags must be waterproof. Some jurisdictions may redesign their entire tag while other jurisdictions may simply place a non-waterproof triage tag into a plastic zip-lock bag and attach it to patients via a plastic bracelet.

Some jurisdictions may refrain from using a triage tag at all unless the patient is serious enough for ambulance transport. The majority of patients who will arrive at the OST3C will arrive walking and thus can be easily identified as Minimal. Those having difficulty will be more obvious in a crowd of walking patients, and should be officially triaged by standard practice.

Tracking Patient Belongings

Each jurisdiction should develop a mechanism for tracking patients' personal belongings. As patients prepare for gross decontamination by removing their clothing, their personal items should be separated as durable or non-durable. Some examples are as follows:

- Durable Non-durable
- Keys Clothes
- Cell phones Shoes and socks
- Electronic devices Jackets
- Purses/wallets

As the goods are separated, they should be bagged according to the proper category, assigned a tracking number, and tagged with the patients' name. After the tracking process is completed, the items should be retained until law enforcement determines that they are not wanted as evidence.

If patients refuse to turn over their belongings, they should report to a police officer to have their items checked for weapons and other paraphernalia before entering the building with their personal items. When the patient is discharged from the Center, the out-processing station can give the patient instructions about cleaning their goods.

In some communities, the authorities may never intend to return non-durable items to the owner. Although it may seem futile for staff to bag and tag non-durable items, there may be evidence in the collected goods.

If a jurisdiction plans to return items, durable or non- durable, then those items must be cleaned before they are given to the respective owner.

Patient Charting

For those patients that are brought to the treatment area, the OST3C must officially document the patient's medical status and collect patient demographic data. Jurisdictions may determine to start official patient charting earlier but the IRP suggests that it begin at the second triage area. As patients are re-triaged and directed toward the appropriate treatment area, Minimal patients could start to fill out the demographic portion of their chart should they need to wait for an available health care provider. Patients that have conditions that are more serious would not be expected to fill out their own chart, and medical personnel should try to capture this information particularly if the patient is transferred to a higher level of care.

The chart will be completed at the out-processing station. Any information that patients or staff were unable to obtain, personnel at this area can fill in while patients review their discharge papers.

Jurisdictions should consider a charting method that they are already accustomed to using. If the charting methods are not practical or applicable for use at the OST3C then jurisdictions should consider implementing a charting system that can already compile the necessary data.

CRITICAL FUNCTIONS WITHIN THE OST3C

Jurisdictions should design their own patient flow at the OST3C. Each location may require a slightly different approach or have different priorities when allocating resources. Each building that emergency planners identify may present particular challenges, such as narrow corridors, or doorways, and stairs that do not allow stretchers or wheelchairs to pass easily. Additionally, inclement weather may influence whether or not a jurisdiction establishes an outside gross decontamination function. *(See Annex D for a general patient flow diagram that* incorporates the critical functions outlined in this section.)

The following section delineates and describes the critical aspects of an OST3C. Each jurisdiction should consider these critical functions when planning their version or application of the OST3C concept. The OST3C, by design, is meant to be modular and flexible, leaving the jurisdiction to determine when and where functions should occur and if they are applicable. *(See* Annex C for a description of the following critical functions and the associated skill sets required to perform the function.)

Perimeter Security

Due to the nature of the incident the alternative health care center may require a full compliment of security efforts. Terrorists may want to target large groups of citizens and emergency workers. Those with knowledge of a community's response plan may see the Center as an ideal secondary target. Perimeter security is needed to maintain order, deter criminal acts, and provide for the safety of the public.

Those providing perimeter security become gatekeepers to the Center. Security will need to ensure that only authorized and properly credentialed staff enters the facility grounds. All entrances should be locked or have security in place to control entry into the building. Security should establish separate entrances for victims and staff. Signs should be posted directing them to their respective entrance.

It will also be difficult for officers to differentiate between patients and others wanting to enter the OST3C. Officers are inclined to decrease their level of suspicion when patients convey an acute medical condition, making it difficult to distinguish between those who are really patients and those whose presence is counterproductive to the operations of the Center. Jurisdictions should create a system that helps security personnel identify staff and patients.

Jurisdictions should also determine if law enforcement agencies are needed to check patient belonging bags for dangerous items (e.g. weapons), when patients refuse to relinquish personal items.

Perimeter security efforts also include directing traffic and controlling traffic patterns. Though most of the OST3C's patients will arrive by bus and/or ambulance from the scene, many citizens may arrive in their private vehicles, taxis, public buses, or foot. Officers must determine ambulance and bus drop off points, and private citizen vehicle parking.

Persons who arrive in their own vehicles may have unknowingly cross-contaminated their vehicles. Jurisdictions must determine if they are going to release contaminated vehicles or if they will be quarantined. Security personnel may need to direct these citizens where to park and then watch over the vehicles so that citizens do not re-enter them. Security may have difficulty with persons who refuse to allow their vehicles to be quarantined. Should security be faced with such a situation, they should strongly direct patients to drive away from the Center without disrupting those who are entering and those who are exiting.

Once patients leave the Center they should not be allowed to re-enter. Patients should be directed away from the Center to avoid re-contamination.

The number of security officers needed, at the OST3C, will depend on the size of the facility/surrounding grounds and the number of functions they are assigned. Local law enforcement should primarily provide perimeter security but other agencies may be able to support their efforts. School crossing guards, private security agencies, traffic controllers for stadium/concert events, and the Department of Public Works may be able to provide barricades, cones, directional signs, and personnel to supplement traffic control efforts. Personnel who may come into contact with contaminated patients should wear Level C personal protective equipment (PPE). Personnel should pay particular attention to wearing butyl rubber gloves instead of latex, given that chemical agents can penetrate the latter.

The IRP recommends that an OST3C establish two or three security checkpoints. Placing officers at the entry point to the grounds and before patients enter the building ensures more control and helps to maintain order. Multiple checkpoints may also make it easier for security personnel to recognize perpetrators posing as patients.

Initial Triage/Registration

Jurisdictions must determine the method of triaging patients and how to track patients as they arrive at the Center. Plans should consider the best method for categorizing patients, but some form of initial categorization should take place as patients enter the Center. Although the OST3C is designed to treat Minimal patients, it is possible that some patients may deteriorate medically during their transfer to the Center. Self-referring patients may show up in a critical state. Jurisdictions should determine if Immediate or Delayed patients should undergo a gross decontamination and be immediately transferred by ambulance to a traditional hospital emergency department. If no transportation is immediately available, then these patients should undergo a gross decontamination and wait in the treatment area until transport is available.

Plans should include how to handle patients that have difficulty ambulating. It is possible that some patients triaged Minimal are not incapacitated from the chemical exposure but just need physical assistance. Those staffing this area may need wheel chairs or assistants to help patients get from one location to another.

Pre-hospital care providers should perform initial triage as they are accustomed to triage tag use, and categorizing patients into groups. Those performing initial triage must wear Level C PPE. Providers should pay particular attention to wearing butyl rubber gloves instead of latex, given that chemical agents can penetrate the latter.

If jurisdictions plan to supply an antidote cache at the OST3C, the initial triage area is an ideal location for the medication. Patients arriving as Immediate or Delayed would benefit from the medication and could be stabilized before undergoing a gross decontamination. Additionally, it is more likely that staff in the Warm Zone will suffer from cross-contamination than staff stationed in the Cold Zone. Thus, if the antidote is strategically located at the initial triage area then both patients and staff would benefit. Gross Decontamination Not all the patients that arrive at the OST3C will have undergone a gross decontamination. Avoiding contamination is important. A gross decontamination station outside the building will prevent most of the contamination from entering the building. Jurisdictions will need to determine if a gross decontamination station is necessary providing that patients can enter a building and obtain a detailed decontamination inside. Some planning considerations for determining whether or not to have a gross decontamination station include:

- Gross decontamination significantly reduces chances of crosscontaminating the building, those staffing the detailed shower area, ambulance personnel, and vehicles used to transport patients.
- Personnel have access to immediate decontamination if they become cross-contaminated in the Warm Zone.
- A gross decontamination does not need to be used on all patients but can be used for critical patients, patients that have difficulty ambulating, and for staff who become cross-contaminated.
- If a gross decontamination station is established for all patients who have not undergone a gross decontamination previously, then it may be easier to have all patients proceed through gross decontamination versus creating an additional category of patients (e.g., Minimal with a gross decontamination and Minimal without a gross decontamination).
- If gross decontamination is required for all patients, then the registration/patient belonging process that has been previously described may be more suitably performed right before patients undergo gross decontamination.

> Jurisdictions can choose to develop the gross decontamination aspect to the OST3C as elaborately as their resources allow. If jurisdictions choose to set up a gross decontamination station, then they should consider the IRP's *Guidelines for Mass Casualty Decontamination During A Terrorist Chemical Agent Incident* as the minimum standard. It indicates that high volumes of water such as that provided by a low-pressure fire hose are essential to providing adequate decontamination. Those performing gross decontamination should follow standard decontamination guidelines and not simply seek to equip this area with garden hoses and/or untrained personnel.

As with any decontamination line, patient privacy is a major concern. Jurisdictions may not have the resources to set up privacy screens as they have limited resources to provide even the most basic decontamination line. Without some privacy it is likely that patients will not be willing to disrobe in full or in part.

The IRP recommends that gross decontamination should consist of patients disrobing down to their undergarments, bagging and tagging their belongings and placing them in 55-gallon drums or similar containers for safe handling *(See Section 8.2 Tracking Patient Belongings for more details regarding this function)*. Then patients should proceed through the decontamination line. Immediate and Delayed patients should proceed through the line before triaged Minimal patients. At the end of the decontamination, personnel should provide patients with a form of bodily cover that allows patients to remove their undergarments. A trash bag that has been altered with holes for their head and arms is the simplest form of cover. By placing the head through the plastic bag, patients can remove their undergarments with some modesty intact, and then put their arms through the side holes before proceeding into the building for a detailed decontamination.

IRP Guidelines pertaining to chemical agent removal states:

Large volumes of water provided by a low-pressure fire hose are essential to providing adequate gross decontamination.

The gross decontamination aspect should be operated by an agency familiar with HAZMAT operations and mass casualty decontamination efforts. Typically, each state has a department of the environment capable of supporting decontamination efforts. Other states have HAZMAT type industries that staff decontamination teams who could support a decontamination effort in a disaster. Some jurisdictions have a small contingent of HAZMAT decontamination specialists as part of their department of public works. Jurisdictions should choose an agency that would not typically be used at the actual incident site to perform decontamination at the OST3C.

INTERNAL SECURITY

The OST3C must be supported by internal security efforts in order to maintain control and foster patient flow through the Center. Patients may become unruly and disruptive if they have to wait in long lines, are unwilling to shower in the detailed decontamination shower, or are unable to locate other family members. It is also possible that those who perpetrated the terrorist incident may present as patients seeking care or it is possible that others responsible for criminal acts will be among the patient population. It may be necessary to establish a detention area for those persons who become particularly disruptive. Simply providing a police presence may deter certain troublesome acts. Internal security shares many responsibilities that external perimeter security provides, such as performing sweeps for secondary devices, or barricading those portions of the building that are off limits; but they must perform these duties within the confines of the internal building in order to prevent cross-contamination.

Internal security must help patients avoid unintentionally re-contaminating themselves. Once patients leave the Center they should not be allowed to re-enter and should be directed away from the Warm Zone of the Center.

Officers stationed at patient entranceways should wear Level C PPE to avoid cross contamination.

DETAILED DECONTAMINATION / RE-DRESS

The two major purposes of the OST3C are to ensure that all patients from a chemical incident receive a complete and thorough decontamination as well as medical screening and treatment. All personnel entering the OST3C system should undergo a thorough decontamination.

The detailed decontamination provides the following aspects of decontamination that are otherwise not available:

- A segregated decontamination area for males and females that provides semi-privacy.
- An enclosed decontamination area away from the elements that also provides semiprivacy (group shower).
- Removal of all remaining clothing worn at the incident scene.
- Decontamination using soap.
- Warm water shower that will help reduce the possible effects of hypothermia associated with outside cold-water decontamination.
- Cool water shower that will help reduce heat stress associated with environmental conditions or wearing PPE apparel.

OST3C personnel should monitor patients as they undergo detailed decontamination to control patient movement and prevent a bottleneck. Patients should disrobe quickly, spend no more than five minutes in the shower, and then quickly re-dress. Some patients may be inclined to spend more time showering, as they may believe that a short shower will not free them from contamination causing a backup in patient flow. Once patients are thoroughly decontaminated they will enter the Cold Zone portion of the Center and re-dress in paper scrub outfits or similar clothing.

Provisions must be made for patients who have difficulty ambulating. Showers are particularly hazardous since they are slippery when wet.

Showers are generally not designed to prevent cross-contamination. Often patients must cross locker rooms to get to the showers and then cross the locker room to exit the area. A jurisdiction may need to assign staff to the shower area to direct patients coming in and going out the same doorway to prevent cross-contamination. Depending on the layout of the facility, privacy screens could be used to segregate hallways off for either the disrobing or redress area.

Jurisdictions must provide patients with some type of body cover before they proceed through the Center. Paper scrub outfits, hospital scrub outfits, clothing from consignment/second hand stores or churches, or Tyvek suits are just a few options. Jurisdictions should also consider providing space blankets and foot covers. The following critical functions make up the OST3C: perimeter security, initial triage, gross decontamination, detailed shower decontamination/redress, re-triage, treatment, transportation to a higher level of care, patient discharge, general assistance, and internal security.

RE-TRIAGE

A critical aspect to caring for patients is that they must continually be re-assessed until they have been thoroughly evaluated and treated. Patients exposed to chemical agents may develop delayed symptomatology. All personnel should be mindful of watching for patients who have deteriorated and assist them accordingly.

Once patients have dressed they are ready to have a medical evaluation. Based on how the treatment area is established, staff members should direct patients to the most appropriate treatment location. Re-triaging patients should not take an extensive amount time but it is a necessary function. Also it is likely that patients will be confused as to where to go next, thus re-triaging patients while simultaneously directing them to a treatment area may help prevent bottlenecks from developing.

Staff must use a formal triage method to assess casualties to determine which treatment area is best. The IRP recommends that jurisdictions use the START Triage system *(See Annex F)* and sort casualties into one of the following four categories: Immediate - those who need to be admitted to a hospital following initial treatment and stabilization. These patients will have the highest priority for transportation to a hospital. Patients who fit this category should be brought to the Immediate Treatment Area.

Delayed - those who require limited medical intervention for stabilization. These patients may eventually be admitted to a hospital or discharged following temporary medical observation. These patients should be brought to the Delayed Treatment Area.

Minimal - those who require a general assessment. These patients should be directed to the Minimal Treatment Area. Deceased - those patients that arrive deceased or die at the OST3C. They will be placed in the temporary morgue.

As patients are triaged and directed to the appropriate location, personnel should hand them a clean, pre-arranged medical chart and pen. One time saving practice is for patients to fill out the demographic portion of their medical chart if they are able and if they must wait for any length of time.

Treatment

The OST3C must evaluate and treat patients who arrive at the Center. Staff should transfer patients that have more critical conditions than the OST3C can treat, to traditional hospital emergency departments.

Treatment at the OST3C is based on what each jurisdiction is able to provide at the Center. At a minimum, the OST3C should provide basic life support (BLS) and if jurisdictions have a small contingent of advanced life support staff and equipment then a sub-area within the treatment area should be made available.

Jurisdictions should consider arranging their treatment area based on the triage categories. For example, if staff use typical EMS triage practices and triage tags then they would name the treatment sections Immediate, Delayed, and Minimal. If they only categorize patients into critical and non-critical then treatment area subdivisions should be named accordingly. Despite categorizing the treatment area, all treatment should take place in the same general area if possible so that stations can share staff and resources. The IRP recommends that jurisdictions use the START Triage method and subsequently use the three corresponding treatment sub-areas.

Comprehensive patient documentation begins when patients arrive in the treatment area. Staff must complete the medical portion of the chart for all patients and the demographic portion of the chart if patients are transferred from the facility. The treatment area should be set up similarly as to how the jurisdiction will re-triage patients. An Immediate Treatment Area will care for critical patients that need a more extensive evaluation and who have a potentially life threatening status. Critical patients must have beds/stretchers on which to lie. Personnel with a minimum of Advanced Cardiac Life Support (ACLS) certification ability should staff this area. Staff should stock each bed with ACLS equipment and medication *(See Annex G for an antidote and medication list for advanced medical providers to administer).* The medical director should specifically provide oversight for these patients. This area is meant to stabilize patients only and arrange for their transport to a higher level of care. Staff will collect patient demographic information, which would normally be captured at an out-processing area. Immediate patients waiting for transport should not be moved to the holding area, as their medical condition is too unpredictable and requires more extensive observation.

Delayed patients will need a more in-depth, subjective cardiac and respiratory evaluation. A Delayed area should also have beds/stretchers and be able to handle more patients then the Immediate area but not as many as the area for Minimal casualties. Ideally, it should have EKG monitors, respiratory flow meters, oxygen, and access to a minimal supply of medication. Optimally, those staffing this area should know how to perform advanced life support (ALS). A Minimal area should use tables and chairs and be capable of processing 12 or more patients at one time. Staff may include nurses, medical students, and pre-hospital care providers. Emergency Medical Technicians (EMTs) and paramedics are particularly good at performing quick and in-depth subjective patient assessments without relying on a patient chart as a prompt.

Patient treatment will be based on the following findings:

- Method of agent exposure (vapor or liquid).
- Symptomatology.
- Vital signs.
- Pertinent medical conditions that may be exacerbated by the chemical agent exposure.
- Medications and medical allergies.

The lead agency must provide caregivers chemical agent guidelines that contain the following information for each type of chemical exposure:

- A fact sheet on the agent including antidote.
- Pertinent medical conditions that are complicated by the agent exposure.
- Actual treatment modalities to include basic life support and advanced life support procedures, and hospital provider treatment.

The treatment area should include a holding area for those patients waiting to be transferred. The holding area should be staffed with personnel who can stay with patients and observe them for any deterioration in their medical status. Generally, a 7:1 ratio of patients to health care providers will be adequate. Staff should gather all demographic information that would normally be collected during patient out-processing, prior to patient transfer.

All Minimal patients that do not need to be transferred to an outlying hospital will continue through the OST3C process.

When specific areas are under used, the IRP recommends that personnel in lead roles/chiefs redistribute staff from slow treatment areas to help in the Minimal or holding areas. Typically the area for critical patients will not be busy if ambulance transport is readily available. Minimal patients however, should not be brought to other areas; instead staff should re-locate to the Minimal area and provide support.

Patient treatment will include more than just physically evaluating casualties. Patients may suffer from severe mental distress after having been a victim of a terrorist incident. The incident may exacerbate any underlying mental illness. The medical director, in addition to mental health support personnel, should be prepared to medically sedate, treat, provide emotional support, and/or transfer these patients to facilities capable of evaluating their condition. Another special consideration is implementing tele-medicine interlinks at the OST3C to support patient treatment. This link may be helpful when physicians are not available to staff the Center directly.

Out-Processing

Once patients have been decontaminated and received treatment, they are ready to be discharged. Staff should obtain patient demographic/tracking data, and then officially discharge patients from the Center. This information should include as a minimum:

- Patient identification number/medical chart number/ triage tag number.
- Name.
- Date of birth.
- Address.
- Phone number.
- Emergency point of contact.
- Social security number.

The discharge process should include as a minimum:

- Staff specifies that the patient could have been exposed to a particular agent.
- Staff informs the patient of signs and symptoms that warrant them re-entering the medical system.
- Staff informs the patients how to re-access care if they become symptomatic at a later time.
- Staff provides the patient written self-care instructions.
- Staff obtains patient's signature, which specifies that the patient is being discharged from the Center, and then staff enters the date and time of discharge.

Patients may make inquires regarding transportation home, how to find other family members, how to best obtain medication re-fills to replace contaminated medication bottles, etc. Staff out-processing patients should direct patients, with these types of inquiries, to the general assistance area.

Jurisdictions should gather patient demographic data with information systems that can compile large quantities of data. Palm pilots, lap top computers, bar code readers, bubble dot forms, are just a few types of systems that can facilitate information gathering.

Additionally, out-processing patients requires a controlled and quiet atmosphere. Patients may need a semi-private setting before they feel comfortable asking questions or relinquishing personal demographic information.

General Assistance

After the staff has officially discharged patients from the Center, patients may still need some basic assistance before they are ready to leave. The jurisdiction should consider the following aspects in addition to providing patients a means of getting home:

- A collection point where patients can gather before they are transferred home or to a Reunification Center.
- A location where family members can reunite.
- A rest point where patients can sit and for the first time rest.
- A family assistance desk where patients can talk to someone regarding individual concerns and gather information.
- A place where patients can make a phone call.
- The ability to obtain metal health support.
- A location where patients can get more appropriate clothing, other than a paper scrub outfit, if it was not provided earlier in the process. All patients will need transportation home. Patients, who drove themselves while they were contaminated, cannot re-enter the same vehicle until the lead agency declares it free of contamination. Other patients who arrived via bus left their vehicles at the incident site. Jurisdictions should plan to transfer all citizens from the OST3C either home or to a Reunification Center.

Jurisdictions should make arrangements with the local phone company to set up a mobile phone bank (out-going calls only) at the OST3C. Patients will want to inform relatives that they are okay and where they can be picked up.

The IRP recommends that a jurisdiction staff pre-hospital care providers in the general assistance area. It is possible that a patient's medical status may deteriorate and require more medical assistance.

Jurisdictions should plan to provide some general assistance for patients since they will have no way of getting home and will only be wearing what the facility has provided them. Some type of family assistance desk or help desk that can assist patients with special needs should be co-located where patients are waiting to be transferred to the Reunification Center or home. Mental health support personnel should staff this desk, as they can interact with patients in a non-threatening manner and begin to engage in "defusing" types of conversations when handing out information packets. Information should include explaining when and how a patient can re-enter the health care system, and phone numbers for hotline/help-line crisis intervention.

Reunification Center

When an incident is so large that it requires the use of an OST3C, jurisdictions should consider standing up a Reunification Center, at a separate location, to support the OST3C as well as the entire incident. Family members need a location where they can meet up with their loved ones or obtain information regarding their location and status. The OST3C may be unable to arrange each individual's ride home but can make sure that all patients get to a Reunification Center. The Reunification Center can become an information hub that collates the status and location of all casualties, and creates a list of missing persons.

Depending on the number and type of functions jurisdictions want the Reunification Center to handle, emergency planners may request the American Red Cross (ARC) to establish it. Typically, the ARC establishes mass care shelters to support individuals displaced from their homes for an extended period due to a catastrophic events. However, the ARC is accustomed to providing lodging, food, clothing vouchers, and emotional support and may be the best agency to initiate a Reunification Center. Jurisdictions should incorporate their ARC Chapter in their OST3C planning and ask them in what way they are willing to support mitigating the consequences of a chemical WMD attack.

Transportation

The OST3C is not designed to provide care equal to that of an emergency department, consequently patients requiring a higher level of care should be immediately transferred to a traditional hospital. The OST3C should have dedicated ambulances to perform patient transfers. It may be difficult for 911 units to provide this service because they will most likely be fully engaged responding to or supporting mutual aid efforts surrounding the incident scene. Jurisdictions may need to use commercial and/or volunteer units.

As patients are sent from the scene to nearby hospitals, the OST3C Transportation Officer must send patients to hospital emergency departments that are not overwhelmed. These hospitals may be over 45 minutes away thereby slowing ambulance turn-around time.

When the Emergency Medical System (EMS) is unable to accommodate transferring patients via routine methods, the Transportation Officer should seek to use alternate methods of patient transport to avoid mass numbers of patients waiting to be transferred. Jurisdictions need to decide acceptable means of patient transportation during disaster situations but some options may include loading two patients in each available ambulance, or potentially staffing two medical providers on a mini-bus with four to six mildly symptomatic patients.

It is possible that there will be more patient transfers than originally anticipated, particularly if the medical staff is instructed to cautiously evaluate patients. The OST3C transportation component must also provide a means of getting patients home or to a Reunification Center. Jurisdictions may develop MOUs with private transportation agencies, or the public mass transit to support this effort.

Temporary Morgue

It is possible that patients will die at the OST3C or will arrive pulseless and apneic. The OST3C will need to make provisions for the deceased. These provisions may include using a refrigerated truck as a temporary morgue, arranging local law enforcement to secure the temporary morgue, maintaining a chain of custody, and filling out specific paperwork. Other procedures should include a physician signing the death certificate, staff documenting the time of death, and staff reporting the death to the lead investigating agency and medical examiner.

Any death that occurs during the same period as the terrorist incident may be case evidence. Jurisdictions should request the input of the medical examiner/coroner as to the best way to handle remains and to preserve evidence.

ENHANCED CAPABILITIES

The following are not critical functions of the OST3C, however they do support specific community concerns. Each jurisdiction may choose to implement the following aspects as well as any other function that lends to caring and comforting the community and/or supporting other facets of the incident.

Law Enforcement Investigation

The OST3C will become a key location for managing casualties from a terrorist incident. It, therefore, lends itself to being an ideal location for law enforcement investigators to interview patients that may be witnesses or have pertinent information regarding the crime.

Gathering information regarding the incident certainly supports the community at large but investigating the crime is not the primary mission of the OST3C. If a jurisdiction determines that the OST3C should include law enforcement investigations then it should take place after patients have been out-processed from the Center. Patient care should not be jeopardized for investigation activities.

Investigators must determine where they can best interview patients and how to determine which patients should be interviewed. Investigators may decide to station an officer, where patients are out-processed, who can ask patients if they have any knowledge regarding the chemical terrorist incident. Depending on the number of citizens that state they have some knowledge of the incident and how quickly detectives are able to interview citizens, the officer may need to prioritize which citizens are interviewed first. If the line to interview citizens is long, then the officer may start to gather some preliminary information, such as name, address, and phone number, allowing detectives to interview only those who present with the most relevant information, at the OST3C.

Another suggestion is that law enforcement can provide out-processing personnel with red flag questions, which they can ask patients after completing the patient chart. If a patient responds, "yes" to any of the questions then they should be directed to the investigation area. Samples of these types of questions are listed below; however investigators should provide the actual questions based on the current incident.

- Did you see/hear anything unusual?
- Did you take any photos or videos?
- Did anyone ask you to bring or carry anything into the event?

Law enforcement investigations should take place in an office or small room. Investigators require a quiet and controlled setting to perform their interview and discuss pertinent information to the case. Once the interview has ended, investigators can direct patients to the general assistance area.

Victim Assistance

Due to the terrorist nature of the incident, patients are prone to stress and anxiety that can affect their emotional well being as well as their physical state. Some patients may become distraught to the point that they can no longer process information, interpret directions, or understand where to go and what to do next.

The IRP recommends that jurisdictions provide mental health counselors who can "buddy" with patients, who are mentally distraught and require assistance, in the Cold Zone of the Center. Other recommendations include providing mental health counselors who can rove the general assistance area looking for patients that are distraught or unable to care for themselves.

They should engage in "defusing" types of conversations, help them when possible, and arrange for further intervention with an outside agency where applicable. Jurisdictions may also choose to organize an official briefing for patients that address the following:

- Announcements pertaining to the incident and what is officially known.
- The whereabouts of family members who have been transported from the Center.
- Hotline phone numbers and crisis intervention numbers.
- Information regarding the chemical agent exposure and when a patient's medical status warrants re-entering the health care system.

- A location or phone number that patients can obtain critical incident stress debriefing counseling or mental health support.
- Critical Incident Stress Defusing that specifies what happened, what symptoms victims may experience in the next few days that are a normal response to stress, and what significant signs of stress warrant psychological intervention. If a jurisdiction provides a defusing for citizens, they should consider implementing the International Critical Incident Stress Foundation (ICISF) model.

Each jurisdiction will determine what enhanced capabilities their OST3C will have.

Pet Management

It is possible that some people will bring their pets to the OST3C expecting personnel to help them. It may be beneficial for jurisdictions to establish some elementary form of decontamination and pet care at the OST3C, particularly if they think that citizens will become unwilling to go through the Center unless their pet is taken care of. Jurisdictions should look to Animal Control or local veterinarians to supply portable kennels, staff, and equipment to temporarily care for animals at the Center. The following principles should be kept in mind when incorporating pet management into the plan:

- Animal drop-off point.
- How to identify animals with their owner.
- Animal decontamination efforts.
- Medical evaluation/treatment regimens.
- Holding animals when an owner has been transferred to a hospital.
- Animal retrieval procedures that prevent re-contamination.
- Handling Seeing Eye Dogs and other specialty dogs to include: if these animals need a more extensive evaluation, if they should be separated from their owner, etc.
- Food and water (depending on the length of time animals are held in kennels).

- Location of kennels with regards to inclement or extreme weather, i.e., placing kennels in shade when temperatures are hot.
- MOUs with pet product distributors/stores for supplies not normally supplied by the local animal control department.

The following issues should be kept in mind when establishing a plan to decontaminate animals:

- Animal handlers should wear the same level of PPE that is required for others in the Warm Zone.
- The method of decontamination may be as simple as spraying animals with water for five minutes or it may be agent and/or animal specific.
- Decontamination efforts should supersede treatment efforts just as in adult treatment because decontamination is treatment when an animal is exposed to a chemical agent.
- Decontamination efforts should have a specific Warm Zone and Cold Zone.

SITE SHUTDOWN

Once all patients have been absorbed into the health care system the OST3C Commander must request permission from the Incident Commander to "stand down" the facility.

- The lead agency should contact the medical examiner to transfer the temporary morgue to his supervision.
- Remove all hazardous waste.
- Arrange to have all durable items that citizens relinquished, to include their vehicles, decontaminated.
- Return all durable items.
- Contact the lead investigating agency regarding the final disposition of contaminated nondurable clothing items, as they may be evidence or may provide investigators information regarding the case.
- Arrange for the Environmental Protection Agency to test for residual contamination before the building is returned to its former utility.

The primary medical mission in a chemical weapons disaster is to provide casualty triage, decontamination, treatment, and transportation to definitive health care facilities, without intentionally overwhelming the health care system. If contamination is still present and it appears that it will be long lasting, the lead agency, in conjunction with local and state authorities, will make a decision as to the building's long-term viability.

CONCLUSION

The OST3C is one tool that a jurisdiction may use when mitigating the affects of a chemical terrorist incident. It is designed to be a flexible, temporary, stand-alone facility that can be replicated when any one Center exceeds its capacity. Multiple OST3Cs can be established throughout the local health care infrastructure. The primary medical mission in a chemical weapons disaster is to provide casualty triage, decontamination, treatment, and transportation to definitive health care facilities, without intentionally overwhelming the health care system. Once victims have been absorbed into the health care system, the OST3C can be disestablished.

5

Chemical Decontamination

Emergency departments (EDs) and emergency medical services (EMS) are responsible for managing potential chemical disasters, whether they result from industrial accidents or terrorist activities. In recognition of this responsibility, the Joint Commission on Accreditation of Healthcare Organizations (JCAHO) and the Occupational Safety and Health Administration (OSHA) require EDs to prepare for hazardous material incidents.

In treating patients with chemical exposures, decontamination is of primary importance provided the patient does not require immediate life-saving interventions. Any plan must include contingencies for contamination sources within the hospital and for ED evacuation. The determination of a workable hazardous materials plan requires careful thought and often professional input from medical toxicologists, hazardous materials teams, and industrial hygiene and safety officers. Using a patient decontamination plan implemented without specific adaptation to the hospital and without practice can result in undesirable outcomes.

Legal requirements apply to hospital-based decontamination. All EDs incorporated in an emergency response plan for hazardous materials incidents must meet OSHA requirements (29 CFR 1910.120q) for both staff training and response to hazardous materials, because they likely will be presented with a chemically exposed patient who has not been decontaminated at the scene. Under these regulations, emergency medical personnel who may decontaminate victims exposed to a hazardous substance should be trained at a minimum to the first-responder operational level.

For response to an unknown hazard, OSHA regulations require level B protection, which includes a positive-pressure self-contained breathing apparatus and splash-protective chemical-resistant clothing.

Chemical decontamination has 2 primary goals. First, decontamination helps prevent further harm to the patient from the chemical exposure. Methods of patient decontamination include chemical dilution and chemical inactivation. Second, decontamination helps protect health care providers and maintains the viability of the ED as a treatment center. Mismanagement may result in illness in health care providers and contamination of the ED; severe ED contamination may necessitate departmental closure, which is potentially catastrophic in a mass casualty incident.

Decontamination is time consuming and requires resources. Nerve agents and substances causing injury to the skin and tissue are easily soluble in, and penetrate many different types of material, which renders decontamination more difficult. If chemical warfare (CW) agents have penetrated sufficiently deep, then toxic gases can be released from the material for long periods. By adding substances that increase the viscosity of a CW agent, its persistence time and adhesive ability can be increased. These thickened agents will thus be more difficult to decontaminate with liquid decontaminants since they adhere to the material and are difficult to dissolve.

The need for decontamination can only be established by means of detection. If detection is not possible, then decontamination must be performed solely on suspicion of contamination.

Before chemical decontamination can occur, chemical contamination must be recognized. The most important tool for assessing a patient for chemical exposure is a careful history. Continue to consider chemical exposures in the differential diagnosis for any mass casualty incident in which multiple ill persons with similar clinical complaints (point-source exposure) seek treatment at about the same time or in persons who are exposed to common ventilation systems or unusual patterns of death or illness.

Personal protective equipment (PPE) is the clothing and respiratory gear designed to protect the health care provider while he or she is caring for the contaminated patient (see CBRNE - Personal Protective Equipment). The minimum protective equipment required by OSHA regulations for healthcare providers caring for patients contaminated with an unknown substance include chemical-resistant suits that guard against splash exposures and positive-pressure full-faced respirators. Using this equipment requires specialized training; therefore, train appropriate personnel in the use of this equipment before they need to use it.

PPE is divided into 3 levels. Level A PPE is required in the area of chemical release if dangerous exposure levels potentially are present. A level A suit is fully encapsulated and chemically resistant to both liquid and vapor exposures. Since this suit is fully encapsulated, it requires self-contained breathing apparatus. The level of protection typically provided to those involved in the decontamination procedure is a level B suit. This suit requires a full-faced positive-pressure respirator, is chemically resistant, and provides protection against splash exposures. Use level C protection when the chemical hazard is known, the concentration is at nontoxic levels, and ambient air oxygen levels are at or above 21% of atmospheric levels. Level C protection involves chemical-resistant clothing and air-purifying respirators to filter airborne contaminants.

If it is suspected that skin has been exposed to liquid agents, then it must be decontaminated immediately (within a minute). All experience confirms that the most important factor is time; the means used in decontamination are of minor importance. Good results can be obtained with such widely differing means as talcum powder, flour, soap and water, or special decontaminants.

If clothes have been exposed to contamination, then extreme care must be taken when undressing to avoid transferring CW agents to the skin. There may be particular problems when caring for injured persons since it may be necessary to remove their clothes by cutting them off. This must be performed in such a way that the patient is not further injured through skin contact with CW agents. During subsequent treatment, ensuring that the entire patient is decontaminated is essential to avoid the risk of exposing the medical staff to the CW agents. ED staff has the following 3 primary goals in treating a patient who has been exposed to a hazardous material and may be contaminated or who has not undergone adequate decontamination before arrival at the hospital: (1) isolate the chemical contamination; (2) appropriately decontaminate and treat the patient(s) while protecting hospital staff, other patients, and visitors; and (3) reestablish normal service as quickly as possible.

- Health care providers caring for the patient should put on the appropriate PPE prior to coming into contact with contaminated patients. In most instances, this is level B PPE.
- Ideally, decontamination occurs outside the hospital by EMS providers. If this does not occur, prepare a decontamination area for the patient. If possible, the ideal location is outdoors.
    - o If indoor decontamination is necessary, a decontamination room is the next ideal location. Indoor decontamination only should occur in cases in which a controlled indoor environment may be maintained safely.
    - o Control volatilization of the chemical to prevent displacement of ambient room oxygen, to prevent combustion, and to prevent levels of the chemical from reaching air concentrations deemed immediately dangerous to life or health for that specific hazard. In order to monitor this hazard effectively, the hospital requires testing equipment capable of identifying the chemical, its ambient air concentration, and ambient room oxygen concentrations.
    - o If such a room is not available, try to isolate the patient in a single large room after removing nonessential and nondisposable equipment. Ideally, this room should be away from other patient care areas. Maintain ventilation to the area in which the patient is located, but be wary of further contaminating the hospital with recycled ventilation.

  - o Establish a secure zone with yellow tape and permit only appropriately protected individuals to enter as needed. Include in the secure zone any area the patient may contaminate while entering the ED.
- Upon arrival of the patient, determine whether the patient requires any immediate life-saving interventions. If these are required, stabilize the patient before or during decontamination.

GENERAL PRINCIPLES

The hot zone, or immediate isolation zone, is the area of immediate contamination. Entry into a hot zone requires special technique and equipment.

It is imperative that the hot zone be isolated immediately and entry restricted to avoid additional unnecessary casualties. Chemical agents are especially likely to spread downwind, creating an at-risk area, protective action zone, which is potentially amenable to evacuation.

Notably, dispersion dynamics are such that "downwind" is rarely a straight line and is more likely to be an expanding plume. Gases spread differently in the atmosphere during day and night. Meteorologic conditions, population concentrations, communication capabilities, the specific agent and amount released, and evacuation routes must be identified and are factors in decisions to either evacuate or shelter in place.

The hot zone must be approached from an upwind direction, an area that is also a potential evacuation and treatment area. The indicators of nerve gas release will resemble the consequences of other weapons of mass destruction (WMD), such as immediate casualties of similar presentation; a suspicious site characterized by a dispersal device, unexplained gaseous clouds, vapors, or odors; or an absence of animal, bird, or insect life.

Alternatively, there may be intelligence based on reports, remote detection, or point use chemical detectors. Victims must be identified, decontaminated, and evacuated, and general and specific therapy administered as rapidly and efficiently as possible. Considerations include triage and prioritization, communication with a central command center, and identification of all potential sources of important resources such as medications, monitors, and life-support equipment. For example, local supplies of drugs, such as atropine, amyl nitrite, and thiosulfate, will be exhausted rapidly in a mass casualty scenario, so alternative supplies need to be identified and efficiently procured.

Casualties will also be individuals who sustained secondary trauma during exposure to chemical agents, falls and blunt trauma, motor vehicle injuries, burns, or aggravation of preexisting comorbidities such as chronic lung disease and myocardial ischemia.

These patients will need to be treated according to established medical principles, including the ABCDs of acute care.

Treatment Area

When responding to a disaster involving hazardous materials and weapons of mass destruction, it is critical that the treatment area be at least 300 yards upwind of the contaminated area.

- Having the patient perform as much of the decontamination as possible is preferable to decrease the amount of cross-contamination.
- Remove the patient's clothes and jewelry and place them in plastic bags.
- Wash the patient from head to toe with soap and water. Avoid vigorous scrubbing to prevent skin breakdown.
- Decontaminate open wounds by irrigation with saline or water for an additional 5-10 minutes.
- Try to avoid contaminating unexposed skin on the patient. Use surgical drapes if necessary.
- Flush exposed areas with soap and water for 10-15 minutes with gentle sponging.
- Irrigate exposed eyes with saline for 10-15 minutes, except in alkali exposures, which require 30-60 minutes of irrigation.
- Clean under fingernails with a scrub brush.
- Ideally, collect runoff water in steel drums if possible.

SPECIAL CONSIDERATIONS FOR THE CHEMICAL WARFARE PATIENT

The best universal liquid decontamination agent for chemical warfare agents (CWAs) is 0.5% hypochlorite solution. It is prepared easily by diluting household bleach to one-tenth strength (ie, 9 parts water or saline to 1 part bleach). Hypochlorite solution works through physical removal and oxidation and/or hydrolysis of the agent; water does this at a much slower rate. Hypochlorite solutions are for use on the skin and soft-tissue injuries, including open lacerations. Do not use it in penetrating abdominal wounds (leads to development of peritoneal adhesions), in the eye (leads to corneal opacities), in open chest wounds, or in open brain or spinal cord injuries (effects unknown). Irrigate these areas with copious amounts of sterile saline solution. After using hypochlorite solution on either the skin or soft-tissue wounds, subsequently irrigate these areas with sterile saline solution.

The military also has access to a universal dry decontaminant known as M291 resin, which is available as pads packaged in small individual packets. M291 resin is a dry black carbonaceous material that decontaminates by absorption and physical removal of the CWA from the victim. M291 resin is used for spot decontamination of skin exposed to CWAs.

ORGANIZATION OF THE MILITARY TREATMENT AREA IN CHEMICAL WARFARE

A full discussion of the military medical team response to a chemical warfare attack is beyond the scope of this article. A basic understanding of the structure of the military's medical treatment facility is important for civilian health care providers, since they most likely will be working with the military in the event of a chemical warfare incident. The military medical treatment facility is divided into dirty and clean sides. The demarcation of the sides is known as the hotline. The concept of the hotline is to keep all contaminated equipment, personnel, and casualties out of the clean side until decontamination is completed.

The dirty side consists of a triage station, emergency treatment station, and decontamination area. The triage station is the single entry point into the medical treatment facility. If the patient has an emergent medical condition that requires immediate medical intervention before decontamination, the patient is sent from triage to the emergency treatment station. The emergency treatment station is equipped to handle contaminated patients with emergent medical issues and stabilize them for either decontamination at the medical treatment facility or dirty evacuation to another facility for a higher level of care. The decontamination area is divided into ambulatory and nonambulatory patient decontamination areas.

The clean side consists of part of the decontamination area and the clean treatment area. The hotline extends through the decontamination area. Patients are decontaminated on the dirty side and are brought to the hotline nude except for their PPE mask. These patients are transferred across the line to a team on the clean side of decontamination area. The clean side decontamination team then brings patients into the clean treatment area.

The clean treatment area is located 30-60 meters upwind of the dirty side. The clean side decontamination team removes the patient's mask prior to transferring the patient to the clean treatment area. In the clean treatment area, the patient can be treated definitively or transferred to another facility if needed.

Saving lives always depends on ensuring the ABCs: adequate airway, ventilation, and circulation. Greater contamination or exposure more likely results in victims who require early intubation and ventilation. Conversely, adequate ventilation may be impossible because of the intense muscarinic effects of certain nerve gas exposures (copious airway secretions, bronchoconstriction). In this situation, administer atropine before initiating other measures. In some patients, large quantities of atropine may be required, rapidly depleting hospital supplies. Administering succinylcholine to assist intubation is relatively contraindicated, since nerve agents prolong the drug's paralytic effects. Benzodiazepines are the mainstays in seizure treatment. Liberal doses are required; titrate to effect. Termination of seizure activity may reflect onset of flaccid paralysis from the nerve agent rather than adequacy of antiseizure therapy. Bedside electroencephalography (EEG) may be required to assess ongoing seizure activity.

Animal data suggest that routine administration of diazepam reduces the incidence of seizures and decreases severity of pathologic brain injury following nerve agent exposure.

CWAs are a diverse group of extremely hazardous materials. Emergency physicians must be familiar with the pathophysiology and various clinical presentations produced by CWAs and the principles and practices of appropriate medical management. Since deployment of CWAs also places emergency care providers at serious risk of exposure, emergency physicians must be familiar with the different levels of PPE, appropriate use, and decontamination procedures.

CWAs, as potential weapons of mass destruction with the capability of causing a catastrophic medical disaster, easily may overwhelm any health care system. Since civilian victims exposed to CWAs are likely to flee to the nearest hospital, emergency physicians provide the first line of treatment and must prepare their EDs for the treatment of persons exposed to CWAs.

Ideally, a hazardous materials team at the scene will be able to provide assistance regarding the specifics of the exposure and the potential treatment. A local poison control center may also be able to provide assistance. The Chemical Manufacturers Association provides 24-hour assistance in the specifics of treating a particular chemical exposure; it can be reached at (800) 424-9300. The Domestic Preparedness Chem/Bio Helpline can be reached at (410) 436-4484. Online information is available at Centers for Disease Control and Prevention.

VERIFICATION AND IDENTIFICATION

In order to reach decisions on the level of protection required, knowing the type of agent present in the area is necessary. However, if that is not possible, then, at a minimum, level B protection should be used.

Development of detection methods today is mainly concentrated on instruments. New manual methods may be developed, but the development mainly concerns instruments for detection and monitoring. In some cases, instruments capable of both tasks are being constructed.

Several lines of development are presently being followed as regards to detection principles. The most common line of development is some form of ion mobility detector ion mobility spectroscopy (IMS). The Chemical Agent Monitor (CAM) also belongs to this group as well as detectors for warning such as the Finnish M86 and the more recent M90. Another principle used is flame photometry, flame photometric detector (FPD). A flame of hydrogen is allowed to burn the sample of air after which the color of the flame is investigated by a photometer. In this way, the presence of phosphorus and sulphur can be demonstrated. Examples of instruments using this principle are the French monitor AP2C and Israeli combined detector and monitor CHASE.

A third principle is to use enzymes, as in the manual methods for nerve agent detection. Detectors operating on this principle have been developed in the United Kingdom, the Netherlands, and the former Soviet Union, among others.

Methods for long-range monitoring using optical methods (IR) are being developed in France and the United States.

A research sector attracting great interest is the use of biologically active molecules as sensors. These biosensors are believed to have extremely great potential, and research is ongoing in several countries. The advantage of biosensors is that, at least in theory, they can be given the sensitivity and specificity desired. This is possible since the biosensor uses the same mechanisms that influence the human body when exposed to poisoning. A simple type of biosensor is the enzyme ticket.

A more general type of biosensor may also be useful in the early detection of potential threats. Instead of studying toxic substances, investigations can be made of which receptors in the body may be sensitive to, such as a toxin. These receptors could then be used in a biosensor.

MANUAL DETECTION METHODS

Detection Paper

Detection paper is based on certain dyes being soluble in CW agents. Normally, two dyes and one pH indicator are used, which are mixed with cellulose fibers in a paper without special coloring (unbleached). When a drop of CW agent is absorbed by the paper, it dissolves one of the pigments. Mustard agent dissolves a red dye and a nerve agent, a yellow. In addition, VX causes the indicator to turn to blue, which, together with the yellow, will become green/green-black.

Detection paper can thus be used to distinguish between 3 different types of CW agents. A disadvantage with the papers is that many other substances can also dissolve the pigments. Consequently, they should not be located in places where drops of solvent, fat, oil, or fuel can fall on them. Drops of water give no reaction.

Detection Tubes

The detection tube for mustard agent is a glass tube containing silica gel impregnated with a substrate (DB-3). Detection air is sucked through the tube using a special pump. The reaction between the mustard agent and substrate is sped up by heating the tube such as with a cigarette lighter. A developer is then added, and the result can be read-off. If the silica gel in the tube turns blue, then the vapor in the sample contains mustard agent.

Detection Tickets

Detection tickets for nerve agents are used in a similar way. The ticket consists of 2 parts: one with enzyme-impregnated paper and the other with substrate-impregnated paper. When the package is broken and the enzyme paper is wetted, the substrate part of the ticket is exposed to the test vapor by means of a pump.

Subsequently, the 2 parts are put together for 2 minutes. If the enzyme part of the ticket has turned a weak blue color, nerve agent is not present in the air. The detection limit is 0.02-0-05 mg/m^3 depending on the number of strokes of the pump. The ticket can also be used without a pump (by waving it in the air), but this gives a slightly poorer sensitivity.

Note that the blue change of color requires an active enzyme—some form of cholinesterase. In the presence of nerve agents, the enzyme is inhibited and no change of color occurs. Detection tickets of this kind cannot distinguish between the different nerve agents.

Evacuation of the ED rarely is indicated. In most situations, isolation of the contamination is all that is required.

Consider evacuation of the ED in the following situations:

- Toxic material spills in the ED
- Nearby hazardous materials that are threatening the hospital
- Patient is contaminated with a volatile toxic or flammable chemical and is decontaminated insufficiently prior to entering the ED

If symptoms start to occur outside of the isolation area or the situation requires urgent decision-making without time to identify the contaminant, consider evacuation. Odor does not predict toxicity reliably.

MINIMUM LEVEL EQUIPMENT

- Staff PPE
  - o Full face shield
  - o Hood or hair covering
  - o Gloves
  - o Water-repelling gown
  - o Rubber boots
- Equipment list
  - o Patient identification and belongings
    - * Waterproof triage tags
    - * Sealable plastic bags, size small and large to accommodate belongings and clothing
    - * Paper bags
    - * Labels
    - * Permanent marker
  - o Cleaning supplies
    - * Mild soap
    - * Sponges
    - * Long-handled brushes
    - * Buckets

- o Water sources/containment devices (use any type below)
  - * Hoses with gentle flow, controlled nozzles with hot and cold water
  - * Shower - Single with flex head (minimal); multiple heads (recommended)
  - * Plastic pallets to prevent slippage (minimum of 3)
  - * Water containment/collection system - Wading pools, barrels, and pump; built-in decontamination collection and storage systems

- Patient privacy
  - o Gowns and/or suits for patient to don post decontamination
  - o Towels and blankets
  - o Self-decontamination "trash bag" kits (optional)
  - o Tents or prefabricated decontamination tents
  - o Modesty screens, portable screens
  - o Ropes and tarps, barrier tapes
- Miscellaneous supplies
  - o Duct tape
  - o Scissors
  - o Traffic cones
  - o Megaphones
  - o Plastic totes for hospital equipment
- Patient education: Laminated decontamination instructions in different languages (community specific) AND interpreter services

Preferred Level Equipment

- Staff PPE
  - o Full face shield
  - o Chemical-resistant gloves*
  - o Chemical-resistant suit*
  - o Waterproof chemical-resistant boots*
  - o Respirator
    - * Air-purifying respirator (APR)

    - * PAPR with loose-fitting hood
    - * Supplied air with loose fitting hood
  - o Appropriate filter cartridge for APR or PAPR
- Equipment
  - o All equipment listed in minimum level PLUS
  - o Ambulation assistance and transportation devices
  - o Instant developer camera for evidence collection or identification of patient belongings (optional)

Note: The use of specific types of cartridges or filters, chemical-resistant suits, gloves, and boots is determined by the contaminant to which exposure is encountered. The type of equipment obtained and utilized by the hospital should be based on the hazard vulnerability analysis and community risk.

Specialized Level Equipment

Level A or B

- Staff PPE
  - o Level A
    - * Vapor protective suit with hood
    - * SCBA
  - o Level B
    - * Chemical-resistant gloves*
    - * Chemical-resistant suit with hood*
    - * Waterproof chemical-resistant boots*
    - * Supplied air respirator or air-purifying respirator
- Equipment
  - o All items listed in minimum and preferred levels PLUS
  - o Chemical-resistant and waterproof litters (ie, Raven, Stokes, Morgue) or gurneys
  - o Plastic (nonporous) backboard

Note: The use of specific types of cartridges or filters, chemical-resistant suits, gloves, and boots is determined by the contaminant to which exposure is encountered. The type of equipment obtained and utilized by the hospital should be based on the hazard vulnerability analysis and community risk.

6

Chemical Detection Equipment

INTRODUCTION

Chemical detection equipment (CDE) is an essential component of hazardous material (HAZMAT) emergency response. This equipment should detect the harmful agent, correctly identify the agent, and define the area of exposure. Rapid detection is essential so that responders and military targets can recognize a threat and don protective gear (ideally in <9 s). It is also important to know the extent of contamination. During several documented chemical attacks, first responder casualties have been vast enough to delay the rescue. During the Tokyo subway sarin attack in 1995, 9% of emergency medical services (EMS) providers suffered the affects of acute exposure. Effective CDE may help prevent these occurrences.

Several different technologies are used today to detect chemical agents (CAs). CAs are defined as chemicals intended to kill or seriously injure human beings. CDE usually detects the most common CAs: nerve agents, blister agents, and arsenical vesicants. A large variety of equipment is available that is capable of identifying liquid droplets of CAs on surfaces and in vapors. Laboratory-based equipment can detect agents in water, food, and human samples. The main challenges with these technologies are ensuring an appropriate sample for analysis and filtering out nonhazardous environmental chemicals that may be present. This article focuses on the technologies and devices that may be used by first responder teams in the field. Laboratory detection techniques are beyond the scope of this discussion.

ENZYMATIC DETECTION TECHNIQUES

Chemical detection paper is a very sensitive technique for detecting CAs. It is one of the least sophisticated and thus least expensive methods of detection. It is used to detect liquids and aerosols and is a common means for defining a contaminated area.

Chemical detection paper is composed of 2 dyes soluble in CAs and a pH indicator integrated into cellulose fibers. When exposed to CAs, it can change color according to the type of agent. If an aerosolized droplet encounters the paper, the diameter and density of the spot can be used to determine the droplet size of the agent and the degree of contamination.

Chemical detection paper lacks specificity and is prone to error because it reacts with contaminants such as brake fluid, antifreeze, and insect repellent, resulting in false-positive readings. False readings are especially undesirable in civilian situations because they may lead to mass panic. Therefore, always use chemical detection paper with another modality for accuracy of detection.

M8/M9 Chemical Detection Paper

M8 and M9 CA detection papers, commonly used by the military, are available commercially to HAZMAT response teams. M8 paper is packaged in 25 perforated sheets, 2.5 in X 4 in, and is blotted on liquids that arouse suspicion. It identifies CAs by changing colors within 30 seconds of exposure: dark green for persistent nerve agents, yellow for nonpersistent nerve agents, and red for blister agents. M9 paper has adhesive backing that allows it to be attached to clothing and equipment. M9 paper detects the same agents as M8 paper but does not change color to enable identification. M9 paper tends to react faster than M8 paper and can be attached to vehicles that are entering areas filled with vapor to determine contamination. Vehicles thus equipped are limited to a speed of 30 km/h.

M256A1 Chemical Agent Detection Kit

The M256 CA detector kit originally was released in 1978 and was modified in 1987 to the M256A1, which is sensitive to lower concentrations of nerve agents. It was used extensively during the Gulf War but also is available commercially. It is another common component of CDE provided to civilian response teams. This portable kit detects nerve gas, mustard gas, and cyanide and usually is used to define areas of contamination. The M256A1 contains a package of M8 paper, detailed instructions, and a vapor sampler (12 enzymatic tickets that contain laboratory filter paper for detecting CA vapors). The vapor sampler employs wet chemistry technology, in which ampoules containing different substrates are crushed so that the liquids interact with strips of filter paper, chromatographic media, and glass fiber filter. These substrates then are exposed to the vapor under suspicion. The reaction causes a color change, alerting the user to the presence of a CA. The reactions typically take 15 minutes to occur.

The M256A1 can detect nerve gas concentrations of 0.005 mg/m^3, hydrogen cyanide concentrations of 11 mg/m^3, and mustard gas concentrations of 0.02 mg/m^3. This is one of the military's most sensitive devices for detecting CAs and detects all agents at levels below those that can kill or injure people. It is prone to false-positive results, similar to other enzymatic detection techniques, but has not been demonstrated to produce false-negative results in real situations.

Colorimetric Tubes

Colorimetric tubes such as those available from Draeger and RAE systems use enzymatic techniques to identify CAs. A hand pump is used to draw a sample into a specific tube, and the concentration of the substance is read from the tube. This is another simple and inexpensive way of detecting and identifying a CA. It is used extensively in civilian response units for this reason, but it has some disadvantages.

Available are 160 substance-specific reagent tubes identifying different agents. For each agent, a different tube must be used. Efficient use of this system demands knowledge of which CA is likely to be present in a given environment. If a tube for vesicants is used to sample the air and the CA is a nerve agent, the tube reports a false-negative result. A tube for each possible CA must be used for thorough detection.

Draegar has made this process simpler by offering a chip measurement system analyzer (CMS). The analyzer integrates an optical system for analyzing the color reaction, a flow controller, a pump system, and 10 capillaries, each capable of detecting an agent. As long as the proper chip is inserted, 10 agents can be detected and measured accurately within 20 seconds using this device. Draegar offers this device as part of an emergency response kit available to the public.

ION MOBILITY SPECTROSCOPY

Ion mobility spectroscopy (IMS) is used in many handheld and stand-alone detection devices that can be used to scan equipment, surfaces, and people for contamination. This technology involves drawing a gaseous sample into a reaction chamber using an air pump. The air molecules then are ionized, most commonly using radioactive beta emitters such as nickel-63 or americium-241. The ionized particles then are passed through a weak electrical field toward an ion detector. Contaminants are identified according to the time it takes to traverse the distance to the detector. This time is proportional to the mass of the molecule. The pattern is compared to a sample of clean air; if the pattern is markedly different and unique to certain types of agents, the alarm sounds. These systems are capable of detecting and distinguishing between nerve gas, mustard gas, and vesicants. Its sensitivity ranges from 0.03 mg/m^3 for nerve gases such as sarin to 0.1 mg/m^3 for mustard gas.

IMS has certain advantages. It is less sensitive to contaminants, because it relies on a clean air sample for calibration. Thus, if an area has a certain baseline nonhazardous environmental vapor present, it is not detected.

Improved Chemical Agent Monitor and other Handheld Devices

IMS is the cornerstone of many devices used today. The Finnish M86 and M90 are handheld devices that use IMS, as is the Improved Chemical Agent Monitor (ICAM). The ICAM was used extensively in the Gulf War, even attached to certain vehicles. It is a handheld device that continuously displays the concentration of nerve agents or mustard agents. The ICAM is prone to erroneous detection in enclosed spaces and areas of strong vapor concentration (eg, heavy smoke). It also can become saturated, requiring recalibration. Versions of the ICAM are available for commercial purchase and are used by many medical response teams.

The APD 2000, manufactured by Smiths Detection, is another common device that uses IMS and is sold commercially to HAZMAT response teams for domestic preparedness. This handheld device can be powered by batteries and can detect mace and pepper spray as well as nerve agents, blister agents, and hazardous compounds. The Sabre 4000 also uses IMS and is manufactured by Smiths Detection. It is in use by first responders because it can use vapor or trace particle samples to detect explosives, drugs such as cocaine and heroin, as well as chemical agents.

Stand-alone detectors - M8A1, Automatic Chemical Agent Alarm, and Fixed Site/Remote Chemical Agent Detector

Many stand-alone detectors also use IMS technology. The military employs the M8A1 detector that consists of a stand-alone detector, which continuously monitors the environment for hazardous vapors and aerosols, and up to 5 alarms that can be dispersed throughout an area. The M8A1 detects nerve agents and blister agents when the concentration is 0.1 mg/m^3 or greater and alarms within 1-2 minutes. M8A1 is an ideal device for protection from off-target attacks, in which a vapor is released upwind from the targets. However, it is less effective for on-target attacks, in which the CA is released in large amounts within seconds. In this situation, the alarm sounds after the personnel have been exposed. This system was used during the Gulf War and has been upgraded to the Automatic Chemical Agent Alarm (ACAA) system. The ACAA is slightly larger and has a communications interface that is useful in combat.

Smiths Detection provides a commercial version of an IMS stand-alone detector called the Centurion. This system detects and identifies nerve and blister agents and offers superior reliability from interference. The alarm information can be transmitted via radio, satellite, or hardwiring. This system can be useful if placed in hospital wards or at victim collection sites to detect contamination.

INFRARED RADIATION DETECTION TECHNIQUES

Infrared radiation (IR) is employed in several CA detectors, including long-range detectors and point detectors. IR can be used to excite molecules, and each agent has a unique infrared pattern referred to as a fingerprint. Several different detection techniques use IR, including photoacoustic infrared spectroscopy, filter-based infrared spectroscopy, forward-looking infrared spectroscopy (FLIR), and Fourier transform spectroscopy.

Photoacoustic Infrared Spectroscopy

This highly selective technique is used to identify CA vapors. It usually is used in point detector devices. Modulated IR is passed through the sample. Since the CA absorbs the radiation, the temperature increases, and per Boyle law, the gas expands. The pattern of expansion or contraction depends on the modulation of the IR, which in photoacoustic spectroscopy is an audible signal. A microphone detects the modulation and alarms when it is similar to a recognizable agent. This technique's selectivity is based on the number of wavelengths transmitted through the sample. As more wavelengths are passed, the chance of contaminants causing false alarms decreases. These devices are sensitive to environmental variables such as external vibration. Like IMS, if these devices are calibrated in the operating environment, detection should be accurate.

Filter-based Infrared Spectroscopy

This technology also is based on comparing the amount of energy absorbed by the sample, using several different wavelengths of infrared light. A series of filters is used to direct the beam through a predetermined path. Concentrations of each vapor component are used to compile trends and identify the vapor.

Differential Absorption Light Detection and Ranging

This infrared technology is used mainly to track CA clouds that already have been identified. Two pulses of laser are transmitted into the distance, and the reflected IR is detected. One pulse is a frequency that is known to be absorbed by the CA; the other is not known to be absorbed. The difference in the intensity of the return signal is used to determine the concentration of the cloud, while the time of return is used to determine the distance from the observers. This technique also is subject to environmental noise but has been used effectively to track CAs.

Passive Infrared Detection

FLIR and Fourier transform infrared (FTIR) are techniques by which IR emitted from CA vapor is detected simply. These technologies commonly are used in stand-alone detection devices that simply alarm when a CA cloud is detected. Both of these methodologies depend on the collection of infrared information; however, the processing is different.

M21 Remote Sensing Chemical Agent Alarm

The military uses the M21 Remote Sensing Chemical Agent Alarm (RSCAAL) based on passive infrared detection. It is the first fielded standoff chemical detection device. This system can detect a vapor cloud from 5 km with an 87% detection rate. The M21 RSCAAL continuously monitors a background and notes the change in spectral information if a vapor cloud obstructs the background. It automatically scans along a 60° angle, allowing the operator to monitor horizontal movement. The M21 can be set up in 10 minutes and is unaffected by low light conditions. However, the M21 is limited in that it must be stationary and can be obstructed by snow and rain.

OTHER DETECTION TECHNOLOGIES

Photo Ionization Detection

Gas vapors can be ionized using ultraviolet light. Photo ionization detection depends on exposing the suspect vapor to ultraviolet energy powerful enough to ionize agent molecules. Specific ranges of ultraviolet light ionize molecules in certain CAs. An ion detector then registers the amount of ionized molecules. Thus, these detectors can determine the concentration and identity of the agent. Handheld detectors produced by RAE systems and Photovac are examples of detectors that use this technology.

Flame Photometry

Another technology employed is flame photometry. In this technique, a flame of hydrogen is used to burn a sample of air. The color of the flame is analyzed by a photometer for concentrations of sulfur and phosphorous (key components in nerve gas and mustard).

Flame photometry is highly sensitive yet is prone to false-positive results by detecting other gases that contain significant concentrations of sulfur or phosphorus but are nonhazardous. Certain analysis algorithms can be employed to make these detectors less prone to error.

If gas chromatography is integrated with flame photometry, the detectors are more accurate. Gas chromatography is a technique used in labs to separate mixtures of compounds. It involves using a carrier gas to separate a volatilized liquid or vapor based on its passage through a column. As each solute exits the column according to its properties and the temperature of the column, a detector records an electrical signal plotted over time.

Miniature Automatic Continuous Agent Monitoring System

The miniature automatic continuous agent monitoring system (MINICAMS) is a system based on combining gas chromatography with flame photometry.

A sample vapor is drawn into the machine and exposed to a heated preconcentrator loop. As each component exudes from the column, it is exposed to flame photometry. This system enables more specific detection. A typical cycle lasts 3-5 minutes, enabling continuous monitoring of the environment.

Surface Acoustic Wave Detection

Surface acoustic wave (SAW) chemical detectors rely on chemically selective coated piezoelectric crystals that absorb target gases. The absorption causes a change in the resonant frequency of the crystal that is measured by a microcomputer.

These detectors are able to identify and measure many CAs simultaneously. These devices are produced inexpensively, making them a popular choice among civilian response units. The SAW

MINICAD mk II is a portable SAW array detector that is lightweight, battery operated, and available commercially. It is used remotely to define areas of decontamination but also can be used for active detection.

The Joint Chemical Agent Detector (JCAD) ChemSentry also uses SAW technology and is produced by BAE. It weighs approximately 2 pounds and is designed to be used by every department of the military and is available commercially.

It can be used as a personal protection detector to be carried by troops as well as to monitor ships, cargo holds, and wheeled vehicles. It uses a preconcentrator to detect low levels of a specific chemical agent requiring 20 minutes for sample collection but simultaneously monitors ambient air for larger concentrations of most chemical warfare agents.

Carbon Nanotube Gas Ionization Sensors

An emerging technology that may soon be used for chemical detection is based on miniaturized carbon nanotube sensors.

The tips of nanotubes generate high electric fields that when exposed to different gases will exhibit different electrical conductances. This difference in conductances can be used to identify gases and mixtures of gases in a similar fashion to the IMS method of detection.

Previous generations of nanotube sensors have been limited by sensitivity to changes in environmental conditions, the inability to identify gases with low energies, and poor charge transfer. One group at RPI has developed a gas ionization sensor that generates high electric fields at low voltages.

Their sensors have good sensitivity and can be compact and battery powered. They have been shown to detect 1% mixtures of ammonia and argon at room temperature in less than 20 microseconds.

This technology offers many advantages over flame photometry, photoionization, and other techniques. These sensors will soon be integrated into detection devices and used to make more compact, portable, and reliable devices.

FACTORS IN SELECTING CHEMICAL DETECTION EQUIPMENT

A market survey of commercially available detection equipment in May 2000 identified 148 detection devices available to the military and first responders. With many different detectors and technologies available, the National Institute of Justice recommends examining 16 factors when choosing a detection device.

The table below lists these factors. The most sensitive detectors tend to be most susceptible to false-positive alarms. Thus, for most practical applications, multiple detectors are needed to verify the findings of the initial detector.

Factors to be Examined When Choosing a Detection Device

Agents detected	Determination of agents most likely to be encountered
Sensitivity	Lowest concentration of CA that results in positive response; ideally, lower than levels necessary for injury to personnel
Resistance to interference	Factors such as smoke, moisture, or other chemicals that prevent the device from accurately providing a response
Response time	Time to collect, analyze, and provide feedback
Start-up time	Time to assemble and deploy the device
Detection status	Vapor, liquid, and/or aerosols
Alarm capability	Audible, visual, or both
Portability	Ease of transport, which encompasses weight and dimensions
Power capabilities	Battery versus alternating current
Battery needs	Quantity and type of batteries
Operational environment	Extremes of conditions under which the device operates
Durability	Amount of abuse the device withstands
Procurement costs	Cost per device needed
Operator skill level	Skill involved in using the device
Training requirements	Number of hours and type of educational background required for operation

CHEMICAL DETECTION EQUIPMENT IN CIVILIAN RESPONSE TO TERRORISM

CDE technology has advanced primarily as a result of military necessity. More recently, the need for civilian preparedness for terrorist attacks with CA has been recognized. Civilian response is different from military response in many ways, and the choice of CDE must take this into account. Key differences include the following:

- Civilian responders tend to be less experienced in chemical attacks.
- Civilian responders have less information concerning the origin and type of attack and may not recognize that it is a CA attack initially.
- Civilian responders have more stringent budget restraints and thus must use cost-effective equipment.
- Civilian responders have less latitude in incorrectly identifying a CA.
- Civilian responders are deployed primarily to provide medical care, leaving detection as a secondary goal.

In the civilian setting, EMS or other medical providers are the first to arrive. Most EMS providers do not carry CDE to detect CAs and thus initially must recognize the potential threat in order to notify specialized HAZMAT response teams.

These teams exist in many cities and are at a minimum equipped with pH paper and combustible gas indicators. This equipment is inadequate in identifying most CAs. Other teams now are equipped with colorimetric tubes. Colorimetric tubes are much less expensive than more technical devices, such as the ICAM, and can be distributed generally.

Major cities in the US have a Metropolitan Medical Strike Response System (MMRS) organized by the Public Health Service. These are highly specialized, fully equipped, deployable teams to combat civilian threats from weapons of mass destruction.

They are primarily medical providers who provide EMS services, decontamination, detection, and treatment. The first such team was organized in 1995 in Washington, DC, and a second was organized for the 1996 Olympics in Atlanta. They are now present in 27 major cities.

MMRS teams are often better equipped to respond to CA attacks than HAZMAT response teams. Even so, wide variability exists in the type of detection devices used. A recent study by the National Guard recognized that no standards regulate the detection devices among different civilian emergency response units. MMRS teams can employ any of the devices and technologies described above. They commonly use inexpensive CDE such as SAW detectors and enzymatic techniques such as M9 paper and the M256 kit. Some teams also use IMS devices such as the APD2000 and a modified ICAM for domestic preparedness.

7

Chemical Warfare Agents

INTRODUCTION

Because of the ongoing risk of chemical attack, emergency physicians must be able to care for victims of chemical weapon agents (CWAs). This article reviews the physical properties and general clinical effects of CWAs. It also describes the medical management of victims of CWAs, including the use of personal protective equipment (PPE), victim decontamination, provision of supportive care, and provision of specific antidotal therapy. To illustrate these principles with specific agents, the properties, clinical effects, and medical management of nerve agents and vesicant agents are reviewed briefly.

Risk of Exposure to Chemical Warfare Agents

Injury from CWAs may result from industrial accident, military stockpiling, war, or terrorist attack.

Industrial accidents continue to be a significant potential source of exposure to the agents used in chemical weapons. Chemicals such as phosgene, cyanide, anhydrous ammonia, and chlorine are used widely and frequently are transported by industry. The accidental release of a methylisocyanate cloud (composed of phosgene and isocyanate) was implicated in the Bhopal disaster in 1984. These accidents continue today, with nearly 9000 occurring in the United States in 2001 alone.

CWAs first were used in 1915, when the German military released 168 tons of chlorine gas at Ypres, Belgium, killing an estimated 5000 Allied troops. Two years later, the same battlefields saw the first deployment of sulfur mustard. Sulfur mustard was the major cause of chemical casualties in World War I. CWAs have been used in at least 12 conflicts since, including the first Persian Gulf War (Iraq-Iran War). The Iraqi military also used chemical weapons against the Iraqi Kurds during the second Persian Gulf War.

Civilians have also been exposed inadvertently to chemical weapons many years after weapon deployment during war. Approximately 50,000 tons of mustard shells were disposed of in the Baltic Sea following World War I. Since then, numerous fishermen have been burned accidentally while hauling leaking shells aboard boats. Leaking mustard shells also have injured collectors of military memorabilia and children playing in old battlefields.

Although a number of international treaties have banned the development, production, and stockpiling of CWAs, these agents reportedly still are being produced or stockpiled in several countries.

Within the last decade, terrorists deployed chemical weapons against civilian populations for the first time in history. The release of sarin in Matsumoto, Japan, in June 1994 by the extremist Aum Shinrikyo cult left 7 dead and 280 injured. The following year, in March 1995, the Aum Shinrikyo cult released sarin vapor in the Tokyo subway system during morning rush hour, leaving 12 dead and sending more than 5000 casualties to local hospitals. A derivative of fentanyl was also used against terrorists holding hostages in a Moscow theater in 2002. Because of a lack of antidote available by the responders, more than 120 casualties among the hostages occurred from asphyxiation.

Several characteristics of CWAs lend themselves to terrorist use. Chemical substrates used in CWAs are widely available, and recipes for CWA production may be found on the Internet. CWAs are transported easily and may be delivered by a variety of routes. Chemical agents often are difficult to protect against and quickly incapacitate the intended targets. Most civilian medical communities are inadequately prepared to deal with a chemical terrorist attack.

GENERAL CONSIDERATIONS

TYPES OF CHEMICAL WEAPON AGENTS

CWAs comprise a diverse group of hazardous substances. Major categories of CWAs include the following:

- Nerve agents (eg, sarin, soman, cyclosarin, tabun, VX)
- Vesicating or blistering agents (eg, mustards, lewisite)
- Respiratory agents (eg, chlorine, phosgene, diphosgene)
- Cyanides
- Antimuscarinic agents (eg, anticholinergic compounds)
- Opioid agents (opioid derivatives)
- Riot control agents (eg, pepper gas, cyanide, CS)
- Vomiting agents (eg, adamsite)

PHYSICAL PROPERTIES

CWAs generally are stored and transported as liquids and deployed as either liquid aerosols or vapors. Victims usually are exposed to agents via one or more of 3 routes: skin (liquid and high vapor concentrations), eyes (liquid or vapor), and respiratory tract (vapor inhalation).

CWAs are characterized by 2 inversely related physical properties: volatility (ie, tendency of liquids to vaporize, which directly increases with temperature) and persistence (ie, tendency of liquids to remain in a liquid state).

In general, volatile liquids pose the dual risk of dermal and inhalation exposure, while persistent liquids are more likely to be absorbed across the skin. The effects of vapors largely are influenced by ambient wind conditions; even a slight breeze can blow nerve agent vapor away from its intended target. Effects of vapor are enhanced markedly when deployed within an enclosed space.

CLINICAL EFFECTS

Depending on the agent and the type and amount (concentration) of exposure, CWA effects may be immediate or delayed. Large inhalation exposures to nerve agents or mustards are likely to be lethal immediately. Small dermal exposures to nerve agents and mustards are particularly insidious and generally require expectant observation for variable periods because of possible delayed effects. Specific clinical effects of CWAs are as varied as the agents.

Medical Management

To appropriately manage CWA exposures, emergency care personnel are required to protect themselves by performing the following:

- Using PPE
- Decontaminating patients immediately
- Providing supportive care
- Providing specific antidotes when indicated

Personal Protective Equipment

The primary responsibility of those who treat victims of CWAs is to protect themselves by wearing adequate PPE. First responders are at serious risk from the chemically contaminated environment (hot zone), either from direct contact with persistent liquid or from inhaling vapor. First responders and emergency care providers also are at risk from handling skin and clothing of victims contaminated with liquid CWAs (secondary skin and inhalation exposure). Conversely, providing care to those exposed only to vapor CWAs poses little risk to emergency care providers outside the hot zone. Regardless, until identification of the substance is made and it is deemed nontoxic, responders should wear their PPE.

Standard protective garments are inadequate for most CWAs. Double layers of latex gloves are useless against liquid nerve and blister agents, and surgical masks and air-purifying respirators are inadequate against nerve agent vapors.

Levels of Personal Protective Equipment

US regulatory agencies mandate the use of appropriate levels of PPE.

- Level A PPE is required for first responders and others working inside the hot zone, where vapor concentrations may be immediately dangerous to life and health. These suits are fully encapsulated, resistant to liquid and vapor chemical penetration, and include a self-contained breathing apparatus. Level A suits are also cumbersome, hot, and very difficult to wear for more than 30 minutes. There has been some move to mandate the use of level-A suits for hospital personnel. This is a hotly debated subject and as yet is unresolved. The use of level-A suits in hospital-based decontamination is probably not warranted.

- Level B PPE is required for hospital personnel involved in decontamination of unknown hazardous materials. These suits provide adequate protection against liquid and vapor chemicals when accompanied by a self-contained breathing apparatus or supplied air respirator.
- Level C PPE is used when chemical agents have been identified and are amenable to removal by an air-purifying respirator. This suit also provides some protection against penetration by chemical liquids and vapors.

Decontamination

- Decontamination is the physical process of removing residual chemicals from persons, equipment, and the environment. Residual hazardous chemicals on those who have been exposed directly are a source of ongoing exposure to those persons and pose a risk of secondary exposure to first responders and emergency care personnel. Immediate decontamination is a major treatment priority for those with CWA exposure.
- Initial decontamination involves removal from the contaminated environment, removal of all contaminated clothes and jewelry, and copious irrigation with water.
- Rinse exposed persons with a 0.5% hypochlorite solution, which chemically neutralizes most CWAs (eg, nerve agents, mustards). A 0.5% hypochlorite solution conveniently is prepared by mixing 1 part 5% hypochlorite (household bleach) with 9 parts water.
- Avoid hot water and vigorous scrubbing, as they may increase chemical absorption.

- Vapor exposure alone does not require decontamination. Fully decontaminate patients with unclear exposure histories. As well, if a nerve agent is suspected, decontamination should be performed as the patient may off-gas significant levels of the agent with the potential of further exposure to both him or her and responders.
- Ideally, decontaminate as close as possible to the site of exposure to minimize duration of exposure and prevent further spread. Hospitals receiving contaminated persons should establish an area outside the emergency department in which to perform decontamination before people and equipment are allowed in. Portable decontamination equipment with showers and run-off water collection systems are commercially available. All hospitals should have the capacity to safely decontaminate at least one person.

Supportive and Specific Therapy

Supportive therapy for victims of CWAs generally follows the universally accepted algorithm of first ensuring the adequacy of airway, breathing, and circulation, with one important exception. Severe nerve agent poisoning may require immediate administration of parenteral atropine. Many CWAs only can be treated supportively. Specific, well-established antidotes are available only for nerve agent and cyanide exposures. Since no laboratory tests are available to rapidly confirm exposure to CWAs, treatment is based on clinical criteria.

NERVE AGENTS - PROPERTIES AND CLINICAL EFFECTS

Mechanism of Action

The 5 nerve agents, tabun (GA), sarin (GB), soman (GD), cyclosarin (GF), and VX, have chemical structures similar to the common organophosphate pesticide malathion. Like organophosphate insecticides, these agents phosphorylate and inactivate acetylcholinesterase (AChE). Acetylcholine accumulates at nerve terminals, initially stimulating and then paralyzing cholinergic neurotransmission throughout the body. Inhibition of AChE may not account for all of the toxic effects of nerve agents.

These agents also are known to bind directly to nicotinic receptors and cardiac muscarinic receptors. They also antagonize gamma-aminobutyric acid (GABA) neurotransmission and stimulate glutamate *N*-methyl-d-aspartate (NMDA) receptors. These latter actions may partly mediate nerve agent–induced seizures and CNS neuropathology.

Physical Properties

Under temperate conditions, all nerve agents are volatile liquids. The most volatile agent, sarin, evaporates at approximately the same rate as water. The least volatile agent, VX, has the consistency of motor oil. This persistence and higher lipophilicity make VX 100-150 times more toxic than sarin when victims sustain dermal exposure. A 10-mg dose applied to the skin is lethal to 50% of unprotected individuals.

All nerve agents rapidly penetrate skin and clothing. Nerve agent vapors are heavier than air and tend to sink into low places (eg, trenches, basements).

Clinical Effects

Nerve agents produce muscarinic, nicotinic, and direct CNS toxicity with a wide variety of effects on the respiratory tract, cardiovascular system, CNS, gastrointestinal (GI) tract, muscles, and eyes. Onset and severity of clinical effects vary widely, since numerous variables determine predominant effects. Agent identity, dose (determined by concentration and duration of exposure), and type of exposure primarily determine nerve agent toxicity. Toxic effects result from dermal exposure to liquid and ocular and inhalation exposure to vapor.

Liquid Exposure

Liquid agents easily penetrate skin and clothing. Onset of symptoms occurs from 30 minutes to 18 hours following dermal exposure.

Minimal liquid exposure (eg, a small droplet on the skin) may cause local sweating and muscle fasciculation, followed by nausea, vomiting, diarrhea, and generalized weakness. Even with decontamination, signs and symptoms may persist for hours.

In contrast, persons with severe liquid exposures may be briefly asymptomatic (1-30 min) but rapidly may suffer abrupt loss of consciousness, convulsions, generalized muscular fasciculation, flaccid paralysis, copious secretions (nose, mouth, lungs), bronchoconstriction, apnea, and death.

Vapor Exposure

Vapor inhalation produces clinical toxicity within seconds to several minutes. Effects may be local or systemic. Exposure to even a small amount of vapor usually results in at least one of the following categories of complaints: (1) ocular (miosis, blurred vision, eye pain, conjunctival injection), (2) nasal (rhinorrhea), or (3) pulmonary (bronchoconstriction, bronchorrhea, dyspnea).

Exposure to a vapor concentration of 3.0 mg/m^3 for 1 minute causes miosis and rhinorrhea. Inhalation of a high concentration of vapor results in loss of consciousness after only one breath, convulsions, respiratory arrest, and death.

For example, breathing 10 mg $/m^3$ of sarin vapor for only 10 minutes (100 mg/m^3 for 1 min) causes death in approximately one half of exposed individuals. Severe vapor exposures also are characterized by generalized fasciculations, hypersecretions (mouth, lungs), and intense bronchoconstriction with respiratory compromise.

Respiratory Tract

Nerve agents act on the upper respiratory tract to produce profuse watery nasal discharge, hypersalivation, and weakness of the tongue and pharynx muscles. Laryngeal muscles are paralyzed, resulting in stridor.

In the lower respiratory tract, nerve agents produce copious bronchial secretions and intense bronchoconstriction. If untreated, the combination of hypersecretion, bronchoconstriction, respiratory muscle paralysis, and CNS depression rapidly progresses to respiratory failure and death. Nerve agents depress the central respiratory drive directly. Thus, early death following large vapor exposure likely results from primary respiratory arrest, not from neuromuscular blockade, bronchorrhea, or bronchoconstriction.

Cardiovascular System

The cardiovascular effects of nerve agents vary and depend on the balance between their nicotinic receptor–potentiating effects at autonomic ganglia and their muscarinic receptor–potentiating effects at parasympathetic postganglionic fibers that innervate the heart.

Sinus tachydysrhythmias with or without hypertension (sympathetic tone predomination) or bradydysrhythmias with or without variable atrioventricular blockade and hypotension (parasympathetic tone predomination) may occur.

Superimposed hypoxia may produce tachycardia or precipitate ventricular tachydysrhythmias.

Nerve agent–induced prolonged QT and torsades de pointes have been described in animals.

In victims of the Tokyo sarin gas attack, sinus tachycardia and hypertension were common cardiovascular abnormalities, while sinus bradycardia was uncommon.

Central Nervous System

Nerve agents produce a variety of neurologic signs and symptoms by acting on cholinergic receptors throughout the CNS. The most important clinical signs of neurotoxicity are a rapidly decreasing level of consciousness (sometimes within seconds of exposure) and generalized seizures. Symptoms such as headache, vertigo, paresthesias, anxiety, insomnia, depression, and emotional lability also have been reported.

Musculoskeletal System

Nerve agents initially stimulate and then paralyze neurotransmission at the neuromuscular junction. With minimal exposure, exposed persons may complain of vague weakness or difficulty walking. More significant exposures resemble the clinical effects that result from succinylcholine, with initial fasciculations followed by flaccid paralysis and apnea.

Ocular

Nerve agent liquid or vapor readily penetrates the conjunctiva and exerts direct muscarinic parasympathetic effects. This results in constriction of the iris (miosis, blurred and dim vision, headache), constriction of the ciliary muscle (pain, nausea, vomiting), and stimulation of the lacrimal glands (tearing, redness). Although miosis is the most consistent clinical finding after vapor exposure to nerve agents (occurred in 99% of persons exposed in Tokyo sarin attack), it may be absent or delayed in dermal exposure. Duration of miosis varies according to the extent of ocular exposure (up to 45 d).

Laboratory Tests

Routine toxicology testing does not identify nerve agents in serum or urine. Measurements of red blood cell (RBC) or plasma cholinesterase activity have been used as an index of the severity of nerve agent toxicity, but this approach is not always reliable. The reference range of RBC cholinesterase activity may vary widely, and mild exposures may be difficult to interpret without baseline measurement. In addition, RBC cholinesterase activity may not correlate with the severity of signs and symptoms following vapor exposure.

In the Tokyo subway sarin attack, 27% of patients with clinical manifestations of moderate poisoning had plasma cholinesterase activity in the normal range. Moreover, different organophosphates variably inhibit RBC and plasma cholinesterase. For example, in mild-to-moderate exposures to sarin or VX, RBC cholinesterase activity is decreased to a much greater extent than plasma cholinesterase activity.

Since plasma cholinesterase is produced by the liver, its activity also may be depressed in certain conditions (eg, liver disease, pregnancy, infections) or with certain drugs (eg, oral contraceptives).

Conversely, a 20-25% reduction in RBC cholinesterase activity tends to correlate with severe clinical toxicity and, despite the exception noted above, activity of both enzymes approaches zero in most severely poisoned victims. Nevertheless, treatment decisions should be clinically based. Never withhold treatment from a symptomatic patient while awaiting laboratory confirmation. Conversely, decreased cholinesterase activity in the absence of clinical signs of toxicity is not an indication for treatment.

NERVE AGENTS - MEDICAL MANAGEMENT

Personal Protective Equipment

First responders are at serious risk of exposure within the contaminated environment (hot zone), either from direct contact with persistent liquid or from inhaling residual vapors. First responders and subsequent emergency care providers outside the hot zone are at risk from handling persons contaminated with liquid nerve agent (through both dermal and inhalation exposure).

Conversely, victims exposed to nerve agent vapor pose little risk to emergency care providers outside the hot zone; residual agent is not present and off-gassing may occur but rarely in significant amounts. In the Tokyo sarin attack, approximately 90% of exposed persons reported to medical facilities by private or public transportation without notable contamination of others. Additionally, secondary injury to hospital staff was minimal and did not necessitate specific treatment.

Unless a clear history of vapor exposure only is obtained, emergency medical personnel should assume that liquid contamination is present and wear PPE. For most nerve agent exposures, first responders require level A PPE inside the hot zone, and hospital personnel involved in decontamination should wear level B PPE.

Decontamination

Decontamination should proceed as described in General Considerations. Decontaminate with a triple wash, including initial irrigation with tepid water followed by 0.5% hypochlorite solution or soap and water (alkaline solutions also neutralize nerve agent) and repeated thorough water rinsing. In survivors, the amount of residual liquid contaminant is likely to be small, because victims with larger exposures probably will die before they reach the hospital. Other than removing clothing and jewelry, decontamination is unnecessary for victims of vapor nerve agent exposure.

Supportive Care

Saving lives always depends on ensuring adequate airway, ventilation, and circulation. The larger the exposure, the more likely victims require early intubation and ventilation. Conversely, adequate ventilation may be impossible due to the intense muscarinic effects of nerve gas exposure (copious airway secretions, bronchoconstriction). In this situation, administer atropine before initiating other measures. The use of succinylcholine to assist intubation is not recommended, since nerve agents prolong the drug's paralytic effects.

Treat seizures with adequate oxygenation and liberal doses of benzodiazepines titrated to effect. Termination of seizure activity may reflect onset of flaccid paralysis from the nerve agent rather than adequacy of antiseizure therapy. A bedside electroencephalograph (EEG) may be required to assess ongoing seizure activity.

Animal data suggest that routine administration of diazepam reduces incidence of seizures and decreases severity of pathologic brain injury following nerve agent exposure.

Specific Therapy

Treatment of victims with nerve gas toxicity is broadly similar to the treatment of those poisoned by organophosphate insecticides.

Atropine Sulfate

Symptomatic patients require immediate treatment with atropine. Atropine blocks muscarinic effects of nerve agents (eg, bronchorrhea, bronchoconstriction), improving ventilation by drying secretions and decreasing airway resistance. Atropine also blocks other muscarinic effects, such as nausea, vomiting, abdominal cramping, bradycardia, and diaphoresis. Atropine does not have nicotinic effects and thus does not reverse toxicity at autonomic ganglia and neuromuscular junctions. Atropine does not prevent or reverse paralysis.

Atropine therapy is guided by clinical signs and symptoms. Titrate dosing to the desired clinical effect. The goals of atropine therapy are to dry secretions and eliminate bronchoconstriction.

Administer more atropine if assisted ventilation remains difficult or secretions persist. Heart rate and pupil size are poor clinical indicators of adequate atropinization. Presence of tachycardia should not dissuade the clinician from initiating or continuing atropine therapy. Miosis may be absent or delayed in dermal exposures and is not reversed by systemic atropine.

- Adults with mild-to-moderate symptoms: 2 mg of atropine IV/IM/ET q2-5min
- Adults with severe symptoms: 5 mg IV/IM/ET
- Children: 0.02 mg/kg (0.1 mg minimum) IV/IM/ET
- Children with severe symptoms: 0.05 mg/kg IV/IM/ET

Up to 20 mg of atropine may be required the first day, unlike with organophosphate insecticide poisoning, where as much as 3000 mg of atropine may be required over 1 day. In the Tokyo sarin attack, only 19% of poisoned patients required more than 2 mg of atropine. Severely poisoned patients required 1.5-15 mg of atropine.

Oxime Therapy

Oximes are nucleophilic substances that bind to the phosphate moiety of the nerve agent more avidly than AChE to reactivate the nerve agent–inhibited enzyme. Reactivation is impossible once dealkylation or "aging" of phosphorylated AChE occurs. Once aging occurs, new AChE must be synthesized. The rate of aging varies among nerve agents. Aging occurs within 2 minutes after soman exposure, 5-8 hours after sarin exposure, and more than 40 hours after tabun and VX exposure.

Pralidoxime chloride (2-PAM) is the only conventional oxime available for clinical use in the US. Administer pralidoxime to symptomatic patients as early as possible, ideally concurrent with adequate doses of atropine. Pralidoxime has its greatest effect at the neuromuscular junction.

- Adult dose: 1-2 g IV
- Pediatric dose: 15-25 mg/kg IV over 30 min

Slowly administer pralidoxime IV to minimize adverse effects such as hypertension, headache, blurred vision, epigastric pain, nausea, and vomiting. When IV access cannot be established, 2-PAM also may be given IM (1 mg with 3 mL sterile saline).

With adequate decontamination and appropriate initial therapy, serious signs and symptoms of nerve agent toxicity rarely last more than a couple of hours. In the unusual event that toxicity persists or worsens clinically, administer repeat doses of 2-PAM at hourly intervals.

In the Tokyo sarin attack, severely poisoned patients required 1-36 g. Since 2-PAM is excreted in the urine, lower repeat doses for patients with renal failure and maintain adequate hydration. If hypertension increases during pralidoxime administration, IV phentolamine may help (adults: 5 mg IV; children: 1 mg IV).

Mark I Kit

Mark I kit was designed for military self-administration in the field. It consists of two spring-loaded IM Autoinjectors containing 2 mg of atropine and 600 mg of pralidoxime, respectively. These antidote kits are not yet available for civilian use.

Hemodialysis

Japanese physicians reported successful use of hemodialysis and hemoperfusion in one severely intoxicated victim of the Tokyo Subway sarin attack who remained unresponsive to pharmacotherapy.

Disposition

Peak toxic effects occur within minutes to hours and resolve within 1 day.

Observe asymptomatic patients exposed to nerve agent liquid for a minimum of 18 hours, since delayed onset of signs and symptoms have been reported (up to 18 h postexposure). Admit symptomatic patients with liquid exposure and monitor them for at least 1 day.

Cholinesterase levels alone should not guide disposition. Some sources recommend observation of asymptomatic patients exposed to nerve gas vapor for 1 hour.

In reality, patients who present after inhaling nerve agent vapor have experienced peak effects long before arriving at the hospital, and no further absorption or worsening is expected. When patients experience no signs or symptoms other than eye findings, they may be discharged. Unlike with organophosphate insecticides, nerve agents have not been associated with delayed neuropathy.

MUSTARDS - PROPERTIES AND CLINICAL EFFECTS

Mechanism of Action

Sulfur mustard (2,2,-dichlordiethyl sulfide) has been used as a chemical weapon since World War I. Nitrogen mustard, a derivative of sulfur mustard, was one of the first chemotherapy agents but never has been used in warfare. These vesicating agents cause blistering of exposed surfaces. Both mustard agents rapidly penetrate cells and generate a highly toxic intermediate episulfonium ion, which irreversibly alkylates DNA, RNA, and protein. This disrupts cell function and causes cell death. The chemical reaction is both temperature dependent and facilitated by the presence of water, which explains why warm, moist tissues are affected more severely. Actively reproducing cells, such as epithelial and hematopoietic cells, are most vulnerable to alkylation.

Mustards also produce cytotoxicity by binding to and depleting cellular glutathione, a free radical scavenger. Glutathione depletion leads to the inactivation of sulfhydryl-containing enzymes, loss of calcium homeostasis, lipid peroxidation, cellular membrane breakdown, and cell death.

Physical Properties

Mustards are oily liquids with odors of mustard, onion, garlic, or horseradish. Highly soluble in oils, fats, and organic solvents, mustards quickly penetrate skin and most materials, including rubber and most textiles. Sulfur mustard is considered a persistent agent with low volatility at cool temperatures but becomes a major vapor hazard at high ambient temperatures. Exposure to mustard vapor, not mustard liquid, is the primary medical concern. More than 80% of mustard casualties in World War I were caused by exposure to mustard vapor. Mustard vapor is 3 times more toxic than a similar concentration of cyanide gas; however, mustard liquid is also quite toxic. Skin exposure to as little as 1-1.5 tsp of liquid (7 g) is lethal to 50% of adults.

Clinical Effects

Mustards injure the skin, eyes, respiratory tract, GI mucosa, and hematopoietic system. The pattern of toxicity depends partly on whether the person is exposed to liquid or vapor. Liquid exposure primarily damages the skin, producing an initial erythema followed by blistering similar to a partial-thickness burn. Vapor exposure preferentially damages the upper respiratory tract (skin usually is not affected).

Mustards penetrate cells and alkylate intracellular components in less than 2 minutes, yet signs and symptoms usually are delayed 4-6 hours (range, 1-24 h). The latent period is shorter with high-concentration exposures, such as those occurring at increased ambient temperature and humidity.

Skin

Chemical burns secondary to mustard often appear deceptively superficial on initial presentation. Earliest symptoms are pruritus, burning, and stinging pain over exposed areas. Moist, thinner skin is affected more severely. Affected areas appear erythematous and edematous. If contamination is more extensive, superficial bullae occur within 24 hours of exposure. Most burns are partial thickness, but full-thickness burns with deep bullae and ulcers may result from exposure to higher concentrations. Severe exposures clinically and histologically may resemble scalded skin syndrome or toxic epidermal necrolysis. Blister fluid does not contain active mustard and is not toxic.

Eyes

Eyes are especially sensitive to the effects of mustard. Ocular symptoms begin 4-8 hours postexposure. Earliest symptoms include burning pain, foreign body sensation, photophobia, tearing, and visual blurring. Clinical manifestations include eyelid edema, conjunctival injection and edema, chemosis, iritis, corneal abrasions, edema and ulceration, and decreased visual acuity. Permanent corneal scarring and blindness may occur with severe exposures.

Respiratory Tract

Mustards primarily damage upper airway mucosa. Inhalation of mustard vapor produces a direct inflammatory effect on the respiratory tract, with damage occurring in a progressive downward pattern. The lower respiratory tract and lung parenchyma rarely are affected. Following a variable latent period of 2-24 hours, injury is characterized by hemorrhagic inflammation and airway erosion.

Upper respiratory tract is affected first, evidenced by sinusitis, sinus congestion, sore throat, and hoarseness. Lower respiratory tract symptoms include cough, dyspnea, and respiratory distress. Direct necrotic effect of mustard on airway mucosa produces epithelial sloughing and pseudomembrane formation, causing small and large airway obstruction.

In severe cases, late pulmonary sequelae include bronchopneumonia and bronchial obstruction. Pulmonary edema rarely occurs, because mustard rarely affects the lung parenchyma and alveoli. Patients with extensive mucosal involvement may suffer fatal respiratory compromise as late as several days after exposure.

Gastrointestinal Tract

Mustard damages rapidly proliferating cells of the intestinal mucosa. GI involvement results in abdominal pain, nausea, vomiting, diarrhea, and weight loss.

Hematopoietic System

Mustards cause unpredictable bone marrow suppression, as leukocyte precursors begin dying 3-5 days after exposure. A leukopenic nadir usually occurs in 3-14 days, depending on the severity of exposure. Anemia and thrombocytopenia are late findings. Complete bone marrow aplasia has been reported.

Laboratory Tests

Diagnosis of mustard exposure is clinical. No laboratory tests identify or characterize acute exposure.

MUSTARDS - MEDICAL MANAGEMENT

Personal Protective Equipment

Liquid mustard contamination poses a dermal contact risk for emergency care personnel. Specialized protective military garments containing a charcoal layer to absorb penetrating sulfur mustard provide protection for up to 6 hours. These protective garments (chemical protective overgarment, battle dress overgarment, mission-oriented protective posture) are not available outside the military. Level A PPE provides the best protection for civilian first responders, and hospital-based emergency care personnel involved in subsequent decontamination should wear level A PPE.

Decontamination

Decontamination within 2 minutes of exposure is the most important intervention for patients with dermal exposure, since mustard rapidly becomes fixed to tissues, and its effects are irreversible. The classic description is an initial lack of signs and symptoms, which does not lessen the urgency to decontaminate patients as soon as possible.

Remove clothing immediately and wash the underlying skin with soap and water. Ocular exposure requires immediate copious irrigation with saline or water. Next, decontaminate the skin with 0.5% hypochlorite solution or with alkaline soap and water, which chemically inactivates sulfur mustard. Because mustard is relatively insoluble in water, water alone has limited value as a decontaminant. Decontamination after the first few minutes of exposure does not prevent subsequent damage but at least protects emergency care personnel from further contact exposure.

Supportive Care

Treatment of mustard exposure proceeds according to symptoms. Since the effects of mustards typically are delayed, persons with complaints immediately after exposure may have an additional injury. Patients with signs of upper airway obstruction require endotracheal intubation or the creation of a surgical airway. Also consider endotracheal intubation for persons with severe exposures. Use the largest endotracheal tube that can pass through, since sloughing epithelium may obstruct smaller tubes. Have patients inhale moist air. Mucolytics also are recommended for those with respiratory complaints.

Avoid overhydration, since fluid losses generally are less than with thermal burns. Monitor fluid and electrolyte status and replace losses accordingly. Mustard-induced burns are especially painful, warranting the liberal use of narcotic analgesia. Adequate burn care is essential, since skin lesions heal slowly and are prone to infection. Severe burns may require debridement, irrigation, and topical antibiotics, such as silver sulfadiazine. Address tetanus toxoid immunity.

Severe ocular burns require ophthalmologic consultation. Eye care typically includes daily irrigation, topical antibiotic solutions, topical corticosteroids, and mydriatics. Treat minor corneal injuries similarly to corneal abrasions. Apply petroleum jelly to prevent eyelid margins from sticking together. More severe corneal injuries may take as long as 2-3 months to heal. Permanent visual defects are rare.

Specific Therapy

Although no antidotes currently are available to treat mustard toxicity, several agents are under investigation, including antioxidants (vitamin E), anti-inflammatory drugs (corticosteroids), mustard scavengers (glutathione, *N*-acetylcysteine), and nitric oxide synthase inhibitors (*L*-nitroarginine methyl ester).

Administer granulocyte colony-stimulating factor to patients with bone marrow suppression following mustard exposure.

Disposition

Patients with significant respiratory tract burns usually require ICU admission and aggressive pulmonary care. Admit patients with significant dermal burns to a burn unit for aggressive wound management, analgesia, and supportive care. Arrange to monitor blood cell counts for 2 weeks following significant exposures. For 12 hours prior to discharge, observe patients who are initially asymptomatic following mustard exposure.

Most patients recover completely. Only a small fraction have chronic ocular or pulmonary damage. Approximately 2% of those exposed to sulfur mustard in World War I died, mostly due to burns, respiratory tract damage, and bone marrow suppression. Sulfur mustard is a known carcinogen, yet a single exposure causes only minimal risk.

CONCLUSION

CWAs comprise a diverse group of extremely hazardous materials. Emergency physicians should be familiar with the pathophysiology and various clinical presentations produced by CWAs as well as the principles and practices of appropriate medical management. Since deployment of CWAs also places emergency care providers at serious risk of exposure, emergency physicians must be familiar with PPE and decontamination.

As potential weapons of mass destruction, CWAs are capable of causing a catastrophic medical disaster, which would overwhelm any healthcare system. Since civilian victims exposed to CWAs are likely to flee to the nearest hospital, emergency physicians play a key role in preparing emergency departments for the treatment of persons exposed to CWAs.

8

Chemical Warfare Mass Casualty Management

SPECIFIC PROCEDURES FOR A CHEMICAL WEAPON RESPONSE

Introduction

This article is for managers who prepare hospital operational plans, for leaders responsible for response activities within a hospital, and for hospital health care providers. It is intended to provide credible source material on how to accomplish numerous concurrent tasks required during a chemical event involving a large number of casualties. More specifically, the intent is to offer possible solutions to a number of tasks comprising the intimidating mission of caring for overwhelming numbers of chemically contaminated casualties.

Although no one article can contain everything a medical treatment facility will require to complete this mission, a number of practical solutions to critical tasks are presented. This information is the product of expertise acquired during the 1991 Persian Gulf War assisting hospitals to prepare, train, and exercise to receive chemical warfare agent casualties; during many years of preparing a hospital response capability for a disaster; and during actual hospital disaster response. It is a work in progress and will be regularly updated.

These recommended actions will be most useful in planning the early response phase of a chemical event but also have relevance for other public health events. It is not meant to supplant other works from either private or governmental sources but rather to provide a complementary perspective on how to approach several key tasks. A number of additional resources are identified to facilitate preparation of plans and procedures; these are identified as references or as web sites in the text.

While the measures discussed are possible actions for an individual health care facility, the inherent nature of a weapon of mass destruction (WMD) demands a community or regional approach (Joint Commission on Accreditation of Healthcare Organizations JCAHO). Each health care organization within the community must define its role and understand the roles and limitations of other treatment facilities to develop viable comprehensive plans to address overwhelming numbers of casualties. Through collaborative planning, community health care institutions capabilities and limitations will be recognized.

The joint community planning extends beyond health care facilities. An event that produces large numbers of casualties will transcend all aspects of emergency response and local government. Police, fire, emergency medical services (EMS), and other emergency operations groups must plan together to identify overlapping capabilities and, more importantly, to recognize limitations and develop interagency communications capability. Many areas have local emergency planning committees (LEPC). These committees would provide an excellent forum to begin or continue planning to protect public health, safety, and the environment from chemical hazards.

A hazard vulnerability analysis (HVA) is a necessary first approach. Defining potential hazards within the local geographic area is essential to prepare all-inclusive realistic plans. The Occupational Safety and Health Administration (OSHA) included examples of HVAs in their publication "Best Practices for Hospital-Based First Receivers" (OSHA, 2005). Developing a HVA in concert with other medical and nonmedical authorities will provide a basis for decision-making and development of coordinated plans. Identification of appropriate staff, development of specialized teams, selection of personal protective clothing, other specific equipment and materials, and necessary pharmaceuticals can only be determined once specific local hazards are recognized.

Environmental conditions will present risks to both casualties and hospital first receivers. Practical solutions are required for cold weather to protect patients during decontamination. Hospital personnel working outside in hot conditions, particularly those in personal protective equipment (PPE), are at risk for heat injury. Environmental factors are particularly important when large numbers of personnel are being triaged and held for treatment. Persons who are chronically ill, elderly, and very young are especially susceptible to heat or cold; an area must be identified to protect them from extreme conditions.

Procedures for a Chemical Weapon Response

Specific measures to handle an incident involving a chemical WMD should be integrated into existing hospital emergency preparedness plans. Although some of these measures are common to disaster response of any nature, the demands that may result from a chemical WMD crisis may require expanding existing hospital emergency preparedness plans, including the protection of employees and the physical plant.

First, a recognized chain of command to direct the hospital staff and to manage critical assets during a mass casualty event will be required to provide an orderly response. The designated leader is responsible for coordinating the activities of the departments and hospital staff in accordance with the emergency preparedness plan. In addition, the leader is responsible for communicating and coordinating activities with outside agencies. This chain of command may be delineated in the health care facility incident command system (ICS; see Hospital Emergency Incident Command System HEICS) or in the emergency operations plan. An excellent alternative to HEICS is the Medical and Health Incident Management System (MaHIM) by Joseph Barbera, MD, and Anthony Macintyre, MD. Regardless of the system chosen or developed, locally, it must be in accordance with the National Incident Management System (NIMS).

One strategy to promote such planning is to have department or clinic chiefs prepare a sequence of objectives for their staff to follow during a chemical incident that is in accordance with the overarching hospital procedure. Include housekeeping, facility engineers, maintenance, administrative, pharmacy, and security staffs. To support the hospital plan, each department or unit must develop a standard operating procedure (SOP) that defines how each task is to be accomplished. The unit's SOP must be simple but all-inclusive; each task must be defined. Cue cards or checklists to address specific tasks or the sequence of tasks can be prepared as appendices to the SOP. The cue cards, distributed at the outset of an event, prevent essential tasks from being overlooked. Laminated wallet cards can be issued pre-event. The SOPs must be consolidated and reviewed closely to identify shortcomings and to ensure a coordinated response.

Staff members must practice frequently to maintain their competency. Also, take into consideration the staffing differences by shift or day of the week. Special attention to training is needed by part-time weekend personnel.

A chemically hazardous environment requires additional safeguards to protect hospital workers and patients. Designate a safety officer. This officer monitors work and/or rest cycles of employees working in PPE, ensures contamination control, and identifies safety hazards that occur during the hospital response. In addition, the safety officer ensures that patients are decontaminated thoroughly before entering the hospital; therefore, the safety officer is the last line of defense for clinical personnel and the facility. Even with the urgent needs of many victims of a chemical attack, the hospital, staff, and patients must not be compromised by chemical contamination.

Establish a plan to handle decontaminated and contaminated victims of a chemical WMD incident. Ideally, hazardous materials (HAZMAT) teams decontaminate people at the incident site before evacuating them to a medical facility, but this cannot be relied upon. However, planners should anticipate that less-injured patients may self-transport to the nearest medical facilities and may contaminate these facilities.

The plan must include ways of diverting these people to a holding and/or treatment area that does not compromise the health care facility. The requirement to remove all chemical contamination from patients delays their entry into the health care system but should not delay lifesaving treatment by staff in appropriate PPE. Finally, do not rely on hasty decontamination done by others outside the hospital. Put patients through a thorough decontamination procedure at the hospital when indicated.

INTEGRATION OF HOSPITAL PLANS INTO COMMUNITY DISASTER PLANS

JCAHO's Environment of Care (EC) standards require organizations to participate with the community in establishing priorities among potential emergencies, defining the organization's role in the community's emergency medicine (EM) program, and linking with the community's command structure (EC.4.10)

Detection, diagnosis, and mitigation of illness and injury caused by biological and chemical terrorism constitute a complex process that involves numerous partners and activities. A large-scale chemical event is not solely a medical issue. Many local and community resources will be called upon to assist in resolving the incident.

Whenever or whatever disaster or mass casualty event occurs, community and local response will be key to survival; communities must look to themselves and adjoining communities for answers (JCAHO, 2005).

Implementation of a plan requires collaboration with state and local public health agencies and groups, including the following:

- Public health organizations
- Poison control centers
- Medical research centers
- Health care providers and their professional networks
- Professional societies
- Medical examiners
- Emergency response units and first responder organizations
- Safety and medical equipment manufacturers
- Federal agencies
- Federal Bureau of Investigation (FBI)

- Local law enforcement
- Emergency management agencies and local emergency planning committees

Establish an early notification system with emergency response units and first responder organizations to notify hospitals when a chemical WMD incident occurs.

Early notification of an event helps a hospital prepare for mass casualties. Preparing a medical facility to receive casualties who may arrive without preliminary decontamination requires considerable effort. Early warning permits initiation of specific procedures and assembly of appropriate staff to receive casualties.

Prepare formal agreements with vendors (ie, hospital suppliers, pharmacies), health departments, EMS, fire and police departments, other local hospitals, laboratories, city officials (eg, transportation and emergency planners), the American Red Cross, and ambulance services to provide the best possible response. Review these agreements annually and practice procedures frequently to maintain proficiency.

Steps to prepare public health agencies for chemical attacks include the following (*MMWR*, 2000):

1. Enhance epidemiologic capacity for detecting and responding to chemical attacks.
2. Enhance awareness of chemical terrorism among EMS personnel, police officers, firefighters, physicians, and nurses.
3. Stockpile chemical antidotes.
4. Develop and provide bioassays for detection and diagnosis of chemical injuries.
5. Prepare educational materials to inform the public during and after a chemical attack.

While these steps are intended primarily for public health agencies, key hospital staff must be aware of the total response environment. Understanding the overall community response is critical to becoming an active and successful member of the community response team.

COMMUNICATIONS

An effective communications network is essential to a coordinated and efficient incident response. Communication equipment and expertise are likely to be among the weakest links in any response to a terrorist incident. During conventional incidents involving only a few casualties, information frequently is inadequate, incorrect, or nonexistent. Backup systems with built-in redundancy inside the hospital are necessary to ensure that communication equipment is available at critical moments. Consider continuous open channels to maintain a flow of information. Communication plans should identify departments, units, or positions rather than individuals because of varying work shifts and rotation of personnel in key positions. Designated channels should be available for law enforcement and other essential contacts.

METHOD OF COMMUNICATION

Select an effective method of communication. Mobile telephone systems may be overwhelmed and become ineffective as the first responders, members of the ICS and health care system, and citizens attempt to keep abreast of the situation. Handheld radios within the hospital are effective and frequently are the communication method of choice. The radios' short range is effective within the medical facility but does not interfere with similar devices a short distance away. Care must be taken with portable communication equipment to avoid interference with patient monitoring devices and other electronic equipment within the hospital.

Coordinate communication plans with external agencies early in the planning phase to avoid conflicts with local regulations and outside requirements. Tailor the methods of communication for each hospital's needs; the methods must also meet the requirements of the surrounding community. Anticipate communication needs that may occur during a crisis and plan for those needs. As a last resort, plan a runner system. Print a supply of messages and request forms for the department's use.

Hospitals should coordinate and practice communication systems to be prepared during a chaotic situation. Anticipate having to shift personnel and move supplies to meet rapidly changing demands. Moving patients within the health care system requires effective communication between the receiving area, clinics, wards, radiology, and expedient patient holding areas so that patients are tracked effectively. Maintain a written log to monitor patients to ensure that they reach the appropriate area for definitive care. If available, a bar code system is a rapid and effective means to accomplish patient tracking. Members of the American Red Cross or another volunteer group may be able to operate a patient locator system and permit hospital staff to be assigned to more critical or complex positions.

Establish procedures to receive calls from family members and friends to keep telephone lines free for operational purposes. Hospitals must be prepared to help families and friends when they inquire about patients' whereabouts and medical status. Plan a family waiting area. Finding and identifying patients is a major undertaking. Patient confidentiality must be maintained during this process.

Information Dissemination

Controlling sensitive information may be a priority among law enforcement officials. Police and the ICS supervisor are more willing to communicate with health care facilities if outsiders cannot access the communication system. The ICS and Unified Command System (UCS) are methods for command, control, and coordination of a response and provide a means to coordinate the efforts of individual agencies as they work toward the common goal of stabilizing the incident and protecting life, property, and the environment. Both HEICS and MaHIM address essential command, control, and organizational functions specific to health care institutions.

An emergency communication plan that ensures rapid dissemination of health information to the public during actual, threatened, or suspected acts of chemical terrorism will be a valuable asset. Announcements to the news media must be coordinated, open, reliable, and current. During a terrorist event, all public communication should be through the designated community or regional spokesperson, even though large medical centers may have communication procedures and a media spokesperson. Gaining public cooperation requires that consistent information from all sources is related by one spokesperson. Effective communication with the public through the news media is essential to limit the terrorist's ability to induce public panic and disrupt daily life. Gaining and retaining public confidence and cooperation is extremely important during a WMD incident.

Address what information to release and by which method. Prepare sample public health advisories and develop repositories of information on anticipated chemical warfare agents and industrial chemicals for use in a crisis. Specific information is available on traditional chemical warfare agents and toxic industrial chemicals at one or more of the web sites identified in this article. Provide the community spokesperson with a fact sheet prepared specifically for the public.

In some instances, the hospital spokesperson may be called upon to comment on the situation. Reliable information from a known and respected community resource can dismiss rumors and inaccurate predictions from self-proclaimed experts. To achieve a more rapid response to warnings, provide the public with enough information to allow everyone to understand the instructions from local officials.

In the hospital's emergency preparedness plans include plans for communicating with the media. The designated spokesperson or security person should assist the reporters and camerapersons but not allow them to interfere with hospital activities. During decontamination and treatment, consider the privacy of patients and prohibit filming of patient areas. Staff members who come into contact with media personnel should refer the reporters to the appropriate hospital spokesperson. The designated spokesperson responds to the media according to hospital policy after coordinating with the regional or community spokesperson.

Improving the Plan

Prepare a formal critique of the event response as an important step in improving the emergency plan. Afford the entire staff the opportunity to present comments through the chain of command. Presenting these comments during the first 24 hours after the event is resolved or an exercise is completed is critical to capture the lessons learned.

Personnel Considerations

Develop a recall roster adapted to local needs. Prioritize and update the sequence of notification of personnel (see the table below). Clinics or support departments may have their own recall roster in addition to maintaining one for key hospital staff. Because actual terrorist incidents are likely to be unannounced, the treatment facility may have little or no time to prepare for receiving casualties. Adding as many key staff members as quickly as possible will facilitate the hospital response. Although the presence of clinical staff members is generally the first priority, support staff members also are necessary. Security, logistics, pharmacy, housekeeping, and patient decontamination personnel are other essential staff in a chemical incident scenario.

Those individuals identified as essential in the event of a mass casualty incident must be aware that they are required to respond with little or no notice. Family considerations and support require advance planning and preparation. Many of today's workers are single parents, and, in many families, both spouses are employed. Essential personnel need to make prior arrangements for family support, child care, and pet care in case the operation continues for hours or up to days. Planning strategies should be developed that account for medication prophylaxis of essential personnel and their families. Training nonmedical support personnel is essential to build confidence, dispel fears, and promote their participation during crises.

Prepare a format to provide critical information to the local poison control center, public health department, and other agencies. Distribute the format to key personnel in the hospital and those agencies. Provide the following information in accordance with local community procedures as it becomes available:

- Number and types of casualties
- Substances involved
- Estimated time of arrival at the hospital
- Time of incident

- Incident site
- Method of contamination (vapor or liquid)
- Necessary decontamination (and extent)
- Hazards to health care providers
- Role of the health care facility in the incident
- Frequently updated information as it becomes available

Enlisting the support of health care providers who usually work outside the hospital is important during an influx of casualties. Physicians and nurses in family practice clinics and urgent care centers may be available to augment the hospital staff. Have a list readily available of community health care providers who are trained and prepared to assist in emergencies. These providers are essential during sustained operations. Consider approving credentials and hospital privileges for these physicians and nurses for emergency situations. Address liability and reimbursement for services. Volunteers may be available to help with specific tasks. Identify in advance people from outside the usual hospital staff who can help in a severe situation and use these people when appropriate. These individuals require an orientation to the disaster plan and should be included in training and exercises to be most effective.

The hospital incident commander must know what staff is available at all times; therefore, maintain a roster of when staff members and volunteers arrive and depart. When they report to work, have key and essential personnel pass through the hospital entry control point. The cue cards discussed earlier can be handed out as staff supervisors enter the facility. This procedure allows the hospital incident commander to identify personnel shortfalls and tasks that need to be reassigned.

CASUALTY MANAGEMENT

A health care facility must develop an area, preferably outside the hospital, for decontamination, and personnel must be trained in patient decontamination. This special area is crucial for the protection of the facility. After the Tokyo sarin attack, local hospitals were overwhelmed immediately with chemical agent casualties; many of whom transported themselves to the hospital. No effort was made to decontaminate them; as a result, health care providers were exposed to sarin vapor that off-gassed from clothing.

Protection of Personnel

The first rule for personnel assigned to decontamination must be that they protect themselves. (Information concerning PPE is presented in CBRNE - Personal Protective Equipment.) OSHA has identified the minimum PPE for hospital-based first receivers (OSHA Best Practices, 2005). Failure to use appropriate procedures or protective equipment places the individual, health care workers, and the medical treatment facility at risk. During a mass casualty incident, many people require medical care; neither health care personnel nor health care facilities can be compromised.

Decontamination Area

The ambulance garage or parking area may be used as a decontamination area. Since the ambulance area frequently is located near the ED entrance, casualties may be sent to the ED or other designated area after they are clean. The garage also may provide adequate storage for decontamination equipment and supplies. This area can be heated for patient protection or cooled to reduce the heat load of PPE worn by the workers; however, even sites with overhead cover only can provide protection from radiant heat. A water source generally used for washing vehicles can be used to decontaminate casualties. Firefighters or facilities engineers can be consulted on how to modify the existing plumbing so that it is conducive to washing both ambulatory casualties and nonambulatory casualties.

Consider the traffic pattern for both ambulatory patients and litter patients. In addition, plan for and prepare sites for the separation of males and females for undressing, washing, and dressing; a heating source for water; and drainage and capture of potentially contaminated water when possible. An effective decontamination site can be erected with limited expenditures by using available structures and equipment. Litters are now available with open mesh fabric that permits effective decontamination, which is not possible with a standard gurney. Conveyor roller units also can make handling nonambulatory patients easier as they are moved through the decontamination lane.

A decontamination site has 3 areas, as follows:

- Hot zone: Incoming traffic, personnel, and casualties potentially contaminate this area.
- Warm zone: Decontamination takes place in this area.
- Cold zone: In this clean area, casualties are triaged again and then moved into the health care facility.

Managing a chemical casualty is a continuum from triage to discharge from the hospital. Only the management principles required to get a chemical casualty safely into a medical treatment facility are discussed.

TRIAGE

The first task is to triage casualties before decontamination and again as they enter the hospital. The purpose of triage is to sort the injured by priority and determine the best use of available resources (eg, personnel, equipment, medications, ambulances, hospital beds). The emphasis is on saving as many people as possible.

Triage must occur at each site because of changes in patient status. In a chemical incident, victims are triaged for 3 purposes at the incident site: decontamination, treatment, and evacuation. Triage at the hospital primarily is for decontamination and treatment. Evacuation to other medical facilities may be necessary to provide specialty care or to distribute the patients throughout the regional health care system.

Triage terminology and methods to identify the different categories vary and are a matter of preference. Military terminology is presented below, but civilian methods such as the Simple Triage and Rapid Treatment/Transport (START) are both rapid and effective methods of separating casualties. To avoid confusion or delays in care, standardize terminology and methods throughout the region. Four triage categories for treatment are described as follows:

- Immediate: Casualties need lifesaving measures performed without delay if they are to survive.
- Delayed: Casualties can wait for definitive treatment without causing additional harm.

- Expectant: Casualties will not survive or will require extensive resources and time if they are to be saved.
- Minor: Casualties are generally ambulatory and are only slightly injured.

Triaging for decontamination is necessary to move the casualties quickly and safely into the health care system. Divide casualties into ambulatory and nonambulatory groups. Ambulatory casualties most often are classified as minor or delayed. However, observe people triaged as minor or delayed for worsening signs and symptoms. Immediately decontaminate casualties who were closest to the point of chemical release, those with liquid contamination, and those who have severe signs or symptoms of chemical injury or severe conventional injuries. Victims may be classified as expectant when they have serious signs and symptoms after initial therapy or are unresponsive to antidotes.

Move deceased casualties to a site that is not observed readily by the public or other casualties. Keep the deceased at this site until law enforcement officers have acquired any available evidence and living casualties have been moved into the health care facility. Deceased casualties require a thorough decontamination before they are moved to the morgue or they are ready for release.

Effective triage requires the presence of a triage officer who is trained to identify the type of casualties that will be sorted. For instance, a person contaminated with a liquid nerve agent who arrives as an ambulatory casualty may deteriorate rapidly once the agent is absorbed. Triage officers are in a key position, and the individual must be capable of making quick and frequently difficult decisions. Also, triage officers must be very familiar with the medical staff and the hospital's capabilities and limitations.

Admission Procedures

Following a chemical event with many casualties, normal patient admission procedures are not effective. A system that initially captures essential information is sufficient. Additional patient information can be captured when time permits. Ambulatory patients and many nonambulatory casualties are able to provide appropriate information. However, identify unconscious casualties before their personal belongings are removed. A plastic driver's license with a photo may be decontaminated and used to accompany the patient. Photo identification is particularly useful for unconscious and deceased casualties.

Additionally, a number can be assigned to each patient; the number then can be placed on the patient and on 2 bags. The first bag contains clothing; the second holds the patient's valuables. Clear bags facilitate identification at a later date. Consider these bags contaminated, keep in a secured location, and preserve as potential evidence as in any criminal investigation. A meticulous practical method of cataloging belongings helps ensure proper return and possibly helps in forensic investigations.

A bar code system is an excellent approach to tracking multiple casualties evacuated from an incident scene to multiple health care facilities. The EMS and hospitals in St Louis use an impressive system on a daily basis that has the capability to expand to meet the patient identification needs for a large-scale event. A comprehensive system that meets routine daily needs is essential. Attempting to institute an unfamiliar system during the confusion of a mass casualty event is difficult.

A secondary triage following decontamination further identifies casualties who require immediate attention and those who can wait for treatment. Move casualties who can wait for treatment to a clean holding area. A nurse, paramedic, or emergency medical technician assigned to the clean holding area can observe these individuals and provide reassurance if necessary. Additional clean holding areas can be established in dining rooms, physical therapy departments, and meeting rooms.

Emergency Treatment

Emergency treatment for immediate casualties depends on the chemical agent(s) used and on the availability of definitive treatment measures. For many toxic agents, no antidotes are available, and treatment is supportive. Administer antidotes judiciously to ensure that they are not wasted on minor casualties who arrive early or on those with no chance of survival.

The requirement for ventilators may exceed availability. Spreading the serious casualties among community hospitals or consolidating ventilators to 1 or 2 major medical treatment facilities are local options. The Strategic National Stockpile (SNS) has ventilators in their inventory and can provide them within a few hours. The specific types that are in the SNS should be identified to train respiratory therapists on the use of the particular models that will arrive. Also, the model information will be important to acquire repair parts and consumables when needed.

Take measures to protect hospital personnel and maintain the integrity of the health care facility. Have emergency procedures for exposure of staff members in place. If the decontamination procedure fails and staff members become contaminated, decontaminate and treat them. Until the cause of the contamination is determined, do not use the treatment facility or the contaminated area of the facility if that can be determined. If decontamination procedures fail, correct them immediately. Place exhaust fans to ventilate contaminated air. Keep doors between clean and contaminated areas closed, except when moving a casualty into a treatment area. Do not let chemical vapor contamination into an area with unprotected health care providers and casualties. Consult with the hospital facilities engineer for heating, ventilating, and air conditioning (HVAC) guidance. Include physical plant personnel in the planning process.

Human remains may provide essential evidence and are important to law enforcement personnel. Unconventional methods may be required to hold the bodies until they can be decontaminated and released. Refrigerated vans may be used to store the remains temporarily. Morticians and funeral directors may need to be given specific directions for handling the remains. Bodies exposed to classic chemical warfare agents can be decontaminated and released to funeral homes. Bodies contaminated by other chemicals require individual evaluation for safety in handling. The National Disaster Medical System has Disaster Mortuary Operational Response Teams (DMORT) to provide victim identification and mortuary services. State authorities may request assistance from these teams.

An important part of the medical response to a chemical terrorism event is dealing with the psychological reactions among health care workers, first responders, and the public. The death of family members, coworkers, and particularly children is traumatic. Plan to provide critical incident stress management support early in a chemical event.

Transportation Issues

Transportation and evacuation of patients are major tasks during a WMD event. Have a community-wide plan, enforced by the local police department, to identify and mark areas of contamination so that hazardous areas can be avoided and traffic does not become congested. Health care providers must be able to identify themselves and use the routes identified by the police to travel to the hospitals. Although many of the victims may arrive early at the medical facilities by various modes of transportation, the more severely injured may be among the last to arrive. Contact the US Environmental Protection Agency for specific guidance on contamination identification and control.

Plan for the movement of equipment, supplies, and pharmaceuticals to support the influx of casualties. Access to critical areas must remain open, and traffic must not be permitted to become congested. A circular movement of traffic in the critical areas facilitates unloading casualties and rapid departure of vehicles. To ensure that vehicles follow the plan, assign a security guard wearing PPE to direct traffic flow. Security personnel in PPE must have training and medical clearance, required by the Occupational Safety and Health Administration (OSHA), when wearing respirators and protective clothing. During warm weather, security personnel must be rotated frequently to avoid heat injury.

A sufficient number of ambulances may not be available to transport hundreds of casualties in a short time. Consider city bus systems or school buses as alternatives. Methods of moving large numbers of victims may vary for different communities. As a general rule, do not mix resources used to move contaminated or potentially contaminated casualties with those used for moving uncontaminated patients.

LOGISTICS AND FACILITY MANAGEMENT

When the number of patients exceeds the treatment capability of a medical treatment facility, resource management becomes crucial. Planning for the availability of essential supplies, equipment, and PPE at critical times requires close coordination between clinical and support personnel.

Maintain a list of the location and quantity of ventilators and establish agreements between vendors and hospitals prior to an incident. These agreements must be reviewed and agreed upon by all health care facilities in the community and not limited solely to agreements between one hospital and a supplier. Develop a respiratory therapy mutual aid plan among multiple hospitals to share equipment, supplies, and respiratory therapists, and include ventilator vendors. Other important equipment requires the same coordination and written agreements.

List vital pharmaceuticals and supplies and prepare them for rapid distribution. An integral part of an emergency plan includes listing specific antidotes and supporting pharmaceuticals for the most likely emergency situations. Such lists permit pharmacists to prepare preplanned push packages to send to the emergency treatment area and save valuable time in meeting the treatment demands of many casualties. Awareness of the stockpile of antidotes maintained by the Metropolitan Medical Response Systems (MMRS), the National Medical Response Teams (NMRT), and the Strategic National Stockpile (SNS) of the Centers for Disease Control and Prevention (CDC) as well as the antidotes' expected time of arrival may alleviate the need for large quantities of antidotes to be stockpiled locally. A regional pharmaceutical mutual aid plan can be developed among hospitals and can include pharmaceutical suppliers.

Floor plans of the hospital and diagrams of the immediate area surrounding the hospital are useful in planning for a WMD event. Floor plans help determine the most appropriate routes for patient flow and vehicle movement. The identification of an area for decontamination with ready access to an emergency treatment area may be much more apparent when looking at a diagram. A large dining facility or waiting area may be prepared quickly to receive decontaminated casualties. Warehouses may provide alternate facilities for initial triage, decontamination, and emergency treatment or serve as a holding area for minor casualties. Alternatives to the usual ways of conducting business and areas allowing for overflow of patients are important components of a comprehensive plan.

Alternate or back-up utilities may be required if the chemical incident site includes the local electrical plant or if electrical power is disrupted. Water systems also may be affected. A medical treatment facility must be self-sufficient for at least 24 hours following a terrorist event or natural disaster.

The influx of both patients and staff requires food service support. If the chemical event continues for hours or days, food service personnel need to provide food and water to meet the increased demands. Additional housekeeping service to remove excess trash, provide linens, and replace expendable items is required. Maintenance workers are needed to keep equipment functioning in treatment areas. Identify areas for the temporary storage of potentially contaminated clothing and other personal belongings that must be identified and stored until final disposition is determined.

SECURITY AND SAFETY PLANS

The normal hospital security plan requires modification to satisfy requirements of the emergency situation and to conform to community plans. Hospital lock-down should be implemented when a mass casualty incident happens. To avoid the risk of the health care facility becoming contaminated and unusable, it must be secured and access limited. At the hospital staff entry point, guards check to ensure that people arriving are listed on the hospital disaster response roster, log those people in, and note their time of arrival. The same procedures apply to personnel leaving the hospital. Identification (ID) badges can be issued at the entry control point. The ID badges may be issued to employees before an event, but invariably, some will not have their ID badges when they arrive. Badges can be color coded to identify a particular unit or service.

Security is necessary at the decontamination point. Guards need to wear PPE; rotate staff frequently in warm weather. Crowd control, casualty flow, and traffic control are critical at the health care facility. Vehicles must not linger in the area, or others may be slowed or denied access. Crowds and media must be kept at a safe distance so that they are not harmed and do not impede the emergency process. Develop a plan to address any breach of security.

A terrorist may plant more than one device. Additional devices may not be the same type as the initial one and may not be at the same site. Investigate and secure the area where casualties or onlookers congregate during an emergency to exclude the presence of additional devices. For example, a terrorist in Northern Ireland exploded a bomb that caused several casualties. Knowing a crowd would form to unload and assist the casualties, the terrorist exploded a second bomb outside the busy emergency treatment area.

Have a safety plan that addresses specific issues in chemical safety and augments the existing emergency preparedness safety plan for other disasters. An existing safety plan may not include contamination control and casualty decontamination requirements.

At least one safety officer who is knowledgeable in the operations being implemented should be at the medical treatment facility. The safety officer has specific responsibility for identifying and evaluating hazards and provides direction with respect to the safety of operations. The safety officer's primary function is contamination control to ensure the safety and welfare of the hospital personnel and to prevent the contamination of the facility. To avoid contaminating treatment areas, constant vigilance is required to ensure that contaminated casualties, staff, and equipment are not permitted to enter the hospital area prior to decontamination. When positioned at a critical location, the safety officer can help prevent the spread of contamination. Safety officers need to work closely with security staff and police to enforce measures to protect personnel and health care facilities.

In addition to preventing contaminated people and objects from entering the health care facility, the safety officer can observe workers while they are performing decontamination. The officer is able to ensure that work and/or rest cycles are implemented and enforced and that PPE is worn appropriately in hazardous areas. Also, safety officers may be appointed as the final approving authority for decontaminated casualties to enter the hospital.

TRAINING AND EXERCISES

TRAINING

OSHA cites specific training requirements for first responders and others who participate at the incident site. Additional information on training requirements may be available at the National Institute for Occupational Safety and Health. Hospital personnel who are designated as safety officers or who are involved in decontamination also should be trained to the appropriate level as specified in the OSHA Hazardous Waste Operations and Emergency Response regulation.

Everyone who participates at an incident site or in receiving contaminated casualties must know the basic hazards, signs, and symptoms of exposure to chemical agents. OSHA has a document titled "Best Practices for Hospital-Based First Receivers" that also addresses training for hospital-based personnel to receive victims from mass casualty incidents involving the release of hazardous substances (OSHA, 2005).

An effective mass casualty plan relies on all staff members knowing their tasks and responsibilities. Most employees are involved in a specific task in one area of the hospital. Becoming familiar with a particular task may require minimal training. Individual training and small team training are appropriate before integrating multiple teams into a training exercise.

Decontamination is not a routine task, and employees require extensive training. Each specific task is not complex; however, the ability to perform the tasks while wearing PPE requires hours of practice. In addition, cross-train the decontamination team in various tasks because they must be capable of changing tasks to assist other team members. Building from single tasks to multiple tasks, learning to function in PPE, and learning to work as a team takes time, but rehearsal can produce an effective team. Physicians, physician assistants, and nurse clinicians designated to provide treatment to chemically contaminated casualties require specific training. A cadre of well-trained health care and public health workers should be available at each health care facility. Local poison control centers should be consulted immediately to acquire the latest information on specific treatment of patients.

The US Army requires that physicians assigned to depots storing chemical warfare agents attend courses in the management of chemical agent casualties in addition to attending advanced cardiac life support (ACLS) and advanced trauma life support (ATLS) courses. The Medical Response to Chemical Warfare and Terrorism teleconference course is available to civilian health care providers via the Internet and is offered biannually at many videoconference sites throughout the country.

Rapid turnover of personnel requires ongoing training programs. Reviewing the appropriate portion of a written plan and viewing a videotape of a previous exercise can facilitate the training process. Videotaping exercises is an excellent method to capture department activities, and videotapes can be produced inexpensively. In addition to being used as training aids, tapes can be observed and critiqued to improve response.

Hospital preparedness for mass casualty incidents increases if hospitals engage in regular ongoing inservice training programs and in readiness drills. Some of the cost for such training can be defrayed through the use of videotapes, CD ROMs, and web-based technologies. In addition to being cost effective, these resources are updated frequently and provide new and revised lists of resources. The American College of Emergency Physicians is preparing a standardized 2-phase curriculum and a set of training materials for mass casualty preparedness. Such initiatives to standardize training reduce individual hospital costs and provide acceptable procedures and educational material.

Components of the educational curricula and course outlines have been developed by several agencies. The typical curriculum is divided into multiple levels. The first level, a brief awareness program, is designed for all workers and describes the threat and basics of how to respond while protecting personal safety. A decontamination procedures course is more extensive and is intended for workers designated as members of the decontamination team. The decontamination course includes presentations on PPE, safety issues, required medical screening, stations in the decontamination line, and physical characteristics of chemical agents. Health care providers are presented a course on the recognition and management of chemical agent casualties.

The clinician's course may use the Medical Response to Chemical Warfare and Terrorism teleconference. To supplement training, some hospitals have developed cue cards that identify a set of tasks for a department or unit. Using a checklist facilitates accomplishing all tasks that are necessary for the operation. In the absence of a trained primary member, another member of the unit can ensure that each task is assigned and completed.

Drills

Following individual and unit training, the hospital should integrate a WMD response into 1 of the 2 annual drills required by the JCAHO. An ideal hospital exercise requires rehearsals through tabletop exercises for supervisors and small unit drills. Both require time and personnel, but, in some cases, they can be as simple as a clinic or unit staff meeting designed for a discussion and walk-through of each portion of the emergency preparedness plan. Hospitals should endeavor to hold more than the 2 annual drills in consideration of their 3 shifts and separate weekend crews to better prepare their staff.

A tabletop exercise for leadership provides an opportunity for senior personnel to coordinate their activities during a mock exercise. An exercise that involves each department chief and requires synchronization of major activities reveals deficiencies in the emergency preparedness plan at the management level. In addition to the overall plan, the communications component can be tested during the tabletop exercise. Internal hospital communications and contacts with designated agencies within the community are both critical to the response. Once the unit training and the tabletop exercise are completed, schedule an exercise to test the overall system and to meet JCAHO requirements.

Biannual (or more frequent) hospital exercises can be videotaped for review, analysis, and future training. The exercises can be extremely valuable in identifying flaws in and minor adjustments to the response plan. A person who happened to be videotaping in a Tokyo hospital recorded the 1995 sarin incident. That videotape has been used many times as an example in training classes and as a tool to improve hospital response.

RECOVERY

Once the event has ended and the patients are within the health care system, the process of returning to normal function begins. Scientifically and logistically, this can be the most difficult aspect of the incident. Numerous areas, equipment, vehicles, and other items may be left contaminated. Identifying the contaminating chemical or chemicals, the preferred methods for decontamination, the chemical's persistency on various surfaces, and the chemical's effect on water and food sources requires considerable review and expertise.

The decontamination area must be cleaned, and contaminated clothing and equipment used during the decontamination process must be cleaned or disposed of appropriately. Final disposition of contaminated articles is in accordance with previously established arrangements and the overall community hazardous waste plan.

Patients' valuables are an important issue. During the patient decontamination process, rings, watches, wallets, purses, and other items such as hearing aids are removed and placed in marked plastic bags.

A security person may be the most appropriate person to ensure that these items are stored in a secure manner. To avoid legal difficulties, follow chain-of-custody procedures to ensure that these valuables are not disturbed. As soon as it is practical, check these items for contamination and clean them as necessary for return to their owners. The agency responsible for declaring items safe for return to their owner may be a city, state, or federal organization, depending on local and state capability. Law enforcement approval must be obtained to return personal clothing and items that may be considered evidence in a terrorism incident.

Capture lessons learned early in the recovery phase. An exercise critique must include each participant at the clinic or unit level. Individual workers and unit supervisors can contribute important comments on specific procedures to improve their respective operations. The activities at this basic level are crucial to the overall plan and must be included to refine and improve the complete plan. Department chiefs then must meet to discuss their consolidated recommendations. The incident leader and hospital administrator can incorporate the needed changes. Lessons learned must be captured within hours after an exercise or incident. Otherwise, hospital staff returns to normal responsibilities, and important information is lost. Allocate a time at the termination of each exercise to obtain these comments and recommendations. The department chiefs can consolidate the comments and recommendations and meet with other chiefs and administrators within 24 hours to discuss their suggestions.

Evaluation of a Chemical Warfare Victim

Chemical warfare is not a popular topic but is one of great concern to civilians, emergency physicians, and prehospital providers given the potential devastation.

As General Pershing noted after World War I, "...the effect is so deadly to the unprepared that we can never afford to neglect the question."

The US government has determined that the likelihood of a terrorist attack within the United States is increasing. This has prompted governmental domestic preparedness training initiatives targeted at physicians and other healthcare providers in the areas of nuclear, biological, and chemical warfare.

Decontamination is time consuming and requires resources. Nerve agents and substances causing injury to the skin and tissue are easily soluble in and penetrate many different types of material. If chemical warfare (CW) agents have penetrated sufficiently deep, then toxic gases can be released from the material for long periods. By adding substances that increase the viscosity of a CW agent, its persistence time and adhesive ability can be increased. These thickened agents will thus be more difficult to decontaminate with liquid decontaminants since they adhere to the material and are difficult to dissolve.

The need for decontamination can only be established by means of detection. If detection is not possible, then decontamination must be done solely on suspicion of contamination. This article focuses on the initial approach to the chemical warfare victim. Detailed information on patient decontamination and the appropriate use of personal protective equipment is described elsewhere on this web site.

TRIAGE OF CHEMICAL CASUALTIES

Patient triage only should be carried out in the hospital setting by those wearing appropriate personal protective equipment. In the simplest form of triage, patients or casualties are separated into 3 groups. The first group consists of those for whom the degree of medical care required exceeds that which is available. In this setting, medical assets are insufficient relative to the presenting illness, or an experienced triage officer deems the patient's injuries irreversible. The medical focus is on comfort care, and the casualty is triaged as expectant. A casualty's classification may change as assets become available or when later reevaluation demonstrates that the casualty's condition was not as serious as first anticipated.

The second group consists of casualties who require immediate intervention for survival. In a conventional situation (ie, noncontaminated environment), these casualties usually have treatable injuries affecting the airway, breathing, or circulation (ABCs). Other examples of immediate interventions include administration of antidotes or spot decontamination.

The third group consists of casualties who have injuries that place them in no immediate danger of loss of life. Medical care is needed but not immediately. For example, casualties in this group may include those with minor injuries who merely require laceration repair or those with extensive injuries necessitating long-term hospitalization who are presently stable.

The triage system commonly used by US military medical departments and by civilian medical systems contains the above categories (immediate, delayed, and expectant) and incorporates a fourth category (minimal). In this scheme, minimal injuries are those that require a quick intervention, do not require a physician or evacuation, and result in a rapid return to duty. Occasionally, as in the North Atlantic Treaty Organization (NATO) *Emergency War Surgery Handbook,* a fifth category, urgent, is added to denote a casualty who requires intervention within minutes to survive. Also, in some schemes, the term "chemical immediate" is used for casualties who require immediate administration of antidotes for survival (as in nerve agent or cyanide poisoning).

Decontamination is the process by which particulate, vapor, and liquid materials are safely removed from an exposed person without further contaminating the casualty, the environment, or rescuers. Decontamination is an important part of all disasters involving hazardous materials and weapons of mass destruction.

Two main goals exist in setting up decontamination at a medical facility:

- To protect the facility and its personnel from becoming contaminated, and thus further casualties
- To facilitate the treatment and triage of contaminated patients as rapidly as possible

Analysis of hazardous materials accidents has shown that up to 85% of the victims arrive at a healthcare facility without prehospital treatment or decontamination. Terrorist events, with their larger number of patients, unknown substances, and large numbers of "worried well," increase the possibility of casualties arriving at a facility contaminated or potentially contaminated.

Immediate Support Measures

Monitor patients who potentially are exposed to chemical warfare agents for changes in their clinical status and provide appropriate supportive measures. First address the patient's ABCs and coexisting life-threatening or limb-threatening injuries. Reassess these injuries throughout the patient's course.

Emergency department management

Potential for Secondary Contamination

Victims who were exposed only to gas or vapor and have no gross deposition of the material on their clothing or skin are not likely to carry significant amounts of chemical beyond the hot zone and are not likely to pose risks of secondary contamination to hospital personnel. However, victims whose skin or clothing are covered with liquid or solid chemical or victims who have condensation of chemical vapor on their clothes or skin may contaminate hospital personnel and the ED by direct contact or by off-gassing vapor. If the victim has ingested a chemical, toxic vomitus may also pose a danger through direct contact or off-gassing vapor.

Decontamination Area

Previously decontaminated patients and patients exposed only to gas or vapor who have no evidence of skin or eye irritation may be transferred immediately to the critical care area. Other victims will require decontamination as described below.

ABC Reminders

Evaluate and support airway, breathing, and circulation. Intubate the trachea in cases of respiratory compromise. If the patient's condition precludes intubation, surgically create an airway.

Treat patients who have bronchospasm with aerosolized bronchodilators; use these and all catecholamines with caution because of the possible enhanced risk of cardiac dysrhythmias.

Patients who are comatose, hypotensive, or have seizures or ventricular dysrhythmias should be treated in the conventional manner.

Basic Decontamination

Patients who are able and cooperative may assist with their own decontamination. Remove and double-bag contaminated clothing and personal belongings.

Flush exposed or irritated skin and hair with plain water for 3-5 minutes. For oily or otherwise adherent chemicals, use mild soap on the skin and hair. Rinse thoroughly with water.

Flush exposed or irritated eyes with plain water or saline for at least 5 minutes. Remove contact lenses if present and easily removable without additional trauma to the eye. If a corrosive material is suspected or if pain or injury is evident, continue irrigation while transferring the patient to the critical care area.

In cases of ingestion, do not induce emesis. Administer 4-8 ounces of water to dilute stomach contents if the patient is conscious and able to swallow. Immediately transfer the patient to the critical care area.

Critical Care Area

Be certain that appropriate decontamination has been carried out.

ABC Reminders

Evaluate and support airway, breathing, and circulation. Establish intravenous access in seriously ill patients. Continuously monitor cardiac rhythm.

Patients who are comatose, hypotensive, or have seizures or ventricular dysrhythmias should be treated in the conventional manner.

Inhalation Exposure

Administer supplemental oxygen by mask to patients who have respiratory complaints. Treat patients who have bronchospasm with aerosolized bronchodilators; use these and all catecholamines with caution because of the potential or possible enhanced risk of cardiac dysrhythmias.

Skin Exposure

If chemical burns are present, treat as thermal burns.

Eye Exposure

Ensure that adequate eye irrigation has been completed. Test visual acuity. Examine the eyes for corneal damage using a magnifying device or a slit lamp and fluorescein stain. For small corneal defects, use ophthalmic ointment or drops, analgesic medication, and an eye patch. Immediately consult an ophthalmologist for patients who have severe corneal injuries.

Ingestion Exposure

Do not induce emesis. If the patient is alert and charcoal has not been given previously, administer a slurry of activated charcoal. If a corrosive material is suspected, administer 4-8 ounces of water; do not give a slurry of activated charcoal. Consider endoscopy to evaluate the extent of gastrointestinal tract injury. If a large dose has been ingested and the patient's condition is evaluated within 30 minutes after ingestion, consider gastric lavage.

Laboratory Tests

Routine laboratory studies for all exposed patients include CBC, glucose, and electrolyte determinations. Additional studies for patients exposed to an unidentified chemical include ECG monitoring, renal function tests, and liver function tests. Chest radiography and pulse oximetry (or ABG measurements) are recommended for severe inhalation exposure.

Disposition and Follow-up

Consider hospitalizing patients who have suspected serious exposures and persistent or progressive symptoms

Delayed Effects

When the chemical has not been identified, the patient should be observed for an extended period or admitted to the hospital.

CATEGORIES FOR TRIAGE OF CHEMICAL CASUALTIES

Immediate

Nerve Agents

A casualty of nerve agents who is in severe distress is classified as immediate. The patient may be unconscious, may be in severe respiratory distress, or may have become apneic minutes before reaching the facility. He or she may be convulsing or immediately postictal.

Often the contents of 3 MARK I kits (or more) plus diazepam and possibly short-term ventilatory assistance is all that is required to save a life. In addition, classify a casualty with signs in 2 or more systems (eg, neuromuscular, gastrointestinal GI, respiratory excluding eyes and nose) as immediate and administer the contents of 3 MARK I kits and diazepam.

Cyanide

A casualty of cyanide who is convulsing or who became apneic minutes before reaching the medical facility and has adequate circulation (still has a pulse) is in the immediate group, assuming that cyanide antidotes are available.

If the ABCs remain adequate, the administration of antidote may be all that is required for complete recovery. Since death usually occurs within 4-5 minutes of exposure to a lethal amount of cyanide unless treatment is immediate, this type of casualty is unlikely to be seen at the medical facility.

Phosgene and Vesicants

Place casualties of phosgene or vesicant agents who have moderate or severe respiratory distress in the immediate group, where intense ventilatory and other respiratory support measures are immediately available.

Incapacitating Agents

Those with cardiovascular collapse or severe hyperthermia are placed in the immediate category following exposure to agents such as 3-quinuclidinyl benzilate (BZ) or Agent 15.

Delayed

Nerve Agents

Place casualties who require hospitalization but have no immediate threat to life in the delayed group.

This generally is limited to a casualty who has survived a severe nerve agent exposure, is regaining consciousness, and has resumed spontaneous respiration. This casualty requires further medical care for the time necessary for recovery.

Vesicants

Triage those with skin injuries of greater than 5% total body surface area but less than 50% as delayed. Other criteria include severe eye involvement or pulmonary symptoms with an onset of more than 4 hours postexposure.

Cyanide

Triage victims of cyanide vapor exposure who are alive after 15 minutes as minimal or delayed.

Pulmonary Agents

Following exposure, triage patients with delayed onset of respiratory distress (>4 h) as delayed.

Incapacitating Agents

Severe or worsening signs after exposure warrant patient triage to the delayed category.

Minimal

Nerve Agents

Patients who are walking and talking can be assessed for the degree of miosis and its potential to interfere with performance prior to return to duty.

CHEMICAL WARFARE AGENTS

Nerve Agents

Nerve agents are organophosphates and therefore cause the characteristic cholinergic toxidrome. Organophosphates inhibit acetylcholinesterase, which results in an excess accumulation of acetylcholine at muscarinic and nicotinic receptors. Clinically, these agents cause increased bodily secretions (SLUDGE; salivation, lacrimation, urination, defecation, emesis), miosis, bronchospasm, increased airway secretions, sudden loss of consciousness, seizures, apnea, muscle fasciculations that progress to flaccid paralysis, and death. The primary cause of death in patients exposed to nerve agents is respiratory failure caused by respiratory muscle weakness, bronchoconstriction, and increased respiratory secretions. Maintain a high index of suspicion of organophosphate and/or nerve agent poisoning whenever presented with a patient who has pinpoint pupils with seizures, muscle fasciculations, or flaccid paralysis.

Depending on the patient's clinical status, treatment with atropine and pralidoxime may be feasible. Atropine dries secretions and relaxes smooth muscle via antagonism of acetylcholine at its muscarinic receptors. Clinically, this results in decreased SLUDGE and improved ventilation by decreasing bronchoconstriction and bronchorrhea. Pralidoxime improves the patient's muscle strength by removing the nerve agent from acetylcholinesterase. The acetylcholinesterase, when freed from the nerve agent, then resumes breakdown of acetylcholine. Pralidoxime's effectiveness decreases with time, because the enzyme/nerve agent complex can age and form an irreversible bond. The time course for this depends on the specific agent and can vary from minutes to hours.

Exposure to nerve agents occurs from either vapor or liquid forms. A patient's vapor or liquid exposure can be classified as mild, moderate, and severe based on clinical criteria.

Vapor Exposure

Mild vapor exposure results in miosis and rhinorrhea. Patients also may develop eye pain, which can be treated with topical homatropine. Patients with only a mild vapor exposure do not require treatment with atropine or pralidoxime. Observe patients with mild vapor exposure and those who are asymptomatic but claim to have been exposed to a nerve agent vapor for 1 hour for development of muscle weakness, respiratory symptoms, or GI symptoms. If these symptoms develop, classify the patient as moderate; he or she requires treatment with atropine and pralidoxime. Severe vapor exposure results in loss of consciousness, seizures, flaccid paralysis, and apnea.

Liquid Exposure

Mild liquid nerve agent exposure results in localized fasciculations and sweating. A mild liquid nerve agent exposure requires 1 dose of atropine and pralidoxime. Patients with mild liquid exposure, those who are asymptomatic but claim to have been exposed to a liquid nerve agent, and those with an unknown form of exposure require an observation period of 18 hours. If patients develop respiratory or GI symptoms, classify them as moderate. Loss of consciousness, seizures, flaccid paralysis, and apnea are manifestations of a severe exposure.

Cyanide

Levels of Exposure

Cyanide binds to ferric state iron found in mitochondria, which prevents the mitochondria from using oxygen. Because of the subsequent anaerobic metabolism, patients develop lactate accumulation with severe acidosis and cellular asphyxiation.

Cyanide can be found in vapor, liquid, and solid salt forms. Cyanide toxicity from chemical warfare typically occurs by inhalation of vapor, but it also may occur by ingestion or dermal contact with a large amount of the liquid form.

Cyanide poisoning at low concentrations produces anxiety, hyperventilation, headache, dizziness, and vomiting. Patients also may develop a cherry red skin discoloration, although this is rare. Since the body normally metabolizes cyanide into thiocyanate, which then is excreted in the urine, patients with mild exposures should improve when removed from the source of exposure and may not require any other intervention.

Cyanide poisoning at higher concentrations begins to produce respiratory distress. Suspect significant cyanide poisoning whenever confronted with a patient who is experiencing respiratory distress with normal oxygen concentration of the blood. This occurs because cyanide prevents the body from using oxygen. Toxicity screens for cyanide are not timely enough to be useful in patients with toxicity. A high venous oxygen level and lactic acidosis may help confirm suspicion of cyanide poisoning. Patients with this intermediate level of exposure may require treatment with amyl nitrite, sodium nitrite, and sodium thiosulfate.

Cyanide exposure at even higher concentrations can produce dramatic results. Patients can progress through anxiety and hyperpnea to seizures within 30 seconds. Within 3-5 minutes of exposure, patients may stop breathing. Finally, patients may experience asystole and death within 6-10 minutes.

Treatment

Treatment of cyanide involves removing cyanide from the cells, detoxifying cyanide, and providing supportive measures aimed at minimizing toxic effects. Treatment details are discussed elsewhere.

Vesicants

Vesicants are chemical agents that cause blistering of the skin. Lewisite and sulfur mustard are the 2 main agents used in chemical warfare. Exposure to either agent can come from a vapor or liquid form. Both agents produce irritation and damage to the eyes, skin, and airway. Chemical decontamination within 30 minutes of exposure is of primary importance, as that is when most of the injury to the patient occurs. Decontamination after that point still is required to prevent cross-contamination of healthcare providers.

Effects of Exposure

Eyes: Eye exposure can produce mild conjunctivitis up to corneal perforation depending on the level of exposure. Treat eye exposures beyond decontamination in conjunction with ophthalmology.

Skin: Skin exposures result in vesicles, which coalesce into bullae. Bullae require surgical irrigation, debridement, and a topical antibiotic.

Respiratory: Airway injury initially damages the upper airway, resulting in epistaxis, pharyngitis, laryngitis, and bronchitis. With a high enough level of exposure, damage may progress to the lower airway. Damage to the lower respiratory tract produces dyspnea from bronchiolitis, which can progress to respiratory failure and death. Treatment of respiratory symptoms is supportive, with use of bronchodilators, oxygen, and mechanical ventilation if necessary.

Mustard also can produce bone marrow suppression beginning 3-5 days after exposure, which can contribute to a delayed cause of death. Time to onset of symptoms from exposure to lewisite is immediate. Conversely, mustard exposure does not produce symptoms until 2-48 hours after exposure. For lewisite exposures, a specific antidote of dimercaprol (British antilewisite agent) can be administered in a dose of 2.5-5 mg/kg IM.

Pulmonary Intoxicants

Pulmonary intoxicants cause lung injury via inhalation of a vapor. Chemical warfare agents in this group include phosgene and chlorine. Phosgene exposure causes a mild transient irritation of the eyes, sinuses, pharynx, and bronchi upon initial exposure. Patients then are asymptomatic until 2-4 hours postexposure, when they begin to develop noncardiogenic pulmonary edema, which should be treated with supplemental oxygen and mechanical ventilation as needed. These patients also may develop hypovolemic shock from loss of fluid into the alveolar space and may require intravenous fluids for hypotension. Since the pulmonary edema is noncardiogenic and the patients are hypovolemic, do not use diuretics.

Chlorine exposure has a pronounced, immediate irritant effect on the upper and lower respiratory tract, which may produce respiratory failure shortly after exposure. If the patient survives the initial exposure, he or she may develop noncardiogenic pulmonary edema and hypovolemic shock within 12-24 hours, similar to that caused by phosgene.

SUMMARY

Triage of casualties of chemical agents is based on many of the same principles as the triage of conventional casualties. Members of the triage team try to provide immediate care to those who need it for survival; they temporarily set aside or delay treatment of those who have minor injuries or do not need immediate medical intervention; and they do not use limited medical assets on the hopelessly injured. Initial triage and treatment of the chemical-exposed patient pose unique medical challenges, since early care must be rendered within the constraints of personal protective clothing. In addition, decontamination, which may be a time-consuming process, must be carried out before the casualty receives more definitive care. Triage is a matter of judgment on the part of the triage team. Ideally, base this judgment upon knowledge of medical assets, the casualty load, and most importantly, an understanding of the toxicology of the chemical agent involved and potential complications of exposure.

9

Reigle Report on Chemical War

INTRODUCTION

In October 1992, the Committee on Banking, Housing, and Urban Affairs, which has Senate oversight responsibility for the Export Administration Act (EAA), held an inquiry into the U.S. export policy to Iraq prior to the Persian Gulf War. During that hearing it was learned that U.N. inspectors identified many U.S. - manufactured items exported pursuant to licenses issued by the U.S. Department of Commerce that were used to further Iraq's chemical and nuclear weapons development and missile delivery system development programs.

On June 30, 1993, several veterans testified at a hearing of the Senate Committee on Armed Services. There, they related details of unexplained events that took place during the Persian Gulf War which they believed to be chemical warfare agent attacks. After these unexplained events, many of the veterans present reported symptoms consistent with exposure to a mixed agent attack. Then, on July 29, 1993, the Czech Minister of Defense announced that a Czechoslovak chemical decontamination unit had detected the chemical warfare agent Sarin in areas of northern Saudi Arabia during the early phases of the Gulf War. They had attributed the detections to fallout from coalition bombing of Iraqi chemical warfare agent production facilities.

In August 1993, Senate Banking Committee Chairman Donald W. Riegle Jr. began to research the possibility that there may be a connection between the Iraqi chemical, biological, and radiological warfare research and development programs and a mysterious illness which was then being reported by thousands of returning Gulf War veterans. In September 1993, Senator Riegle released a staff report on this issue and introduced an amendment to the Fiscal Year 1994 National Defense Authorization Act that provided preliminary funding for research of the illnesses and investigation of reported exposures.

When this first staff report was released by Senator Riegle, the estimates of the number of veterans suffering from these unexplained illnesses varied from hundreds, according to the Department of Defense, to thousands, according to the Department of Veterans Affairs. It is now believed that tens of thousands of U.S. veterans are suffering from a myriad of symptoms collectively labelled either Gulf War Syndrome, Persian Gulf Syndrome, or Desert War Syndrome. Hundreds and possibly thousands of servicemen and women still on active duty are reluctant to come forward for fear of losing their jobs and medical care. These Gulf War veterans are reporting muscle and joint pain, memory loss, intestinal and heart problems, fatigue, nasal congestion, urinary urgency, diarrhea, twitching, rashes, sores, and a number of other symptoms.

They began experiencing these multiple symptoms during and after — often many months after — their tour of duty in the Gulf. A number of the veterans who initially exhibited these symptoms have died since returning from the Gulf. Perhaps most disturbingly, members of veteran's families are now suffering these symptoms to a debilitating degree. The scope and urgency of this crisis demands an appropriate response.

This investigation into Gulf War Syndrome, which was initiated by the Banking Committee under the direction of Chairman Riegle, has uncovered a large body of evidence linking the symptoms of the syndrome to the exposure of Gulf War participants to chemical and biological warfare agents, chemical and biological warfare pre-treatment drugs, and other hazardous materials and substances. Since the release of the first staff report on September 9, 1993, this inquiry has continued. Thousands of government officials, scientists, and veterans have been interviewed or consulted, and additional evidence has been compiled. This report will detail the findings of this ongoing investigation. Since the Banking Committee began its inquiry, the position of the Department of Defense regarding the possible causes of Gulf War Syndrome has altered only when challenged with evidence that is difficult to dispute. Yet, despite the vast resources of the Department of Defense, several independent and congressional inquiries with limited resources continue to uncover additional evidence of hazardous exposures and suspicious events.

The Department of Defense, when first approached regarding this issue by Committee staff, contended that there was no evidence that U.S. forces were exposed to chemical warfare agents. However, during a telephone interview on September 7, 1993 with Walter Reed Army Medical Center commander Major General Ronald Blanck, Committee staff was informed that the issue of chemical and biological warfare agent exposure had not been explored because it was the position of "military intelligence" that such exposure never occurred.

Then, during a November 10, 1993 press briefing at the Pentagon, the Department of Defense acknowledged that the Czech government did detect chemical agents in the Southwest Asia theater of operations. After analyzing the results of the Czech report, the Department of Defense concluded that the detections were unrelated to the "mysterious health problems that have victimized some of our veterans." According to former Secretary of Defense Les Aspin, in some cases the wind was wrong and the distances too great to suggest a link. For instance, Seabees serving to the south and east of the detection site have complained of persistent health problems; but according to the Pentagon, the wind was blowing in the other direction at the time of the detections and the concentrations were too low to do harm over that kind of a distance.

The fact is, no one has ever suggested that there was a link between the Czech detections and what occurred during the early morning hours of January 19, 1991 near the Port of Jubayl. (These two events will be described in detail in Chapter 2.) Former Defense Secretary Aspin said at the briefing that this incident could not have been from the Coalition bombings of the Iraqi chemical weapons facilities because the winds were blowing to the northwest. Yet according to available Soviet documents, the dispersal of chemical agents and other hazardous substances is controlled by other factors in addition to surface wind direction and velocity, such as topography, temperature, precipitation, vertical temperature gradient, and atmospheric humidity. These factors all contribute to the size and type of dispersal that will be observed. Unclassified visual and thermal satellite imagery confirms that the fallout from the bombings of Iraqi targets during the air and ground war moved to the southeast, with the weather patterns and upper atmospheric wind currents, towards Coalition force positions. (See Chapter 3.)

According to a knowledgeable source who has requested confidentiality, the Czechs believed that the detections were caused by the weather inversion which occurred that day (January 19, 1991) as the weather front moved southward. The Czechoslovak chemical detection unit reported this information to U.S. command officials immediately, but the responding units were unable to confirm their findings when they arrived, according to the Pentagon. Nonetheless, at the November 10, 1993 briefing, the Department of Defense admitted that the Czech detections were believed to be valid. The Department of Defense failed to disclose that the Czechoslovak chemical detection team also detected yperite (HD) that morning. The presence of both of these agents in such close proximity could only reasonably be the result of one of two possibilities: (1) direct Iraqi mixed agent attack, or (2) fallout from the Coalition bombings of Iraqi weapons facilities and storage bunkers.

Defense Department officials, having had possession of the Czech report for over a month, were at a loss to explain the chemical mustard agent detected by the Czechoslovak chemical detection team in the Saudi desert near King Khalid Military City on January 24, 1991. This despite the fact that both the Czechs and French claim that this detection was reported to U.S. command authorities during the Persian Gulf War. Additionally, during the Gulf War, the Czechs claimed that they detected Chemical nerve agent after a Scud missile attack. These statements, heretofore only reported in the press, have been confirmed by a member of the U.S. 1st Cavalry Division and by an entire platoon of a U.S. Army chemical detection unit who trained with the Czechoslovak

Chemical detection unit near King Khalid Military City. These reports have not been addressed publicly by the Department of Defense and will be addressed in this report in Chapter 3.

The contents of this report supports the conclusion that U.S. forces were exposed to some level of chemical and possibly biological warfare agents during their service in the Gulf War. Any review conducted by the Pentagon must extend far beyond the information being reported by the Czech Ministry of Defense. The Czech information, while important, represents just a small fraction of the evidence currently available, only some of which will be detailed in this report.

It is now the position of the Department of Defense that it has no other evidence that U.S. forces were exposed to chemical agents. Yet this report contains descriptions and direct eyewitness accounts that provide evidence which suggest that gas was detected, along with many other events which may have been actual attacks on U.S. forces.

This report supports the conclusion that U.S. forces were exposed to chemical agents. The assertion that the levels of nerve agents detected by the Czechs and others were not harmful is flawed. In subsequent requirements for chemical detection equipment, the Department of the Army acknowledges that the principal chemical agent detection alarm deployed during the war, the M8A1 was not sufficiently sensitive to detect sustained low levels of chemical agent and to monitor personnel for contamination. Further, U.S. Army Material Safety Data Sheets (MSDS) indicate that chronic exposures to levels of over .0001 mg/m3 for Sarin (GB) is hazardous and requires the use of protective equipment. (See appendix A.) The minimum level of chemical agent required to activate chemical agent detection alarm M8A1, commonly in use during the war, exceeds this threshold by a factor of 1,000. (See appendix A.) As the chemical agent alarms began to sound during the "air war," French, Czech, and many U.S. commanders confirmed that they were sounding from the fallout from the bombings. Over time, even at these levels, after repeatedly being told that there was no danger, many U.S. forces failed to take precautionary measures. Other report that the alarms were sounding so frequently that they were turned off.

M8A1 alarms do not detect blister agents. The findings of this report prepared at the request of Chairman Riegle detail many other events reported by U.S. servicemen and women that in some cases confirm the detection of chemical agents by U.S. forces. In other cases these reports indicate the need for further detailed investigation. But still the question remains: Is exposure to these and other chemical agents the cause of Gulf War Syndrome? We have received hundreds of reports that many of these symptoms are being experienced by family members. Numerous developments have taken place over the last several months which suggest that, while chemical agents and other environmental hazards may have contributed to the Gulf War illnesses, bacteriological, fungal, and possibly other biological illnesses may be the fundamental cause. This position is supported by the following.

First, Dr. Edward S. Hyman, a New Orleans bacteriologist, has treated a small number of the sick veterans and several of their wives for bacteriological infections, and has developed a protocol of treatment that has resulted in symptom abatement in many of his patients.

Second, during the November 10, 1993 unclassified briefing for Members of the U.S. Senate, in response to direct questioning, then Undersecretary of Defense John Deutch said that the Department of Defense was withholding classified information on the exposure of U.S. forces to biological materials. In a Department of Defense- sponsored conference on counter-proliferation, held at Los Alamos National Laboratory on 6-7 May, 1994, Dr. Deutch admitted that biological agent detection is a priority development area for the Department of Defense, since there currently is no biological agent detection system fielded with any U.S. forces anywhere in the world.

Third, the Department of Defense has named Dr. Joshua Lederberg to head its research team into the causes of Gulf War illnesses. Dr. Lederberg, among his other credits, is a Nobel Laureate and an expert in the fields of bacteriology, genetics, and biological warfare defenses.

Fourth, in detailed informational interviews conducted of 400 Gulf War veterans, it has been learned that over 3/4 of their spouses complain that they have begun to suffer from many of the same debilitating symptoms. (See Chapter 4.)

This report, like the one which preceded it, will discuss the relationship between the high rate of Gulf War illnesses among Group I individuals (those possibly exposed to a direct mixed agent event), and the lower rates among those in Group II (individuals exposed to the indirect fallout from coalition bombings of Iraqi chemical, biological, and nuclear targets) and Group III (individuals who suffered severe adverse reactions to the nerve agent pre-treatment pills). Despite the varying rates of illness between the groups, however, the symptoms are similar. While other possible causes of the Gulf War Syndrome such as petrochemical poisoning, depleted uranium exposures, and regionally prevalent diseases, have been discussed elsewhere and must be pursued, there is a great deal of compelling evidence which indicates that all of these possibilities must now be seriously considered. We believe, however, that no other explanations prove as compelling as the ones which will be presented in this report.

This report includes a great number of first-hand accounts and other documentary evidence in addition to the anecdotal information that appeared in the print and electronic media during the Gulf War. It establishes convincingly that the Department of Defense assertions are inaccurate. We believe there is reliable evidence that U.S. forces were exposed to chemical and possibly biological agents. But regardless of whether U.S. forces were exposed or not, the entire official body of information, including all classified or heretofore unpublished information, available research data sets, case histories, and diagnostic breakdown information must be made available to independent civilian medical researchers in order to further the research into the causes of and treatments for these illnesses. Absent a release of information by the Department of Defense of the science which forms the bases for their theories, the Department of Defense position must be viewed by qualified scientists as anecdotal and unsubstantiated.

Given that there is also a growing body of evidence indicating that spouses and children of Gulf War veterans are vulnerable to similar illnesses, the Department of Defense must now share all of its information with civilian, non-governmental researchers.

These family members are civilians who may be at risk. This illness was first reported over three years ago.

On February 9, 1994, Chairman Riegle sent a letter to Secretary of Defense William Perry asking that he release all U.S. military personnel from any oath of secrecy they may have taken regarding classified information specifically pertaining to chemical or biological warfare agent exposure in the Persian Gulf theater. This request was based on a recommendation of the National Academy of Sciences, National Institute of Medicine in their 1993 publication Veterans at Risk: The Health Effects of Mustard Gas and Lewisite. On May 4, 1994, the Secretaries of Defense, Health and Human Services, and Veterans Affairs responded to the Chairman's letter stating that there was no classified information on chemical or biological detections or exposures. This directly contradicts the statement of Deputy Secretary Deutch in his November 10, 1993 unclassified briefing to Members and staff.

Why isn't the Department of Defense aggressively pursuing the answers to the questions surrounding of the events which may have caused illnesses being suffered by many Gulf War veterans? One possible explanation lies in a 1982 article. Then Senate Armed Services Committee Chairman John Tower wrote, "Chemical training in the United States armed forces is, at best, perfunctory. It is rarely conducted in a simulated contaminated environment and stocks of individual protective equipment are too limited, and therefore too valuable, to risk them in the numbers necessary to allow troops to operate in them for realistic training. As a result, most U.S. personnel are relegated to a minimal and highly artificial exposure to the problems and hardships entailed in performing their respective combat missions should they have to 'button up'." As numerous U.S. General Accounting Office (GAO) reports have noted, the U.S. was not much better prepared prior to the Gulf War than it was when Senator Tower wrote in his article.

IRAQI CHEMICAL AND BIOLOGICAL WARFARE CAPABILITY

Over the last ten years, Iraq, a signatory to both the Geneva Protocols of 1925 (prohibiting the use of poisoned gas) and the Biological Warfare Convention of 1972 (banning biological weapons), has expended an enormous amount of research and energy in developing these and other prohibited weapons.

Iraq was believed to have been manufacturing mustard gas at a production facility in Samarra since the early 1980s. It also began an extensive program to produce nerve agent precursor chemicals, taking advantage of its own natural resources. Phosphate mines/industries are at Akashat, Al Qaim, and Rutbah. The Iraqi Al Fallujah gas warfare complex was believed to be capable of producing up to 1,000 tons per month of Sarin, as well as the nerve agent VX. In addition, with the assistance of foreign firms, Iraq developed the capability to experiment with hydrogen cyanide, cyanogen chloride, and lewisite. By the start of the Gulf War, Iraqi forces had developed chemical delivery capabilities for rifle grenades, 81mm mortars, 152mm, 130mm, and 122mm artillery rounds; bombs; 90mm air-to-ground rockets; 216 kilogram FROG and 555 kilogram SCUD warheads; and possibly land mines and cruise missiles.

On July 30, 1991, Ambassador Rolf Ekeus, director of the United Nations Special Commission on Iraq (UNSCOM), charged with overseeing the elimination of Iraq's chemical and nuclear arsenals, told the Security Council that the U.N. inspectors had found chemical warheads armed with nerve gas. Mr. Ekeus claimed that some warheads found were already fitted onto the SCUD missiles.

Iraq's chemical warfare capability was known to the U.S. government before the war. A month before the war began, then Central Intelligence Agency (CIA) director William Webster estimated that Iraq possessed 1,000 tons of poisonous chemical agents, much of it capable of being loaded into two types of missiles: the FROG (Free Rocket Over Ground) and the SCUD B(SS-1). Jane's Strategic Weapons Systems lists warhead capabilities for the FROG-7 as high explosive (HE), chemical, or nuclear, and for the Iraqi versions of the SCUD as probably HE or chemical.

Status of Iraqi Readiness to Use Chemical Weapons Against Coalition Forces

In March 1991, Molly Moore reported from Jubayl, Saudi Arabia that Marine Commanders found no indications of chemical weapons stockpiles on the battlefields of Kuwait. According to a Washington Post report that day, (March 7, 1991), U.S. intelligence analysts claimed that these weapons "never got distributed down to the battlefield" from storage sites north of the Euphrates River. A U.S. military intelligence source stated in March 1991 that "it was a matter of not deploying chemical weapons, rather than not having them, ...my guess .... is they never managed to get it down to division level."

Regarding the presence of chemical weapons and Iraqi readiness to use them against Coalition forces, Committee staff has received the following information:

Dale Glover, of the 1165th Military Police Company, was with the 7th Corps, approximately 75 miles inside Iraq, when they came upon a destroyed artillery site. They entered a bunker that was half uncovered by the bombing. Inside there was a very strong ammonia smell. They discovered leaking chemical munitions inserts packed inside aluminum casings. A test confirmed a blister agent. They went back to their unit and reported what they had found. Mr. Glover recalled that "they didn't get back to us for 2- 3 hours, then told us it was a false positive, nothing to be concerned about." However, he said, within hours they were ordered to move from the location where they were camped, about three miles from the bunker. Mr. Glover recalled that they had been at that position only a couple of weeks and had not expected to move that soon. When questioned if the site they discovered was south of the Euphrates, he confirmed that it was.

Another source who identified himself to the Committee but wishes to remain anonymous has informed Committee staff that he also was with the 7th Corps in southern Iraq. Somewhere between As Salman and Bashra (in a position south of the Euphrates River), his unit came upon bunkers containing crates of substances that "made you choke, made you want to throw up, burned your eyes. It smelled like ammonia, only a lot stronger." He could not approach the crates without experiencing immediate breathing problems. He said these crates were leaking.

Chris Alan Kornkven was a Staff Sergeant with the 340th Combat Support Company during the Persian Gulf War. He reported to Committee staff that a U.S. military doctor at the 312th Evacuation Hospital told him that doctors at the hospital had been speaking with Iraqi officers. According to these doctors, the Iraqi officers said that they had chemical weapons at the front, and had authorization to use them, but that the winds in their area were blowing the wrong way.

Several press sources carried reports of encounters with chemical mines by the 2nd Marine Division during the initial mine field breaching operation early on February 24, 1991. According to the Chicago Tribune, which interviewed officers and enlisted Marines involved in the operation, a FOX vehicle confirmed positive readings for a nerve agent and for a mustard gas. A second detecting device gave the same positive reading. General Keys, the 2nd Division commander, and Colonel Livingston, commander of the 6th Marine Regiment, told reporters they believed it was possible that a chemical mine was blown up or hit. General Schwarzkopf told reporters he considered the reports "bogus."

British troops also discovered Iraqi chemical mines on the Gulf battlefield, according to Gannett News Service. A British official (not further identified) said the incident was reported to Prime Minister John Major's war cabinet; no details were given.

Press reports indicate Iraqi readiness to use these weapons against Coalition forces. The British Sunday Times reported on January 27, 1991, that American intelligence detected greatly increased activity at Iraq's main chemical plant at Samarra in the last week of December, and the British Ministry of Defense said that the Allies believe that Iraq "may have as many as 100,000 artillery shells filled with chemicals and several tons (of bulk agent) stored near the front line." According to the Times report, a British Ministry of Defense official said: "The plant was at peak activity and the chemicals were distributed to the troops in Kuwait and elsewhere in theatre." The Times reported that an unnamed Pentagon source said that Hussein had given front-line commanders permission to use these weapons at their discretion, and that "it was no longer a question of if, but when."

Iraqi soldiers captured by the British units also informed the allies that before the war started, Iraq distributed substantial supplies of chemical weapons along the front lines to be held for the ground war. According to Newsweek, U.S. intelligence sources had reported that Saddam Hussein had ordered his commanders to fire chemical weapons as soon as the allies launched a ground offensive. A British signals officer was reported to have said that "we were tuned into the Iraqi command radio net. We heard them give the release order to their front-line troops to use chemical weapons against Rhino Force if it crossed the border."

DESTRUCTION OF IRAQ'S CHEMICALS AND CHEMICAL WEAPONS BY THE UNITED NATIONS

In April 1993, weapons inspectors from the United Nations charged with locating all of Iraq's nuclear, chemical and biological weapons by U.N. Resolution 687, confirmed that in Muthanna, 65 miles northwest of Baghdad, Iraq manufactured a form of mustard gas as well as Sarin and Tabun, both nerve agents. This vast desert complex was the nucleus of Iraq's chemical weapons program. During the allied bombing in the early days of the Gulf War, Muthanna was a priority target. It was repeatedly attacked and production sites were destroyed. As United Nations inspectors attempted to destroy Iraq's chemical weapons arsenal, they discovered bombs, missiles, and chemical weapons of mass destruction spread out across this immense complex. Of particular concern were the chemical warheads of Al-Hussein modified SCUD missiles, each filled with five gallons of Sarin. Twenty-eight of these warheads have been drained and destroyed by the U.S. inspectors. These weapons were not destroyed during the bombings at Muthanna because they had been removed to other locations before the Gulf War started. Their relocation and transfer back to Muthanna was described by U.N. inspectors as a painstaking process. According to Brigadier General Walter Busbee, U.S. Army Chemical and Material Destruction Agency, Aberdeen Proving Grounds, these warheads were exported to Iraq from the former Soviet Union. Chemical warfare agents which either survived the allied bombing or were inventoried and returned to the Muthanna facility for destruction include:

- 13,000 155-mm artillery shells loaded with mustard gas;
- 6,200 rockets loaded with nerve agent;

- 800 nerve agent aerial bombs;
- 28 SCUD warheads loaded with Sarin;
- 75 tons of the nerve agent Sarin;
- 60-70 tons of the nerve agent tabun; and,
- 250 tons of mustard gas and stocks of thiodiglycol, a precursor chemical for mustard gas.

U.N. inspectors have concluded that the Muthanna plant was capable of producing two tons of Sarin and five tons of mustard gas daily. The plant was also capable of manufacturing VX, a nerve gas and one of the most toxic chemicals ever produced.

In addition to Muthanna, chemical agents were destroyed at two airbases: one located 40 miles west of Baghdad and the other located near An Nassiriyah, where a number of 122mm rockets loaded with Sarin (GB) were blown in place. According to UNSCOM sources, many of these weapons were hastily deployed prior to the air war and later returned for destruction. The U.N. has destroyed hundreds of tons of bulk chemical agents and tens of thousands of chemical munitions. In addition, hundreds of thousands of liters of key chemical precursors which have been identified and destroyed include: 14,600 liters of DF; 121,000 liters of D4 and 153,983 liters of thiodiglycol. According to UNSCOM, the Iraqis were capable of employing both binary and mixed agent weapons. Binary weapons identified used DF. When combined with appropriate chemicals, GB and GF are produced.

UNSCOM also discovered, at various locations, evidence of research into certain biological agents, including botulinus toxin, anthrax, an organism responsible for gas gangrene (clostridium perfringens) and others as identified below. The evidence discovered by the group suggested that this was primarily an offensive biological warfare program. On February 13, 1994, a clandestine radio service in Iraq, the Voice of the Iraqi People, reported that Saddam Hussein's government was still attempting to hide chemical and biological weapons from international inspectors by repeatedly relocating them. Citing unidentified individuals, the radio reported that the banned weapons were being hidden in the oil pipelines that have been "out of operation because of the international embargo."

CHEMICAL WARFARE DOCTRINE AND THE USE OF COMBINED AGENT WARFARE

There is substantial evidence to suggest that in the use of chemical weapons, as in other military areas, the Iraqi military adhered, at least in part, to Soviet military doctrine. Soviet military doctrine suggested that chemical warfare should be conducted with mixed agents. Mixed agents, often referred to as "cocktails," are intended to enhance the capabilities of nerve agents and defeat the precautions taken by the enemy. Use of mixed agents could account for the wide variety of symptoms displayed by the Gulf War veterans. Mixed agents can be made by combining a variety of biotoxins, nerve agents, vesicants, blister agents and some biological agents — such as bacteria and fungi, and others described briefly below.

According to some sources, Iraq used mixed agent weapons combining cyanogen, mustard gas, and tabun against the Kurds. Saddam Hussein stated on April 2, 1990, that Iraq had "double combined chemical" weapons since the last year of the Iran-Iraq War. It was also believed that in 1984 Iraq may have used mixed agent weapons with biological tricothecenes and mycotoxins against Majnoon Island during the Iran-Iraq War.

The utility of chemical weapons and the possibility of exposing one's own troops to indirect chemical weapons effects is an issue which has been seriously debated by both U.S. and Soviet military planners. Soviet doctrine questions the utility of initiating chemical warfare, since chemical weapons produce secondary effects that could obstruct troop advances. U.S. Military doctrine warns that according to its calculations, the use of a nerve agent against a target area of no more than a dozen hectares (a hectare is about 2.47 acres) can, under certain weather conditions, create a hazard zone downwind of up to 100 kilometers in length. Within this downwind area, friendly military units would have to take protective measures.

According to the official military announcements made in the last half of January 1991 and based on the quantity of chemical agents observed by UN inspectors after the war, the scope of coalition bombing against these facilities involved hundreds — if not thousands — of tons of bulk chemical nerve agents, mustard gas, as well as tens of thousands of pieces of chemical munitions. This quantity of chemical warfare agents vastly exceeds the amounts that might be expected to be deployed by a military force in a single chemical attack.

The dispersal of the chemical agents and other hazardous substances is controlled by factors such as topography, wind velocity, direction, temperature, precipitation, vertical temperature gradient and atmospheric humidity. These factors all contribute to the size and type of dispersal pattern which will be observed. In addition, as confirmed by unclassified U.S. satellite imagery, debris from the Coalition bombings were upwardly dispersed, rather than downwardly dispersed as would occur in offensive use, causing chemical agents to be carried by upper atmospheric currents and distributed as "traces" of chemical fallout over "down weather" positions. Czech and French officials confirmed the detections of these chemicals during the war. (See Chapter 3.)

In considering the consequences of the placement of troops in areas downwind (where non-lethal exposure to chemical warfare agents might be expected), it must be remembered that chemical nerve agents, such as Sarin and Soman and other agents, have cumulative effects — often explained as slow rates of detoxification.

Chemical Nerve Agents

Nerve agents kill by disrupting the metabolic processes, causing a buildup of a chemical messenger (acetylcholine) by inhibiting the production of acetylcholine-esterase, a key regulator of neurotransmission. Lethal exposure to chemical nerve agents is generally characterized by drooling, sweating, cramping, vomiting, confusion, irregular heart beat, convulsions, loss of consciousness and coma.

According to a material safety data sheet (MSDS) for Soman (GD), and VX prepared by the U.S. Army Chemical Research, Development and Engineering Center, Aberdeen Proving Grounds, Maryland, "the inhibition of cholinesterase enzymes throughout the body by nerve agents is more or less irreversible so that their effects are prolonged. Until the tissue cholinesterase enzymes are restored to normal activity, probably by very slow regeneration over a period of weeks or 2 to 3 months if damage is severe, there is a period of increased susceptibility to the effects of another exposure to any nerve agent. During this period the effects of repeated exposures are cumulative; after a single exposure, daily exposure to concentrations of nerve agent insufficient to produce symptoms may result in the onset of symptoms after several days. Continued daily exposure may be followed by increasingly severe effects. After symptoms subside, increased susceptibility persists for one to several days. The degree of exposure required to produce recurrence of symptoms, and the severity of these symptoms depend on duration of exposure and time required to produce recurrence of symptoms, and the severity of these symptoms depend on the duration of exposure and the time intervals between exposures. Increased susceptibility is not specific to the particular nerve agent initially absorbed." (See appendix A for MSDS on Soman, Sarin, Tabun, and VX).

Some of the symptoms commonly associated with acute exposure to chemical nerve agents include myosis, frontal headaches, eye pain on focusing, slight dimness of vision, occasional nausea and vomiting, runny nose, tightness in chest, sometimes with prolonged wheezing, expiration suggestive of broncho-constriction or increased secretion and coughing. Following systemic absorption, these symptoms are identified as typical: tightnesss in chest, wheezing, anorexia, nausea, vomiting, abdominal cramps, epigastric and substernal tightness, heartburn, diarrhea, involuntary defecation, increased sweating, increased salivation, increased tearing, slight bradycardia, myosis, blurring vision, urinary urgency and frequency, fatigue, mild weakness, muscular twitching, cramps, generalized weakness, including muscles of respiraton, with dyspnea and cyanosis, pallor and occasional elevation of blood pressure; giddiness, tension, anxiety, jitteriness, restlessness, emotional lability, excessive dreaming, insomnia, nightmares, headaches, tremors, withdrawal and depression; bursts of slow waves of elevated voltage in EEG (especially on over ventilation), drowsiness, difficulty concentrating, slowness on recall, confusion, slurred speech, ataxia, coma (with absence of reflexes), Cheyne-Stokes respirations, convulsions, depression of the respiratory and circulatory centers, with dyspnea, cyanosis and fall in blood pressure.

The majority of automatic chemical agent detection alarms (M8A1) deployed during the war were not sufficiently sensitive for detecting sustained low levels of chemical agent and monitoring personnel for contamination. U.S. Army Material Safety Data Sheets (MSDS) indicate that chronic exposure to levels of over .0001 mg/m3 for Sarin (GB) is hazardous and required the use of protective equipment. (See appendix A). The minimum level of chemical agent required to activate the automatic chemical agent detection alarm M8A1, commonly in use during the war, exceeds this threshold by a factor of 1,000. As the chemical agent alarms began to sound during the "air war," French, Czech, and many U.S. commanders confirmed that they were sounding from the fallout from the bombings. Over time, even at these levels, after repeatedly being told that there was no danger, U.S. forces failed to take precautionary measures. Others report that the alarms were sounding so frequently that they were turned off.

This increased susceptibility associated with prolonged exposures to non-lethal dosages of nerve gases, suggests that the synergistic effects of the fallout from the bombings of the chemical warfare agent facilities and the administration of the cholinesterase inhibiting drug, pyridostigmine bromide, should be further researched as factors contributing to the symptoms being described by the Gulf War veterans.

The following is a listing of a number of agents which the Iraqi government could have combined or which could have been combined in the atmosphere as a result of Coalition bombings:

Sarin (GB) - A colorless and practically odorless liquid, Sarin dissolves well in water and organic solvents. The basic military use of Sarin is as a gas and a persistent aerosol. A highly toxic agent with a clearly defined myopic effect, symtoms of intoxication appear quickly without any period of latent effect. Sarin has cumulative efffects — that is, a slow rate of detoxification independent of its method of entry into the body. According to Joachim Krause and Charles K. Mallory in Chemical Weapons in Soviet Military Doctrine: Military and Historical Experience, 1915-1991, the progressive signs of initial Sarin intoxication include myosis (contraction of the pupil), photophobia, difficulty breathing and chest pain.

Soman (GD) - A neuro-paralytic toxic agent. Soman is a transparent, colorless, involatile liquid smelling of camphor. Soluble in water to a limited degree, Soman is absorbed into porous and painted surfaces. Soman is similar to Sarin in its injurious effects, but more toxic. When it acts on the skin in either droplet or vapor form, it causes a general poisoning of the organism.

Tabun (GA) - A neuro-paralytic toxic agent. Tabun is a transparent, colorless liquid. The industrial product is a brown liquid with a weak sweetish smell; in small concentrations, it smells of fruit, but in large concentrations, it smells of fish. Tabun dissolves poorly in water but well in organic solvents; it is easily absorbed into rubber products and painted surfaces. Injury occurs upon skin contact with Tabun vapor and droplets. The symptoms of injury appear almost immediately . Marked myosis occurs.

VX - This colorless, ordorless, liquid has a low volatility and is poorly soluble in water, but dissolves well in organic solvents. The danger of pulmonary VX intoxication is determined by meteorological conditions and the delivery method used. VX is thought to be very effective against respiratory organs when in the form of a thinly dispersed aerosol. The symptoms of VX intoxication are analogous to those of other nerve agents, but their development is markedly slower. As with other nerve agents, VX has a cumulative effect.

VESICANTS AND BLOOD AGENTS

Lewisite - A vesicant toxic agent, industrial lewisite is a dark brown liquid with a strong smell. Lewisite is a contact poison with practically no period of latent effect. Lewisite vapors cause irritation to the eyes and upper respiratory tract. According to the Center for Disease Control, lewisite would cause stinging and burning. Its smell, generally characterized as the strong smell of geraniums, could be confused with the smell of ammonia (the reaction to which is regulated by pain fibers rather than smell). Iraqi stores of lewisite were not located after the war according to the Department of Defense.

Cyanogen Chloride - The French first suggested the use of cyanogen chloride as a toxic agent. U.S. analysts have reported that it is capable of penetrating gas mask filters. Partially soluble in water, it dissolves well in organic solvents. It is absorbed easily into porous materials; its military state is a gas. Cyanogen chloride is a quick acting toxic agent. Upon contact with the eyes or respiratory organs, it injures immediately. Lethal exposures result in loss of consciousness, convulsions and paralysis.

Hydrogen Cyanide - A colorless liquid smelling of bitter almonds, hydrogen cyanide is a very strong, quick acting poison. Hydrogen cyanide affects unprotected humans through the respiratory organs and during the ingestion of contaminated food and water. It inhibits the enzymes which regulate the intra-cell oxidant-restorative process. As a result, the cells of the nervous system, especially those affecting breathing — are injured, which in turn leads to quick death. An important feature of hydrogen cyanide is the absence of a period of latent effect. The military state of hydrogen cyanide is a gas. The toxic and physiologic properties of hydrogen cyanide permit it to be used effectively in munitions — predominantly in rocket launched artillery. Death occurs after intoxication due to paralysis of the heart. Non-lethal doses do not cause intoxication.

Blister Agents

According to the material safety data sheet (MSDS) for sulfur mustard gas (HD) prepared by the U.S. Army Chemical Research, Development and Engineering Center, Aberdeen Proving Ground, Maryland, "Chronic exposure to HD can cause skin sensitization, chronic lung impairment, cough, shortness of breath, chest pain, and cancer of the mouth, throat, respiratory tract, skin, and leukemia. It may also cause birth defects. (See appendix A for MSDS sheets on sulfur mustard agents HD and T.) The U.S. Army Chemical and Biological Defense Command lists the current detector sensitivity threshold for the M256A1 kits, a commonly used piece of chemical agent detection equipment in the Gulf War, as 2.0 mg/m3. According to the Material Data Safety Sheets for sulfur mustard, total weight average exposures of greater than .003mg/m3 over an 8 hr. period requires the use of protective equipment. (See appendix A.) Therefore, the detection kit would not detect the agent until the amount of agent present exceeded the safety threshold by a factor of over 660. The M8A1 automatic alarms do not detect blister agent.

Mustard Gas - This is a colorless, oily liquid which dissolves poorly in water, but relatively well in organic solvents, petroleum, luricant products, and other toxic agents. The injurious effect of mustard gas is associated with its ability to inhibit many enzyme systems of the body.

This, in turn, prevents the intra-cell exchange of chemicals and leads to necrosis of the tissue. Death is associated mainly with necrosis of the tissue of the central nervous system. Mustard gas has a period of latent effect (the first signs of injury appear after 2-12 hours), but does not act cumulatively. It does not have any known antidotes. In military use it can come in gas, aerosol, and droplet form. It therefore acts through inhalation, cutaneously, perorally and directly through the blood stream. The toxic and physico-chemical properties of mustard gas allow it to be used in all types of munitions.

RELATED CHEMICAL AGENT INFORMATION

Committee staff has learned that Iraq may have acquired any one of a number of the Soviet binary novachok ("newcomer") series of chemical warfare agent compounds or information relevant to the development of those compounds. This series of chemical warfare agents reportedly contains both lethal and debilitating agents. According to a confidential Committee source, if the Iraqis had obtained samples of these compounds they could be easily analyzed and produced with readily available materials. Several of these compounds are described as agents that even in microdoses can have long lasting effects.

These agents are described as inducing myosis, vomiting, memory loss, involuntary motions and internal organ dysfunction. Many of these materials are also described as having mutagenic effects. These materials are, according to the source, stored in the lipids (body fats) and have no known antidotes. In addition, according to the Committee source, the Soviets were believed to have conducted research in a number of dioxin-based chemical warfare agents, and on at least one agent that could be used to contaminate drinking water supplies. Committee staff is conducting further inquiries to determine if Iraq may have had access to any of these compounds

Biotoxins

Biotoxins are natural poisons, chiefly of cellular structure. A distinction is made between exotoxins which are given off by an organism while it is alive, and endotoxins which are given off after a cell's death. The exotoxins cause the injurious effects of biological weapons, but endotoxins guarantee the effects of chemical weapons and do not cause the widespread disease outbreaks associated with biological warfare. Some examples of biotoxins include botulinus toxin and staphylococcic enterotoxin.

Biological Warfare Capability

According to the U.N., the Iraqi biological warfare program was initiated in mid- 1986 at Salman Pak. UNSCOM inspectors discovered evidence of research into certain biological agents including botulinus toxin and anthrax — as well as organisms responsible for gas gangrene, tetanus and brucellosis, components of a biological weapons program which was not defensive in nature. In four years of work prior to the war, only 10 papers were published. These research programs focused on Iraqi efforts to isolate the most pathogenic spores. They also did research on the aerosolization and on the environmental survivability of some of these biological materials according to the United Nations.

While the Department of Defense maintains that the Iraqi military did not weaponize its biological warfare program, UNSCOM is less certain, reporting that their degree of confidence that weaponization did not occur is low. In fact, readily high performance agricultural aerosol generators could easily be converted to both decontaminate areas in which chemicals are used and to aerosolize biological and chemical warfare agents.

Other ways in which biological materials could have been weaponized include the use of Iraqi 250 and 500lb bombs, aerial rockets, unmanned aerial vehicles, FAW ground-to-ground missiles, helicopters and Iraqi aircraft. The Committee has received several reports of Iraqi helicopters penetrating Saudi airspace during the war by flying at low levels through the wadis and of Iraqi aircraft penetrating the area over the northern Persian Gulf.

According to UNSCOM, indications that suggested that the program was offensive in nature include:

- No declared links between the BW defense program and medical corps research.
- No links between aerosolization research and research on defensive filters.

The United Nations said that the Biological Inspection was initiated on August 8, 1991 at Salman Pak. The inspection was delayed because of the need to extensively immunize the members of the inspection team. The Salman Pak facility was razed one week prior to the arrival of the inspection team.

The United States is aware of the Iraqi potential for using biological weapons. The employment of biological agents in a "cocktail" mix with chemical warfare agents is consistent with Soviet military doctrine.

It is clear that biological weapons are much more difficult than chemical weapons to detect and defend against. Some of the symptoms experienced by veterans suffering from Persian Gulf Syndrome are consistent with biological warfare agent use. Verification will require sophisticated medical diagnosis, which to date has not been publicly undertaken.

The question of whether U.S. forces were attacked with a biological agent is problematic. According to Chemical/Biological Program: A Department of Defense Perspective, "it has been recognized that our biological defense program was inadequate. Creditble analysis indicated that optimal employment of biological agents could result in a significantly large hazard area."

It further cites a memo from the Chairman of the Joint Chiefs of Staff to the SECDEF (Secretary of Defense) noting: "inadequate ability to counter BW (biological warfare) attack/BW defense is a priority requirement.

The inadequacy of the current biological defense and detection program was also supported by Deputy Secretary of Defense John Deutch in an unclassified May 6, 1994 address delivered at a Department of Defense sponsored counterproliferation conference at the Los Alamos National Laboratory. According to Deputy Secretary Deutch, the United States has "no biological detection capability deployed with any forces, anywhere."

Novel BW agents created by altering DNA plasmids and vectors are specifically intended to avoid detection. As noted below, several shipments of biological materials that might have been used to carry out such a program were licensed for export from the United States to the Iraq Atomic Energy Commission. In such a program, common intestinal flora such as e. coli could be altered to produce viral, bacterial, or other toxins and would be difficult to treat.

If Iraq was successful in developing such agents, diagnosis will continue to elude physicians testing for traditional illnesses. Novel BW agents would certainly elude biological detection devices. There is evidence, based on the nature of the materials imported, that this type of research was being conducted. Since the Iraqi government managed to dismantle much of its biological warfare program prior to the UNSCOM inspections, we can only speculate on how advanced this program might have been.

It has been suggested that if these problems the veterans are experiencing are Gulf War related, then we should be seeing even more serious problems among the Iraqis. Since beginning this investigation we have learned that many Iraqi enemy prisoners of war (EPW) suffered skin rashes, sores, nausea, vomiting, coughing and other medical problems while they were being detained in Saudi Arabia.

Many members of units who had close contact with these individuals are now reporting to the Committee symptoms consistent with those being suffered by other Gulf War veterans. In addition, Iraq has claimed a dramatic rise in reported cases of communicable diseases since the end of the Gulf War including typhoid, brucellosis, hepatitis and cholera.

Further, reports of Gulf War illnesses being reported are no longer limited to veterans of the Gulf War. Others reporting manifestation of these symptoms include:

- Department of Defense civilians who served in the Persian Gulf War.
- Department of Defense civilians working at the Anniston (AL) Army Depot and the Sharpsite (CA) Army Depot decontaminating equipment which was returned from the Persian Gulf.

- Spouses, particularly the spouses of male veterans, are reporting the following symptoms: chronic or recurring vaginal yeast infections, menstrual irregularities (excessive bleeding and severe cramping), rashes, fatigue, joint and muscle pain, and memory loss.
- Children born to veterans prior to the Gulf War. In many cases both male and female children born prior to the war have experienced symptoms similar to those of the veterans and their spouses.
- Children born following the Gulf war. Some reports have been published which suggest a high rate of miscarriages in the families of Gulf War veterans. Further, several reports have surfaced which suggest that there has been a high rate of physical abnormalities in children born to Gulf War veterans since the war.

Bibliography

Anthony, J. Parel : Gandhi, Freedom, and Self-Rule, New Delhi, Vistaar, 2002.

Arend, A.: International Law and the Use of Force, London, Routledge, 1993.

Azad, Maulana Abul Kalam: India Wins Freedom, New Delhi, Orient Longman, 1959.

Bellamy, C.: Knights in White Armour: The New Art of War and Peace, London, Random House, 1997.

Brierly, L.: The Law of Nations, New York, Oxford University Press, 1955.

Chandra, R.: Judicial System in India, Lucknow, Print House (India), 1992.

Damrosch, L.F.: Law and Force in the New International Order, Boulder, Westview Press, 1991.

Davies .A.: Telecommunications and Politics. The Secentralised Alternative, London, Pinter, 1994.

Dixit, Prabla: Communalism: A Struggle for Power, New Delhi, Orient Longman, 1981.

Friedman, G.: The Future of War: Power, Technology and American World Dominance in the 21st Century, N.Y., Random House, 1996.

Greer P.: Transforming Central Government: the Next Steps Initiative, Buckingham, Open University Press, 1994.

Heimanson, Rudolph: Dictionary of Political Science and Law, N.Y.: Oceana Publications, 1967.

Holsti, K.: The State, War, and the State of War, Cambridge, Cambridge Univ. Press, 1996.

Huntington, S.P.: The Soldier and the State, N.Y., Vintage Books, 1964.

Janowitz, M.: The Professional Soldier: A Social and Political Portrait, N.Y., The Free Press, 1960.

Jones, W.H.: The Government and Politics of India, London, Hutchinson, 1971.

Keane J.: Democracy and Civil Liberty, London, Verso, 1988.

Kelly, John B.: Britain and the Persian Gulf 1795-1880, Oxford, Clarendon Press, 1968.

Majumdar, R. C.: An Advanced History of India, New York, St. Martin's Press, 1967.

Mary, W.: Asian Power and Politics: the Cultural Dimensions of Authority, Cambridge, Belknap Press, 1985.

Morris, W.H.: The Government and Politics of India, London, Hutchinson, 1971.

Nair, A. M.: An Indian Freedom Fighter in Japan, Bombay, Orient Longman, 1983.

Noorani, A.G. : Indian Political Trials : 1775-1947, New Delhi, Oxford University Press, 2005.

Posen, B.R.: The Sources of Military Doctrine, Ithaca, 1984, Cornell Univ. Press.

Prahlad, K.: Governance and Public Administration for Poverty Reduction, Salvador, Brazil, 1997.

Rosen, P.: Societies and Military Power: India and its Armies, Ithaca, Cornell University Press, 1996.

Rosen, P.: Societies and Military Power: India and its Armies, Ithaca, Cornell University Press, 1996.

Simon, D. : Public Administration, New York, Knopf, 1950.

Victor G. : Law as a Political Instrument, New York, Random House, 1955.

Ziring, L.: An Introduction to Asian Politics, N.J., Prentice-Hall, 1977.

Index

A

Administration, 84, 144, 146, 177, 185, 208, 214, 216, 224, 239, 248, 252, 259, 275.
Advantages, 101, 108, 121, 194, 199.
Agency, 84, 139, 140, 141, 143, 144, 146, 147, 148, 149, 150, 151, 161, 162, 166, 169, 170, 171, 173, 175, 176, 239, 246, 267, 270.
Application, 30, 50, 52, 75, 116, 157.
Assistant Secretary, 14, 72.

B

Biological Weapons, 5, 22, 28, 30, 40, 43, 266, 270, 271, 279, 280.

C

Casualty Management, 135, 223, 233.
Chemical Battlefield, 85, 99, 126.
Chemical Decontamination, 177, 178, 256, 259.
Chemical Detection, 191, 192, 197, 199, 200, 201, 262, 263.
Chemical Warfare, 1, 2, 3, 4, 5, 9, 14, 15, 16, 17, 18, 20, 21, 23, 26, 30, 35, 38, 46, 47, 48, 52, 65, 73, 74, 75, 76, 77, 78, 79, 80, 81, 82, 83, 84, 85, 86, 87, 88, 89, 90, 93, 96, 102, 103, 106, 112, 130, 141, 142, 143, 144, 194, 198, 199, 215, 218, 219, 237, 254, 264, 271, 276, 277, 279, 280, 282.
Chemical Wars, 6.
Chemical Weapons, 1, 2, 5, 6, 9, 12, 14, 15, 17, 19, 20, 22, 23, 24, 25, 26, 27, 30, 39, 46, 48, 49, 62, 64, 72, 73, 83, 120, 124, 126, 129, 130, 131, 132, 135, 137, 176, 203, 204, 261, 267, 268, 269, 270, 272, 275, 279, 280.
Cold War, 22, 33.
Combination, 35, 57, 71, 130, 210.
Commander, 21, 22, 26, 42, 43, 44, 52, 54, 55, 56, 58, 79, 85, 87, 88, 92, 99, 100, 103, 108, 111, 112, 114, 115, 120, 125, 127, 141, 143, 144, 147, 151, 175, 233, 261, 269.
Commission, 177, 224, 267, 281.
Committee, 14, 75, 76, 77, 259, 260, 261, 266, 268, 269, 278, 279, 281.
Communications, 9, 142, 143, 148, 195, 224, 229, 245.
Community, 21, 131, 135, 136, 137, 145, 149, 150, 172, 189, 190, 224, 227, 228, 229, 230,

231, 232, 233, 237, 239, 240, 241, 245, 246.

Conditions, 6, 25, 55, 58, 59, 76, 88, 103, 110, 112, 116, 137, 156, 163, 165, 166, 167, 181, 197, 199, 200, 205, 209, 212, 225, 272, 276.

Considerations, 130, 160, 181, 183, 205, 213, 232.

D

Department, 12, 16, 23, 52, 57, 74, 75, 76, 77, 78, 80, 82, 87, 92, 93, 104, 116, 117, 118, 124, 125, 126, 130, 131, 133, 135, 141, 146, 148, 158, 159, 161, 162, 170, 175, 199, 208, 225, 226, 232, 239, 244, 245, 246, 247, 249, 259, 260, 261, 262, 263, 264, 265, 266, 276, 279, 280, 281.

Deployment, 9, 17, 20, 54, 126, 149, 151, 185, 204, 222.

Designations, 5, 24.

Developments, 6, 22, 24, 73, 93, 264.

E

Electronic Media, 265.

Emergency, 10, 23, 89, 94, 95, 130, 131, 132, 133, 134, 135, 137, 138, 139, 141, 146, 148, 150, 154, 157, 159, 165, 166, 168, 170, 171, 177, 183, 184, 185, 191, 194, 202, 203, 206, 207, 208, 213, 219, 220, 221, 222, 224, 225, 227, 228, 230, 231, 233, 237, 238, 240, 241, 242, 243, 244, 245, 247, 248, 249.

Energy, 196, 197, 267, 281.

Environment, 4, 14, 47, 71, 79, 106, 108, 121, 125, 126, 128, 162, 180, 193, 195, 196, 198, 200, 206, 207, 213, 224, 226, 227, 228, 230, 248, 249, 266.

Evaluation, 152, 153, 154, 164, 165, 166, 174, 238, 247.

Evidence, 14, 20, 28, 44, 99, 135, 156, 171, 175, 190, 236, 237, 238, 246, 250, 260, 261, 263, 265, 271, 272, 279, 281.

F

Falklands War, 26.

Finance Administration, 144.

Forces, 6, 7, 15, 19, 21, 26, 28, 43, 46, 60, 69, 85, 110, 121, 122, 126, 261, 263, 264, 265, 266, 267, 268, 269, 275, 280.

G

Gas Warfare, 15, 21, 46, 47, 48, 51, 54, 62, 63, 72, 73, 76, 77, 78, 79, 80, 81, 82, 83, 85, 86, 87, 89, 91, 93, 94, 96, 98, 99, 114, 115, 118, 124, 125, 126, 127, 128, 267.

Governments, 18, 22.

Gulf War, 26, 193, 194, 195, 204, 223, 259, 260, 261, 262, 263, 264, 265, 266, 267, 268, 270, 272, 275, 277, 281, 282.

I

Implementation, 7, 12, 227.

Information, 20, 22, 24, 33, 46, 48, 51, 68, 72, 75, 80, 86, 87, 88, 92, 93, 120, 132, 136, 138, 141, 142, 144, 145, 146, 147, 149, 150, 151, 156, 166, 167, 168, 169, 170, 172, 173, 175, 185, 195, 197, 201, 223, 229, 230, 231, 232, 233, 234, 236, 238, 243, 247, 262, 263, 264, 265, 266, 268, 278.

Institute, 20, 21, 23, 24, 48, 51, 200, 237, 243, 266.
Instruments, 91, 185, 186.
Intelligence, 9, 14, 20, 21, 47, 51, 58, 63, 68, 181, 261, 267, 268, 269, 270.
Investigation, 138, 172, 221, 227, 237, 260, 261, 264, 281.
Iran-Iraq War, 272.

J

Justice, 200.

L

Laboratory Tests, 208, 212, 219, 251.
Leaders, 21, 49, 127, 128, 223.

M

Management, 130, 135, 137, 139, 140, 141, 174, 185, 203, 206, 213, 219, 221, 222, 223, 225, 228, 235, 239, 244, 245, 249.
Mechanism, 155, 208, 217.
MEDICAL MANAGEMENT, 213, 219.
Medical Management, 140, 185, 203, 206, 213, 219, 222.
Military Treatment, 183.
Mission, 10, 77, 94, 123, 132, 137, 151, 172, 176, 220, 223.

N

National Laboratory, 264, 280.
Nerve Agents, 1, 4, 11, 20, 22, 24, 26, 27, 47, 129, 178, 184, 187, 191, 192, 193, 194, 195, 203, 205, 207, 208, 209, 210, 211, 212, 213, 214, 215, 216, 247, 252, 253, 254, 263, 270, 272, 273, 274, 276.
Network, 27, 86, 125, 130, 143, 229.

O

Operations, 45, 47, 61, 65, 84, 86, 97, 98, 108, 122, 123, 124, 130, 131, 141, 142, 144, 145, 147, 150, 158, 161, 224, 225, 233, 242, 243, 246, 261.
Opportunity, 103, 231, 245.
Organisms, 1, 5, 279.
Organization, 25, 27, 75, 77, 80, 82, 84, 85, 86, 87, 92, 109, 112, 140, 183, 224, 246, 248.

P

Patient Tracking, 154, 230.
Performance, 23, 145, 147, 254, 279.
Pet Management, 174.
Pharmacology, 84.
Plantations, 45.
Policy, 23, 47, 231, 259.
Production, 1, 2, 14, 15, 23, 30, 35, 58, 60, 61, 71, 75, 76, 82, 83, 84, 126, 127, 204, 259, 267, 270, 273.
Project, 22, 52.
Protection, 9, 10, 23, 38, 40, 67, 68, 69, 94, 95, 101, 102, 106, 108, 113, 175, 178, 179, 185, 186, 196, 200, 208, 220, 221, 226, 234, 235, 240.

R

Relationship, 265.
Research, 1, 2, 4, 9, 14, 20, 22, 23, 24, 48, 68, 75, 76, 77, 78, 84, 186, 227, 259, 260, 264, 265, 267, 271, 273, 277, 278, 279, 280, 281.

S

Safety Officer, 141, 226, 242.
Safety Plans, 241.

Security, 140, 142, 157, 158, 159, 162, 164, 168, 226, 231, 232, 239, 241, 242, 246, 267.
Society, 40, 132, 133.
Soldiers, 7, 18, 25, 34, 43, 44, 46, 50, 51, 53, 57, 64, 67, 70, 71, 72, 79, 85, 95, 100, 101, 102, 110, 111, 113, 116, 117, 118, 123, 126, 127, 269.
Spectroscopy, 186, 194, 196.

T

Technology, 2, 20, 22, 23, 24, 40, 78, 133, 149, 154, 157, 202, 204, 205, 207, 208, 209, 210, 211.
Temperature, 66, 196, 198, 199, 205, 217, 218, 262, 273.
Terrorism, 23, 26, 129, 131, 133, 134, 149, 201, 227, 228, 230, 238, 244, 245, 246.
Terrorist, 26, 28, 130, 131, 132, 133, 134, 135, 137, 139, 140, 154, 161, 162, 167, 171, 172, 173, 176, 177, 201, 203, 204, 229, 230, 232, 241, 242, 247, 249.
Thermal Dissemination, 8, 9.
Transportation, 130, 131, 132, 133, 134, 139, 142, 143, 144, 145, 150, 159, 164, 168, 169, 170, 171, 176, 190, 213, 228, 239.
Treatment, 1, 11, 21, 25, 34, 46, 74, 77, 84, 92, 93, 94, 104, 105, 116, 117, 118, 125, 130, 131, 132, 133, 134, 136, 137, 138, 142, 144, 145, 148, 149, 150, 152, 153, 154, 155, 156, 159, 162, 164, 165, 166, 167, 174, 175, 176, 178, 179, 181, 182, 183, 184, 185, 201, 207, 208, 212, 213, 214, 220, 222, 223, 224, 225, 226, 231, 232, 234, 235, 237, 238, 239, 240, 241, 242, 243, 249, 252, 254, 255, 256, 257, 258, 260, 264, 265.

W

Wave Detection, 198.
Weapons, 1, 2, 5, 6, 9, 12, 14, 15, 17, 19, 20, 22, 23, 24, 25, 26, 27, 28, 30, 31, 35, 36, 38, 39, 40, 43, 46, 48, 49, 52, 53, 56, 62, 64, 71, 72, 73, 83, 85, 91, 97, 113, 120, 124, 125, 126, 128, 129, 130, 131, 132, 135, 137, 156, 158, 176, 181, 182, 185, 201, 203, 204, 222, 249, 259, 261, 262, 267, 268, 269, 270, 271, 272, 275, 279, 280.
Welfare, 242.
World War I, 2, 6, 7, 12, 17, 18, 20, 46, 47, 48, 49, 56, 57, 62, 67, 70, 79, 85, 108, 112, 116, 124, 125, 126, 128, 204, 217, 221, 247.
World War II, 19, 20, 22.